Lewis and Clark

VOICES FROM THE TRAIL

Lewis and Clark

VOICES FROM THE TRAIL

Michael Kerrigan

Photography by Rudi Holnsteiner

BARNES
&NOBLE
BOOKS
NEW YORK

A Note on the Text

Neither Lewis nor Clark was by background, temperament, or interest what we might call a "literary" type, but few would dispute the status of their journals as great literature. Even so, they have had to be edited for modern publication. In the first place, their sheer bulk (and the degree of duplication between the two sets) makes selection necessary. The explorers' astronomical observations, and the detailed botanical, geological and other data they kept, make for indigestible reading in any quantity. We have tried to offer a taste of the method and scope of their scientific researches, but no more.

The *Journals* were produced under unusual (and often very difficult) conditions, written up nightly by the campfire on the trail. The result is a punchy brevity of style, at times even a certain breathlessness, which add greatly to the excitement of the reader. The text used in this book, based on Reuben Gold Thwaites' edition of 1904–05, respects the stylistic integrity of the originals. While abbreviations have been filled out for the sake of clarity, only in a very few places (where hasty composition had left the actual meaning of the text unclear) has any extremely slight alteration been made to the actual words of the explorers.

Spelling is another matter: Lewis and Clark wrote in an age when spelling was not yet standardized, even in everyday English. The same writer might spell the same word in different ways—even on the same page! What's more, Lewis and Clark were, in many cases, recording words that had never previously been written down in English (or, for that matter, in any other tongue). For today's reader, though, it is simply a distraction to have to keep in mind that the Native people referred to as the "Arikara" in one journal entry are the same as those called the "Ricarees," "Rickerrees," or even simply "Rees" elsewhere. We have therefore felt free to regularize such spellings as far as possible.

The task of writing daily records would have afforded Lewis and Clark a few minutes' time out each day and an opportunity for reflection, although the explorers must have found this chore onerous at times. Most important of all, however, there was the exhilarating sense of writing in witness of great discoveries: an excitement that comes across in every line of the *Journals*.

This edition published by Barnes and Noble, Inc., by arrangement with Saraband

2004 Barnes & Noble Books

M 10 9 8 7 6 5 4 3 2 1

ISBN: 0-7607-5314-8

Library of Congress Cataloging in Publication Data available

EDITOR: Sara Hunt
ART AND PRODUCTION EDITOR: Deborah Hayes

Printed in China

Acknowledgments and Photo Credits:
The publisher would like to thank the following people for their help in the preparation of this book: M. Jane Taylor for editing, Lone Nerup Sorensen for compiling the index, Phoebe Tak-Yin Wong for graphic design and cartography, and Marilyn Holnsteiner for her extensive research.

All photographs in this book are © **Rudi Holnsteiner** unless otherwise listed here. Grateful acknowledgment is made to the following individuals and institutions for permission to reproduce illustrations and photographs:

© 2002 **Arttoday.com, Inc.**: 7b, 10, 11, 22t, 23, 37, 43, 59t, 92, 106, 168, 169, 172, 173, 191, 196b; © **Ed Cooper:** 16, 78; **Corbis-Bettmann:** 186; © **Corbis Corporation:** 98–9 (background); © **Terry Donnelly:** 72–3, 74, 80b; **Library of Congress, Prints and Photographs Division:** 9t, 13, 17 (both), 42 (both), 46, 47, 54 (both), 55, 58, 61 (both), 63t, 64 (both), 66t, 67, 70t, 71 (both), 76, 80bl, 81, 83r, 84, 89, 111, 112, 116, 120, 127, 131, 134, 138t&m, 142b, 146b, 148, 149, 154, 156, 157, 160, 175, 180, 189, 195, 197; **Maps by Phoebe Tak-Yin Wong:** 7, 25, 45, 75, 101, 133, 165, 183; © **Missouri Historical Society, St. Louis:** 1 and 15l (Clark Family Collection, William Clark Papers), 15r, 20, 161b (Clark Family Collection, William Clark Papers), 199; **Montana Historical Society, Helena:** 196 (inset); **Collection of Frank Oppel:** 12b; **Saraband Image Library:** 59b; **Courtesy of the Yale University Map Collection, photograph © Joseph Szaszfai:** 9b, 184–5.

Page 1: Clark's journal, opened to his entry of October 26, 1805, held by the Missouri Historical Society, St. Louis.
Page 2: Big Hole River, near Wisdom, Montana. Lewis and Clark passed here on their return, July 6, 1806.

CONTENTS

———✳———✳———

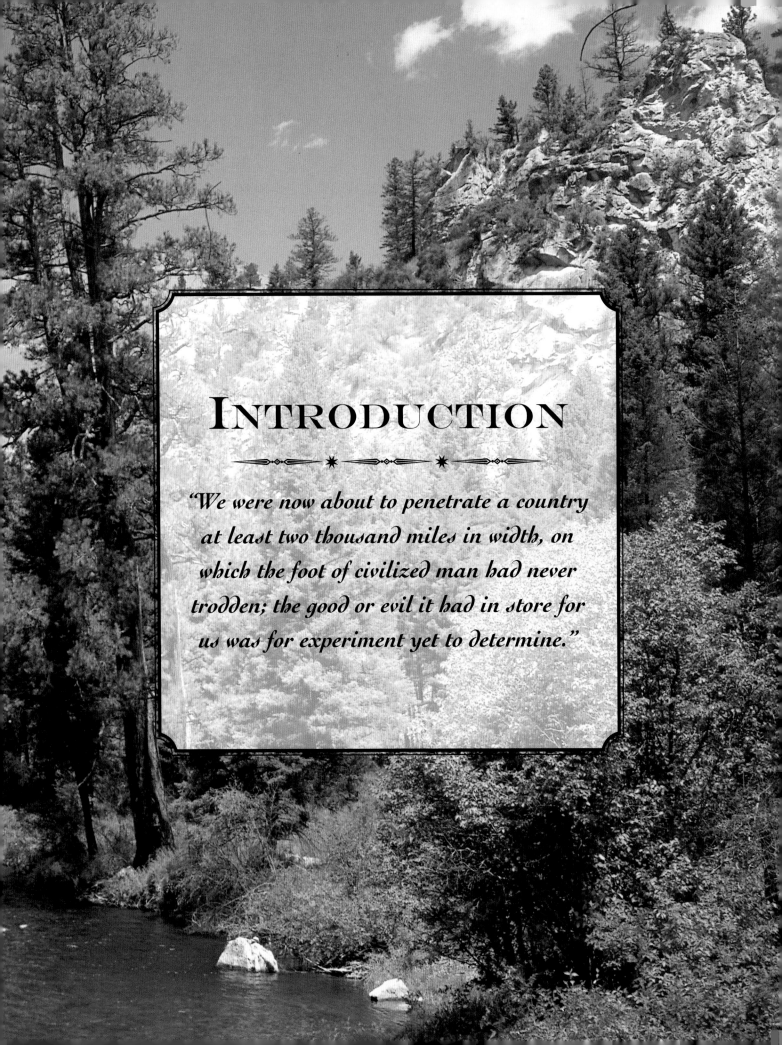

INTRODUCTION

"We were now about to penetrate a country at least two thousand miles in width, on which the foot of civilized man had never trodden; the good or evil it had in store for us was for experiment yet to determine."

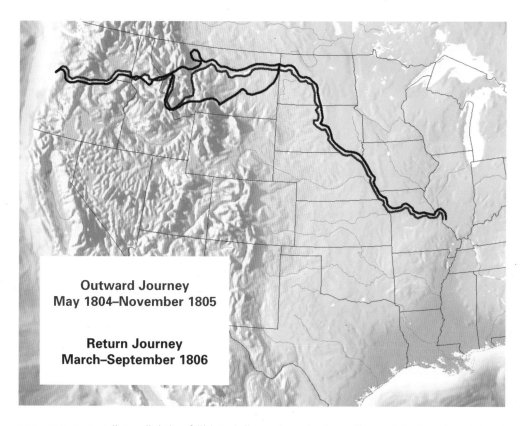

Outward Journey
May 1804–November 1805

Return Journey
March–September 1806

Opposite: *"Leave your stress behind!" the tourist website urges prospective visitors to the Bitterroot National Forest today; there was no chance of Lewis and Clark or their companions unwinding when they camped in these woods at Spring Gulch, outside Sula, Montana, 200 years ago. Wearied by months of travel, nerves frayed by hunger and mounting anxiety, they were growing desperate to find game to hunt or natives with horses to trade for their onward journey. With all its hardships, though, their expedition did much to establish that deep love of the western wilderness which has become so important a part of the American identity.*

We talk too lightly of "historic" events: Just about anything that happens may have its place in history, though few events can really be seen as deciding the destinies of countries or continents—still less the world. Major wars or natural disasters are an obvious example, scything down vast populations or shattering cities, their sheer violence the measure of their impact on the lives of nations. Journeys of exploration, by contrast, are conducted altogether more quietly—yet their implications may be incomparably more far-reaching. A small party of explorers can quite literally redraw the map; Columbus and his crew really did discover a "New World" in 1492. That the Americas had been settled many centuries before by peoples now established as indigenous did nothing to diminish the epoch-making significance of their voyage.

On the successful homecoming of the Lewis and Clark Expedition in 1806,

America's self-appointed national bard Joel Barlow penned an extravagant poem in praise of Lewis. He compared his hero's achievements with those of Columbus—and was roundly derided for his pains. No more than his verse deserved, perhaps:

Left: *In the exciting aftermath of Columbus' first voyage, King Ferdinand of Spain points the way westward to the New World, from an engraving of 1493.*

*Let the Nile cloak his head in the
clouds, and defy
The researches of science and time;
Let the Niger escape the keen trav-
eler's eye,
By plunging, or changing his clime.*

*Columbus! Not so shall thy bound-
less domain
Defraud thy brave sons of their right;
Streams, midlands and shorelands
illude us in vain,
We shall drag their dark regions to
light…
With the same soaring genius thy
Lewis descends,
And, seizing the car of the sun,
O'er the sky-propping hills and high
waters he bends
And gives the proud earth a new
zone.*

Yet, as bad as his poetry may have been,
Barlow was hardly exaggerating his sub-

ject's achievements. Two hundred years
on, if Lewis and Clark's exploits as explorers
seem heroic as ever, the historic significance of what they accomplished seems
immeasurably greater. Crossing the continent of North America for the first time,
they showed their countrymen and -women
the panoramic prospects to be seen to
westward—the space, the scenery, the
endless natural resources. They made their
way through a landscape of indescribable
sublimity, brought back news of an extraordinary flora and fauna, and—most important of all, perhaps—established contact
with many as yet unknown native peoples.
All these different discoveries would be
incorporated into America's vision of what
it was, and what it might become; still
more crucial, though, was the explorers'
indomitable spirit. Their courage and enterprise would be emulated over and over
again in the two centuries that followed, as
Americans built the greatest nation the
world has ever seen.

*Below: The sun rises
over the Missouri at
Niobrara, Nebraska,
where the Expedition
stopped September 4–5,
1804. The Niobrara River
joins its "parent" river
here, the merging of
the streams producing
eddying currents and
shifting sandbanks,
making navigation
very difficult—even
hazardous—then
as now.*

THE NEW REPUBLIC

The United States that had declared independence in 1776 was not the vast "America" we know today: Its destiny to span the continent was by no means manifest. As yet confined to the thirteen former colonies along the eastern seaboard, plus a few frontier territories beyond, it was still very much in the habit of looking eastward. And no wonder: Revolution might have broken the bonds of colonial government by brute force, but the ties of sentiment and culture were both more elusive and more enduring. In any case, the new country could hardly hope to escape the influence of Europe when the European powers still played so active a role in the rule of North America. The British might have been sent packing from their possessions between Massachusetts and Georgia, but they were still very much a presence in Canada to the north. France, though broken as an imperial power after defeat by Britain in the Seven Years' War of 1756–63, was under new and revolutionary management. Those territories surrendered to Spain after the Treaty of Paris (1763) had recently been recovered by France under a secret treaty, though others—notably Ohio, Illinois, Indiana, Kentucky, and Tennessee—had remained in British hands, and upon American independence they became frontier possessions of the United States. Spain, though hardly the superpower that had dominated the Western Hemisphere for so long, still laid claim to an enormous area of western territory sweeping all the way from Texas to the Canadian border.

LOUISIANA

"La Louisiane," as it was called by its first French colonizers in the early eighteenth century, was named for King Louis XIV of France. It extended far beyond the boundaries of the state that bears the name today. Just about the entire Mississippi and Missouri basins were included—in other words, most of the modern Midwest—though areas east of the Mississippi were seized by Britain after the French defeat of 1763. The remainder, which stretched from the Gulf Coast all the way up to the Dakotas and eastern Montana, was ceded to the Spanish, Britain's allies in the Seven Years' War. In 1800, however, Napoleon bullied Spain into handing back the lands of Louisiana by a secret treaty: After forty years, France was back on the North American scene.

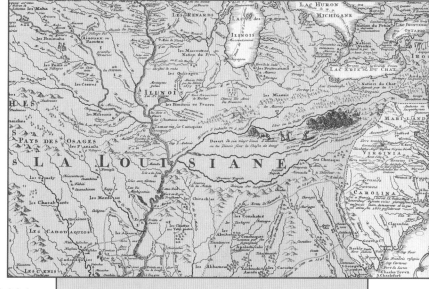

Top: The Pilgrims set up camp ashore at Plymouth, Massachusetts, December 11, 1620. Above: "La Louisiane," as depicted in the late seventeenth century by the German cartographer Johann Baptiste Homann.

THE LOUISIANA PURCHASE

Yet if the United States was a small nation beset by great powers, it did have the inestimable advantage of remoteness—and the European countries were increasingly preoccupied by events then unfolding far closer to home. The French Revolution and the rise of Napoleon had set in motion an explosive chain reaction of international anarchy and conflict that eventually engulfed the entire continent of Europe. France, the epicenter of the upheaval, had far more important things to occupy it than its newly recovered North American territories: Napoleon seems barely to have batted an eyelid before signing "La Louisiane" away.

THE MAN WHO GAVE THE WEST AWAY

Napoleon Bonaparte was born on the Mediterranean island of Corsica, a possession of France, in 1769. He enlisted in the French Army's artillery at the age of sixteen. His early military career was overshadowed by the tumultuous events of the French Revolution of 1789, and the "Reign of Terror" that ensued

in the years that followed as the Royal Family and its aristocratic supporters were sent to the guillotine before jeering crowds. Yet the revolutionary regime was soon under pressure from the people to deliver something more substantial than bloody entertainments—and like many another government, they sought to distract attention with a series of foreign wars. A leader of courage and charisma, and a tactician of extraordinary genius, Napoleon won victories for France from Austria to Egypt. Such was the popular adulation he received that he had soon surpassed the government he nominally served. His solution was simple: to crown himself Emperor. In the end, he took on too much. In 1812 he invaded Russia, taking Moscow, but was compelled to retreat, the pride of the French army mauled by the forces of "General Winter." The alliances mustered against him finally proved too formidable even for him to see off: He was brought down in 1814 and exiled to the Mediterranean Island of Elba. He gave Europe a fright a year later when he returned to lead France in war again, only to be narrowly—yet decisively—defeated at the Battle of Waterloo. This time he was sent to another island much farther afield: St. Helena, in the South Atlantic. He died there in 1821.

In 1803, Thomas Jefferson bought Louisiana—over 800,000 square miles of territory—for $15 million, a sum that seemed laughably low even by the standards of the time. Realistically, though, the French will not have felt too bad about receiving such a sum for a far-flung territory that would inevitably have proved hard to hold onto as time went by, and at a moment when France had much bigger geopolitical fish to fry. Yet it was obviously an extremely good deal for the United States, which had just about doubled in size at the stroke of a pen.

Mere paper proprietorship would not do, Jefferson realized, if encroachment by outside interests was to be prevented: America had to assert an actual presence in the West. Trading companies from Britain were already crowding in upon the northwestern parts of the Louisiana Purchase, while Spanish traders were busy on its southern borders. During the 1790s, Alexander Mackenzie had made his way across Canada to the Rockies and on down the Fraser and Mackenzie rivers to the Pacific Ocean. His journals were published in 1801. To Jefferson they appear to have served not only as an inspiration but also as a warning: Would the United States be left behind in the race for the West?

The price of such a failure was unthinkable. For Jefferson, the newly acquired territories of Louisiana offered not just an immense tract of as yet unexploited land to the west, but the possibility of a viable trade route to the Pacific. Whether even the President, in his hunger for territory, had actually got as far as envisaging an America that spanned the continent from the Atlantic to the Pacific remains unclear. What is certain, however, is his long-held conviction that U.S. agriculture and industry needed a doorway to the markets of Asia, and his sense that, were a way to be found up the Missouri and over the mountains, that doorway would be opened. What he clearly hoped to find was a sort of inland "Northwest Passage"—the way around North America's coasts to the Orient long sought by Old World mariners. The sea route around South America and Cape Horn was extremely hazardous; the way around the Cape of Good Hope inordinately long. There were rich prizes to be had for the country that controlled a more practicable commercial corridor.

THOMAS JEFFERSON: DEMOCRACY AND DISCOVERY

The third president of the United States is most famous as the author of the Declaration of Independence, but his scientific curiosity was equal to his idealism. "There is not a sprig of grass that shoots uninteresting to me," he famously said, and the resume of his writings and researches in everything from science and technology to geography and literature would suggest that this was no exaggeration. At his country retreat of Monticello, Virginia, Jefferson (1743–1826) was able to pursue these interests in peace and quiet, yet study for him was a way of engaging with the world, not of leaving it behind. The Lewis and Clark Expedition—very much his brainchild—typified Jefferson's approach. Real as its scientific objectives were, its diplomatic and economic implications had been thought through extremely shrewdly, the likely long-term interests of the United States assessed with the greatest care.

So it was that the idea of the Corps of Discovery was born. The main object of its mission was, in Jefferson's own words,

"To explore the Missouri River, and such principal stream of it, as, by its course and communication with the waters of the Pacific Ocean, may offer the most direct and practicable water communication across this continent, for the purposes of commerce."

AMERICA FROM THE OTHER SIDE

The Western interior may have been unexplored when Jefferson assumed the presidency, but the Pacific Coast was by no means an unknown quantity. A series of Spanish, British—and eventually American— navigators had prospected it over the years.

✳ 1542 Juan Rodríguez Cabrillo lands near present-day San Diego, becoming the first European to set foot in "Alta California."

✳ 1543 Bartolomé Ferrello sails up the coasts of northern California, Oregon and Washington, claiming them in the name of the Spanish Crown.

✳ 1768 In response to Russian forays across the Bering Strait and the start of settlement down the coast of Alaska and northwest Canada, the Inspector General of Baja California, Jose de Galvez, sends out several parties of settlers to start colonizing the as yet neglected Spanish territories to the north.

✳ 1775 Peruvian-born navigator Francisco de Bodega y Quadra explores the Pacific Coast from California as far north as Alaska, claiming the territories he finds on behalf of Spain.

✳ 1778 In the course of his third and final (indeed, fatal) expedition, English explorer Captain James Cook sails up the coast as far as the Bering Strait, in hopes—not to be realized—of finding a passage to the Atlantic.

✳ 1792 George Vancouver of England explores the Pacific Coast of North America; by agreement he meets Bodega y Quadra at Nootka Bay, Vancouver Island, to discuss demarcation between the territories of Britain and Spain. This same year U.S. trader Robert Gray discovers the mouth of the Columbia River.

VIRGIN TERRITORY?

Jefferson also gave detailed instructions on other things the members of the Corps should record along their way, from "the soil and face of the country, its growth and vegetable productions" to climatic conditions, and any "volcanic appearances." They were to map the territories they crossed in as much detail as was practicable, taking special equipment for this express purpose, and keep detailed records of everything they saw.

They were to take particular care in their observations of the human inhabitants of the Louisiana Purchase—for Jefferson knew well that this was by no means the empty wasteland that most ordinary Americans imagined. "In all your intercourse with the natives," he instructed,

> "treat them in the most friendly and conciliatory manner which their own conduct will admit; allay all jealousies as to the object of your journey, make them acquainted with the position, extent, character, peaceable and commercial dispositions of the U.S., of our wish to be neighborly, friendly and useful to them...."

He required that his explorers make themselves acquainted as far as possible with every aspect of the life of the native communities they encountered, including:

> "the names of the nations and their numbers;
> the extent and limits of their possessions;
> their relations with other tribes or nations;
> their language, traditions, monuments;
> their ordinary occupations in agriculture, fishing, hunting, war, arts and the implements for these;
> their food, clothing and domestic accommodations;
> the diseases prevalent among them, and the remedies they use.
> moral and physical circumstances which distinguish them from the tribes we know;
> peculiarities in their laws, customs and dispositions;
> and articles of commerce they may need and furnish, and to what extent."

Opposite, top: Clark's Nutcracker, a member of the crow family, and one of several new animal and plant species discovered by Lewis and Clark. Opposite, below: "A View of the Habitations in Nootka Sound," from Cook's A Voyage to the Pacific Ocean (1785). Below: An Oglala war party, captured in photogravure by Edward S. Curtis, 1907.

THROUGH THE LENS

Between 1896 and 1930, the photographer Edward Sheriff Curtis (1868–1952) made his leisurely way through the West, creating a unique pictorial survey of the Native American peoples and their lifeways. Visiting eighty different tribes, he produced photogravure images of astounding quality—not just in their technical accomplishment but in their aesthetic beauty and haunting human depth. Sadly, within a generation, this record of a still-surviving—though hard-pressed—culture had become the monument to one that was almost entirely gone. This, of course, only made Curtis's collection the more precious. His photographic odyssey was in its way as significant as the explorations of Lewis and Clark; it is fitting that his unforgettable images should help illustrate this account of their explorations.

As ever, we find in Jefferson's thinking a combination of sheer scientific curiosity and canny calculation: The better America knew these peoples, the more easily it might expect to manage them.

Far from being an empty wilderness, in fact, the West wasn't even empty of Europeans: The Spanish were now actively opening up their longstanding colonies in California, however belatedly. Meanwhile, in Louisiana itself, French trappers and "independent traders" had been working quietly away for generations, making their own commercial contacts with native communities—sometimes even taking native wives. Such men need not be seen as sinister French "fifth columnists"—their independence was genuine enough; the companies they worked for mainly British. Several would join Jefferson's Expedition as hunters and general hands, temporarily enlisting in the U.S. Army for the purposes of doing so. If Lewis and Clark complained about the idle and unhelpful Toussaint Charbonneau (his Shoshone wife Sacagawea was another matter), they found men like François Labuche and Peter Crusat far more to their liking. The indispensable George Drewyer had very likely been born Georges Drouillard.

NORTHWEST PASSAGES

What the Holy Grail was to the medieval knight, the Northwest Passage was to the navigators of modern times—ever since Christopher Columbus found his way to China blocked by the Americas.

✻ John Cabot, the Italian commander of an English expedition, seeks to sail to Asia far to the north of Columbus' route in 1497, and again in 1498. He thinks he has succeeded in reaching Asia, but has in fact only discovered Labrador.

✻ Sir Martin Frobisher, a courtier of the English Queen Elizabeth I, believes he has discovered an entrance to the fabled Northwest Passage in 1476: He has really only traveled as far as what is now known as Frobisher Bay, Baffin Island.

✻ England's explorer extraordinaire, Captain James Cook, attempts to find a way through from the Pacific end in 1778. He too has ultimately to turn back disappointed.

✻ Sir John Franklin comes close to finding the passage in 1845–48, but he never knows it: He and his men are tragically lost in the Arctic ice.

✻ Norwegian Roald Amundsen becomes the first explorer to negotiate the Northwest Passage, 1903–06.

In 1969, a U.S. tanker with ice-breaking bows became the first large vessel to find a way through; ironically, the passage may now at last be opening up of its own accord, thanks to global warming.

THE "CORPS OF DISCOVERY"

THE LEADERS

Lewis and Clark themselves have come down to us as a sort of brand name, a joint personality, and they did to some extent put aside their separate egos on the trail. They were distinct individuals, though, each with his own background and biography, however close their relationship on the trail.

Born in 1774, at Locust Hill, Virginia, a close neighbor of Jefferson's and a protégé from boyhood, Meriwether Lewis grew up to look after the family estate, but jumped at the chance to serve with the militia when the "Whiskey Rebellion" of 1794 erupted. His continued career as a soldier was interrupted when in 1801 he was summoned to the White House by his old mentor who

HERE BE MONSTERS...

Among all the eminently sensible and scientific instructions issued by Jefferson to his Expedition leaders, one more peculiar request may easily pass unnoticed. In their general observations of the West's animal species, he says, they are to look out especially for "the remains and accounts of any which may [be] deemed rare or extinct." What the paleontologist–president had in mind was the possibility that they might find the fossil remains of woolly mammoths or mastodons of the kind that had been discovered in the East. He even seems seriously to have entertained the hope that, in the remoter reaches of the western wilderness, they might come upon living specimens of these extraordinary beasts. He had high hopes too that they might find what, on fossil evidence, he had called the "megalonyx" ("great claw"), a kind of giant tiger—though later paleontologists have concluded that it was in reality a giant sloth. Fortunately, perhaps, for them, the explorers drew a blank in this particular search: The extant hazards of the West were surely quite daunting enough.

wished him to serve him as secretary and aide-de-camp. Lewis's duties were general, but from the first the president seems to have had him in mind as the best possible leader for the expedition he had been planning. As Jefferson wrote in a letter to his friend Benjamin Rush, the distinguished physician, Lewis was:

"Brave, prudent, habituated to the woods and familiar with Indian manners and character. He is not reg-ularly educated but he possesses a great mass of accurate observation on all the subjects of nature...."

Above: A mammoth, sculpted by Doug Van Dowd.
Below: The elkskin-bound journal of Clark, open at the page for October 26, 1805, and the "Method of head-flattening and adults with Skull Deformation," January 30, 1806.

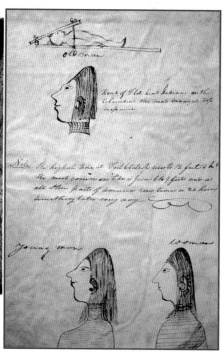

THE MISSION TRAIL: JUNÍPERO SERRA AND GASPAR DE PORTOLA

If the demands of high-minded scientific enquiry and national advantage coincided conveniently in Jefferson's exploratory vision, piety and politics dovetailed neatly in the missionary program of Junípero Serra and Gaspar de Portola. Though active enough in those areas we now know as the American Southwest, Spain had done little to explore, let alone colonize, the lands it claimed in "Alta California"— "Upper California." Only when Russian traders started pushing down the coast from Alaska did the authorities in Mexico's "Baja California" ("Lower California") wake up to the reality that their possession might at any moment be snatched from beneath their noses.

Hence, in 1769, the dispatch of Father Junípero Serra and soldier and sometime Governor of Baja California Gaspar de Portola to found a chain of missions farther north. Twenty-one would be built in all, between San Diego and Sonoma along what became known as the "Camino Real" or "Royal Road." Serra set up nine of these himself, traveling an estimated 24,000 miles in the fifteen years before he died. His personal sincerity need not be doubted—but in historical hindsight it is clear that the building of such missions was an extremely quick and easy way of establishing a colonial presence in what had been a neglected territory.

The shortcomings in his education would be addressed by friends of Jefferson, including Rush himself, who would coach him in everything from medicine and mineralogy to navigation and native history.

Lewis was given the president's authority to start organizing his Corps of Discovery sometime toward the end of 1802, and there were a thousand and one plans and preparations to be made. But he had an energetic helper in the president himself, for whom provisioning his expedition seems to have been the next best thing to actually going along. In between more pressing affairs of state, Jefferson was happy to spend hours working out how much ink might be needed for so many months of record-keeping, how many guns would be required, and how much shot. And with limited carrying capacity, there were tough decisions and trade-offs to be made. How, for instance, was the need for lanterns or blankets to be balanced out against that for soap or saws—or for beads and cloth to be traded with the native peoples?

Personnel was clearly going to be a key issue, but Lewis was hampered in his choice of companions by his need for secrecy: He could not come clean with those he approached about where his expedition would actually be going. William Clark was a comrade from militia days— they had served together only for a few weeks, in 1795, in the course of the Ohio Valley Indian Wars, but even in that brief time the two had become firm friends. Clark had less backwoods experience than Lewis, but he had a real feel for the lie of the land and great flair as a mapmaker; he was a man of great practical abilities—what we might now call a "problem solver." Four years older than his friend, but with much more experience as a military officer, he would find it easier both to command Corps members and to deal with the natives the Expedition encountered. The suggestion cannot be backed up with anything in the way of independent testimony, of course, but it seems to have been the case that, while his journals betray a certain brusque impatience with many of the ways of Louisiana's natives, they themselves appreciated his brisk forthrightness of manner.

Lewis certainly needed no convincing of Clark's qualities: Indeed, he insisted from the first that he be his co-leader rather than his second-in-command. This was not a suggestion that pleased the military hierarchy. Lewis's attempts to get Clark a captaincy to match his own were unsuccessful, but out in the wilderness who was going to complain? He consistently called him "Captain Clark"— and so, accordingly, do we. In other respects, however, Lewis was happy enough to maintain military discipline: He knew how dangerous it might be if standards were to be too much relaxed once the Expedition was beyond the reach of civilization.

THE MEN

The Corps of Discovery was in fact built around a nucleus of professional soldiers: Lewis was authorized to choose up to twelve noncommissioned officers and privates from the forts at Massac, on the Ohio, and Kaskaskia, on the Mississippi. Lewis asked the commander at the latter to provide a sergeant plus "eight good men who

understand rowing a boat." He did well with his four sergeants— John Ordway, Charles Floyd, Nathaniel Pryor, and Patrick Gass (though Gass's commanding officer had been most reluctant to let him go). The men he was sent were less impressive, and Lewis was in any case conscious that men who understood rowing a boat might not necessarily understand setting a trap, hunting a deer, or any of the other myriad skills that might be required of them out in the wild woods and mountains of Louisiana. The Expedition would need men skilled in carpentry, blacksmithery, and boat and gun repair; there would have to be experienced fishermen and competent cooks. Lewis looked for the skills he needed wherever he thought he could find them— several of his new recruits were not regular soldiers and a few were French. Yet whatever their origins, they were to be—at least for the duration of the Expedition—enlisted into the U.S. Army. The discipline and coherence of the Corps were not to be placed in jeopardy.

Yet as Clark drilled the men outside St. Louis before departure, it was already clear that those new to the military life were finding the adjustment irksome, while even the career soldiers may have had the sense of being somehow "on leave" from their normal disciplines and routines. There was a minor mutiny

Opposite: The garden at the San Diego de Alcala mission, established by Junípero Serra himself in 1769. Top: Meriwether Lewis (1774–1809). Below: William Clark (1770–1838).

ESSENTIAL ITEMS

A meticulous record was kept of everything the Expedition was to take with it. The list below includes only a very few:

6½ lbs. strips sheet iron
12 dozen pocket looking-glasses
2¼ dozen lockets
4,600 needles assorted
2,800 fish hooks assorted
3½ dozen tinsel bands assorted

The above—everything from iron to earrings— were taken as gifts for the native communities they met along the way. For the Expedition's own use, an enormous inventory included:

125 large fishing hooks
2 dozen table spoons
package 12 lbs. Castile soap
6 brass kettles from 1 to 5 gallons
2 handsaws
1 spirit level
1 metal sextant
176 lb. gunpowder
500 rifle flints
¼ lb. Indian ink
50 dozen bilious pills to order Benjamin Rush
1 set dentist's instruments.

when, while both Lewis and Clark were away on Expedition business, Privates Reuben Field and John Shields refused to obey an order from Sergeant Ordway; They would take orders only from their captains, they said. Another group—John Colter, John Boleye, Peter Wiser, and John Robinson—defied Ordway to go "hunting." Their insubordination would have been bad enough, from Sergeant Ordway's point of view, had hunting indeed been their purpose—but they were, of course, going off on a major drunk. Apprised of what had happened on his return, Lewis could not but be outraged, but his obviously sincere expressions of disappointment in the men seem to have proved more effective than a sterner punishment might have done. Not that he or Clark would flinch from inflicting such a punishment if it were considered necessary, as Private John Henry Newman would find when, well into the Expedition's journey, he was found to be stirring up mutinous feeling among his comrades. Yet there was a balance to be struck: This was no ordinary undertaking. These men would be striking out far beyond the boundaries of what

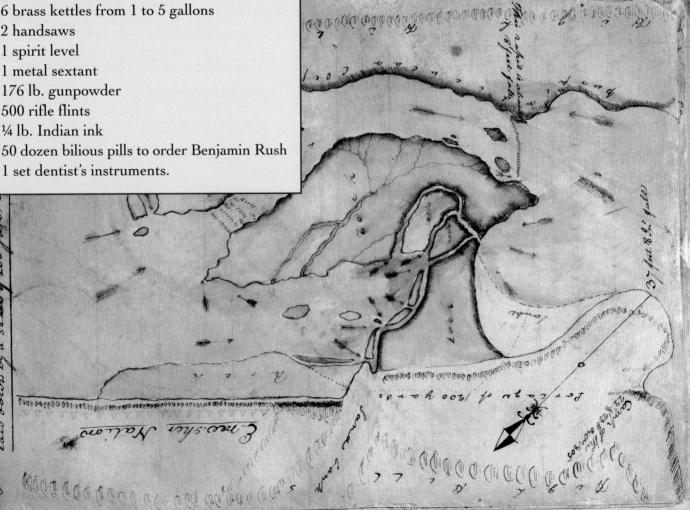

Previous pages: Sunrise at Slaughter River, Montana, where the Expedition camped May 29, 1805. Opposite: Clark's map of the "No. 2 Great Falls of the Columbia River," made in his journal, October 22–3, 1806. Above: The Expedition's one fatality, Sergeant Charles Floyd, is commemorated not only by this impressive obelisk, but by the name of his burial place, "Sergeant Bluff," Sioux City, Iowa.

they knew as civilization. They would need to act on their own initiative in situations for which no regular training could have prepared them and which could not conceivably be covered by Army rules. If their *esprit de corps* was vital to the success of their mission, then so was their sense of themselves as individuals; their sense of having been singled out for a special purpose.

Lewis and Clark would fine-tune the organization of the Corps of Discovery as they made their way upriver. Despite early hiccups, however, the arrangements made in St. Louis on the eve of departure seem to have served them well through a long and grueling—and often very dangerous—journey. Lewis appears intuitively to have found the right balance between firmness and flexibility in the command of a unique company that differed from the normal military unit not only in its goals but in its membership. Even the soldiers in the Corps were a sundry group of very varied age, experience, and attitude—abruptly thrown together for the purpose of this one Expedition. And around this military nucleus, as we have seen, clustered a motley crew of "engagés" enlisted for the duration, several of them neither career soldiers nor Americans. Along the way, indeed, the multicultural complexion of the Expedition would be increased by the addition of the interpreter Toussaint Charbonneau and his Shoshone wife Sacagawea.

This is one aspect of the Expedition that has caught the imagination of modern Americans most vividly: the paradigm it can be seen to offer for a society in which different races live and work together cheerfully in a common cause. And so, up to a point, it does: The respect Sacagawea was accorded as guide, and the status Clark's African-American slave York enjoyed as equal participant were real enough—though this only happened out in the wilderness, where the usual rules and conventions did not apply. At the Expedition's outset, York's place as his master's possession was so unquestioned that it does not appear to have occurred to anybody that he should be enlisted as a member of the Corps in his own right. Inspiration or outrage? The melting pot half empty or half full? The Lewis and Clark Expedition can be seen as representing American racial attitudes at both their best and worst.

But then that is what in the end makes its story so compelling—more so than the most extravagant fictional adventure yarn could ever be. The Expedition's true-life protagonists faced true-life challenges; the odds were quite genuinely stacked against them; they could—quite easily—not have made it back alive. And if they showed real qualities of courage and endurance, they also betrayed real flaws: They took wrong turnings, made misjudgments, on occasion fell short of their own high standards. What they never did was doubt their duty, to each other and to their country—a country that will forever be in their debt.

DOG OF DESTINY

Seaman, a big black Newfoundland dog bought by Lewis in Pittsburgh before the Expedition started, was "very active, strong and docile," according to his master. His "sagacity" would be admired by the Nez Percé. On the way down the Ohio to St. Louis, Seaman made himself useful by plunging into the river to catch squirrels swimming across in the course of their migration, which Lewis then fried, but there is no indication that he performed any similar service once the Expedition was under way. His nocturnal barking helped warn off prowling grizzlies and blundering bison, but for the most part Seaman seems to have been taken merely as a pet, with no specific duties to carry out. He is believed to have weighed in at almost 150 pounds, and must have taken some feeding, but there is no indication that his presence was ever resented by other Expedition members. Neither does it seem that when, out West, dog meat started figuring regularly in the explorers' diet, it ever occurred to anyone—however hungry—that Seaman should be next. A close companion to Captain Lewis (who was plainly moved when the dog was found after a brief disappearance on the trail), Seaman survived everything from spiky needle-grass to theft by hostile Wahclellah in the Oregon Gorge.

Below: Where next? "Decision Point," near Loma, Montana, presented Lewis and Clark with a real quandary (June 2–12, 1805): Which was the Missouri, and which its tributary?

POINT OF DEPARTURE, ST. LOUIS

St. Louis is just a few years older than the United States itself, having been founded by French trappers as a trading post in 1764. It was ideally situated, just below the confluence of the Missouri and Mississippi Rivers. They named the new settlement after their country's Crusader King Louis IX, who had reigned from 1226 until his death in 1270, and shortly after been canonized for his determined (though ultimately unavailing) attempts to win back Arab-occupied Jerusalem for Christendom. The city of St. Louis passed from ruler to ruler, being handed to the Spanish under the terms of the Treaty of Paris, then wrested back by Napoleonic France in 1800. In 1803, for the first time, it became an American city—the ideal starting point for an expedition up the Missouri. Clark writes of St. Louis as a "village" at one point, with no apparent intention of delivering a slight: Its population at that time seems to have been only around one thousand. It would rise dramatically over the decades that followed, however, as the lands of the Louisiana Purchase began to be opened up for settlement, and St. Louis found its role as Midwestern metropolis. Today that role finds symbolic expression in the breathtaking grace of the 630-foot Gateway Arch (1961–66), which was commissioned as a monument to Jefferson and the explorers who opened up the West.

SETTING OUT UPRIVER

*"At 12 o'clock, after bidding an affectionate
adieu to my hostess, ...we set forward...
in order to join my friend, companion and
fellow laborer Captain William Clark."*

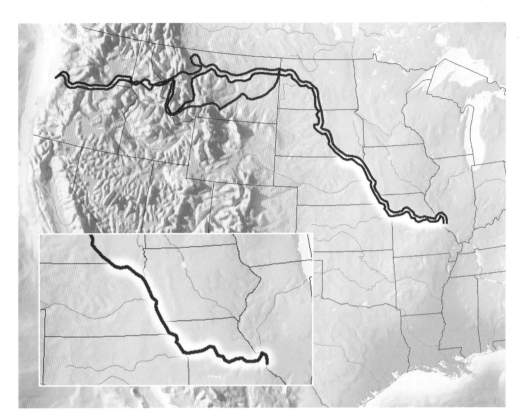

Departure, for the Corps of Discovery, meant committing their fortunes to the Missouri—the great waterway to the West, in Jefferson's ecstatic vision. As yet, the river's full significance could only be a matter of conjecture, but it is not hard to understand the President's epic expectations. The Missouri has many moods but, fair or foul, it is no ordinary river: to stand where it meets the Mississippi is to sense the presence of an awesomely powerful force. On average, 75,000 cubic feet of water per second pour into the "parent" river at this point, some 17 miles above St. Louis—and the flow is far heavier after spring snowmelt or spells of heavy rain upstream. But the water is just the start of it: this torrent brings with it a staggering sediment load whose murky trail can be seen stretching for many miles downriver, only gradually mingling with the clear waters of the Mississippi.

Mud is a considerable part of what the Missouri is all about. "The Big Muddy," many people call it; the local people called it "Nishodshre," which means much the same. (The word "Missouri" itself does not mean "muddy," as has sometimes been suggested, but comes from the Algonquian word for those who inhabited its lower valley: the "Missouria," or "People with dugout canoes.") Every river has its share of silt—topsoil washed into it by streams, or worn away from its own banks by the force of its current—but you could be forgiven for thinking that the Missouri was more mud than water. In 1879, it was estimated, the Missouri brought 11 billion cubic feet of sediment past St. Charles—an amount which, heaped up together in one place, could have covered a square mile of ground to a depth of 200 feet. The sheer scale of the river system is a factor: at almost 2,500 miles in length, the Missouri is one of the world's great rivers—despite being technically no more than a tributary of the Mississippi. But the nature of the terrain it traverses is a factor, too. Rising in the Rockies, the Missouri plunges down a series of whitewater rapids (now largely tamed by damming) before pushing southeastward across the vast expanse of the Great Plains: Much of its 529,000-square-mile basin is, accordingly, open grassland, whose topsoils are notoriously erosion-prone. In forested areas, tree roots help bind the earth up tightly so that it retains its integrity in just about all weathers; on the plains, by contrast, the earth is at the mercy of the elements. Soils seared into dust by drought are washed away by sudden downpours: eventually, it all ends up in the Missouri.

Today, much of the runoff from the Great Plains is trapped behind the series of dams that now regulate the river's progress far upstream. These deposits cause constant headaches for the Corps of Engineers. The amount of sand and silt carried by the current has also been reduced by nineteenth- and twentieth-century "channelization" works, which have straightened bends, dredged deep channels, and strengthened banks to assure a more even flow and easier navigation. Such projects have cut the overall length of the river by 72 miles and, more important for waterborne traffic, helped ease the sort of treacherous conditions of which Lewis and Clark complained. "The water excessively swift today," noted Clark on May 23, 1804. On June 5, the problem was a "very bad sand bar of several miles in extent." Floating logs and branches; eddying currents; concealed

Below: Today it is the picture of tranquillity, but here in what is now the Indian Cave State Park, outside Shubert, Nebraska, on July 14, 1804, the Expedition's keelboat came close to foundering in a storm.

shallows; unstable banks: the river could throw up any number of challenges—and did so every day. Forced to make their way against the current, without the assistance of engines or charts, Lewis and Clark and their men could have been under no illusions as to either the arduousness or the perils of the journey that lay before them. We easily forget how formidable an enemy the river could be to the Expedition: However convenient it may have seemed as a westward route, the Missouri was still a mysterious, powerful, and essentially ungovernable monster.

A great river is often taken as a symbol of eternity: Generations may come and go, but the river keeps on flowing. This is true, so far as it goes, yet the river's is a distinctly paradoxical sort of permanence, its continuity characterized by extraordinary instability. What we call the Missouri once ran far northward of its present course, draining away toward what is now Hudson Bay. Successive Ice Ages over the last two million years forced it to change its course. The encroaching ice sheets—the last of which is thought to have reached its greatest extent around 20,000 years ago—were up to a mile thick in places. Moving with colossal force, they pushed piles of rock and earth before them as they bulldozed their way steadily southward. These remained as ridges when the ice retreated and stood as an insurmountable barrier to the river, which was forced to find a new course south to the Gulf of Mexico.

Even then, however, the restless wanderings of the Missouri were by no means over. Rather than proceeding in a direct

line, any mature river tends to bend back and forth, or meander, as it makes its way along its open floodplain—a phenomenon that is not clearly understood but perhaps relates to the earth's rotation. Whatever its ultimate cause, the meandering effect is reinforced by the actions of the current itself, which scours away ceaselessly at its outside bends while depositing silt or sediment in the slacker reaches on the inside. Over years and centuries, the entire river may move sideways—sometimes drifting many hundreds of yards across its floodplain—with the occasional landslip, earthquake, or other cataclysm complicating the routine cycles of erosion and sedimentation. A time-lapse film of the lower Missouri down the millennia would show it in a condition of more or less constant flux, thrashing about like a fitful sleeper in an uncomfortable bed.

In the course of their preparations at Camp Dubois, Lewis and Clark had taken pains to question experienced Missouri trappers and traders about the river and its ways, yet for much of its length it remained an unknown quantity. That it held its hazards was only too obvious; that it was capricious only too clear—yet no easier corridor to the West was immediately apparent. The lands of the Louisiana Purchase and beyond were, to all intents and purposes, undeveloped wilderness, wholly untouched by civilization—at least as Americans and Europeans would understand that term. There were certainly no roads, and thus no possibility of taking wagons. Had glory alone been the expedition's object, a smaller band might have made the journey across country, traveling light, on foot and on horseback. Yet if such a party might have been able to plant a flag upon the Pacific shore, it could never

have conducted the sort of sustained program of scientific and ethnographic observation and research that had been key components in the project from its inception. Lewis and Clark were setting out to record practically everything they saw in this alien territory, and considerable quantities of equipment and instruments would be needed for this task. They would also have to be able to survive and fend for themselves in a wide variety of different environments—and they had to be armed against any threat, whether from wild animals or Native Americans. But even if none of these requirements had existed, another imperative demanded that the Corps of Discovery make its way by water, its reasoning spelled out in the President's "Instructions" to Captain Lewis:

"The object of your mission is to explore the Missouri River, and such principal stream of it as, by its course and communication with the waters of the Pacific Ocean, may offer the most direct and practicable communication across this continent, for the purposes of commerce."

If the West was to be opened up—not just for travel, also but for trade—some means of bulk transportation was going to be required: it was vital that the possibilities offered by the region's rivers should be explored. The Missouri was, accordingly, rather more than a means to an end: This great river was central to the whole purpose of the Expedition.

Above: *Re-created in modern replica, Camp Dubois, near Hartford, Illinois, was the base from which the Expedition set out on May 13, 1804. But this departure represented the culmination of many weeks of preparation on the ground: Lewis and Clark had been hard at work here since the previous December.*

UNDER WAY

The actual departure of the Expedition marked an end as well as a beginning, the culmination of months of planning and preparation. Captain **Clark's** journal entry for **May 13** gives a sense of the awesome logistics involved in an enterprise of this scale and significance—and of the doubts that still nagged him over whether, even now, his companions were adequately equipped for the challenges they were to face:

I dispatched an express this morning to Captain Lewis at St. Louis, all our provisions, goods and equipage on board of a boat of 22 oars, a large pirogue of 71 oars, a second pirogue of 6 oars, complete with sails, etc., etc. Men completed with powder cartridges and 100 balls each, all in health and readiness to set out. Boats and everything complete, with the necessary stores of provisions

BY WATER

The main objective set for the Corps of Discovery was to find a water route to the Pacific: The hope was that it would be able to make progress along one river or another just about all the way. Its three boats were, accordingly, essential items of equipment; without them, an expedition on such a scale could hardly have been conceived of. Biggest of all was the keelboat, believed to have been 55 feet long and 8 feet 6 inches wide; it would have weighed 7 tons empty, and been able to carry a 10-ton cargo. On the advice of experienced Missouri navigators, this load was concentrated toward the stern. This meant that the vessel's bow, riding high, could more readily clear the sort of "snags" in which the river abounded. Floating branches and other debris remain a hazard to river traffic even today. This boat, as Clark records, had twenty-two oars, but it also had a sail for when the winds were favorable; at other times it would have to be pushed along with poles, or even towed with a rope from the bank.

Had the "large pirogue" really had the seventy-one oars Clark says it did, it would have had to be crewed by almost twice as many men as the Corps of Discovery totaled! In fact, both these vessels were significantly shorter than the keelboat. The larger, "Red Pirogue," is believed to have been just over 41 feet in length, and the "White Pirogue" a couple of feet shorter than that. Imitations of the dugout canoes used for generations by Missouri Indians, these pirogues were flat bottomed and had no keel. This meant that, though less stable than the keelboat, and unable to carry much in the way of cargo, they were able to operate in much shallower water. As a result, they were invaluable for exploring little inlets, creeks, and tributaries along the way.

and such articles of merchandise as we thought ourselves authorized to procure—though not as much as I think necessary, for the multitude of Indians through which we must pass on our road across the continent.

Latitude 38°–55'–19"–6/10 North of equator
Longitude 89°–57'–45"–West of Greenwich

May 14, 1804

Rained the fore part of the day. I determined to go as far as St. Charles, a French village 7 leagues [21 miles] up the Missouri, and wait at that place until Captain Lewis could finish the business which he was obliged to attend to at St. Louis and join me by land from that place, 24 miles. By this movement I calculated that if any alterations in the loading of the vessels or other changes [should be] necessary, that they might be made at St. Charles. I set out at 4 o'clock p.m. in the presences of many of the neighboring inhabitants, and proceeded on under a gentle breeze up the Missouri to the upper point of the first island (4 miles) and camped on the island which is situated close on the right (or starboard) side, and opposite the mouth of a small creek called Coldwater. A heavy rain this afternoon.

Above: *The site at Pelican Island, where the Expedition spent the night of May 15, 1804.*
Opposite: *The sun rises over the Missouri—and over boats of the sort used by the Expedition, reconstructed to the dimensions given by Lewis and Clark.*

A ROUSING SEND-OFF

If Captain Clark's embarkation had taken place amid a flurry of practical concerns, his partner's journey to join him was an altogether more stately—almost ceremonial—affair. Though the Expedition's historic importance could still scarcely be guessed at, Americans understood that something out of the ordinary was about to take place, and St. Louis' social elite turned out to speed the travelers on their way. The ladies were left at home, in deference to the rugged terrain to be traversed and the unknown dangers to be faced in the course of the outing, but in the sendoff event their menfolk enjoyed every civilized amenity. As **Lewis** describes it in his journal for Sunday, **May 20**, his journey began with what amounted to a society picnic—a genteel parody of the epic adventure still to come:

The morning was fair, and the weather pleasant. At 10 o'clock a.m., agreeably to an appointment of the preceding day, I was joined by Captain Stoddard, Lieutenants Milford and Worrell, together with Messrs A. Chouteau, C. Gratiot, and many other respectable inhabitants of St. Louis, who had engaged to accompany me to the village of St. Charles. Accordingly, at 12 o'clock, after bidding an affectionate adieu to my hostess, that excellent woman the spouse of Mr. Peter Chouteau, and some of my fair friends of St. Louis, we set forward to that village in order to join my friend, companion and fellow laborer Captain William Clark, who had previously arrived at that place with the party destined for the discovery of the interior of the continent of North America. The first 5 miles of our route led through a beautiful, high, level and fertile prairie which encircles the town of St. Louis from NW to SE. The lands through which we then passed are somewhat broken, less fertile. The plains and woodlands are here indiscriminately interspersed until you arrive within three miles of the village when the woodland commences and continues to the Missouri. The latter is extremely fertile. At half after one p.m. our progress was interrupted by the near approach of a violent thunderstorm from the NW and concluded to take shelter in a little cabin hard by until the rain should be over. Accordingly, we alighted and remained about an hour and a half and regaled ourselves with a cold collation which we had taken the precaution to bring with us from St Louis.

"Set out at half past three o'clock under three cheers from the gentlemen on the bank...."

The clouds continued to follow each other in rapid succession, insomuch that there was but little prospect of its ceasing to rain this evening. As I had determined to reach St. Charles this evening, and knowing that there was now no time to be lost, I set forward in the rain. Most of the gentlemen continued with me: we arrived at half after six and joined Captain Clark; found the party in good health and spirits.

May 21, 1804 (Clark)

Set out at half past three o'clock under three cheers from the gentlemen on the bank and proceeded on to the head of the island (which is situated on the starboard side), 3 miles. Soon after we set out today, a hard wind from the west-southwest accompanied with a hard rain, which lasted with short intervals all night. Opposite our camp, a small creek comes in on the larboard [left, or port] side.

HARD GOING

May 23, 1806

We set out early, ran on a log and [were] detained one hour; proceeded the course of last night 2 miles to the mouth of a creek on the starboard side called Osage Woman's River [Femme Osage River], about 30 yards wide, opposite a large island and a settlement. On this creek 30 or 40 [American] families are settled.

Many people came to see us; we passed a large cave on the larboard side (called by the French the "Tavern")—about 120 feet wide, 40 feet deep and 20 feet high. Many different images are painted on the rock at this place: the Indians and French pay homage. Many names are wrote on the rock. Stopped about one mile above for Captain Lewis, who had ascended the cliffs which is at the said cave, 300 feet high, hanging over the waters. The water excessively swift today.

This evening we examined the arms and ammunition; found those men's arms in the pirogue in bad order. A fair evening. Captain Lewis near falling from the pinnnacles of rocks 300 feet; he caught at 20 feet.

May 24, 1804

Set out early; passed a very bad part of the river called the Devil's Race Ground: this is where the current sets against some projecting rocks for half a mile on the larboard side.

The swiftness of the current wheeled the boat, broke our tow-rope and was nearly over-setting the boat. All hands jumped out on the upper side and bore on that side until the sand washed from under the boat and wheeled on the next bank. By the time she wheeled a third time, got a rope fast to her stern and by the means of swimmers was carried to shore, and when her stern was down whilst in the act of swinging a third time into deep water near the shore, we returned to the island where we set out and ascended under the bank which I have just mentioned, as falling in.... This place I call the "retrograde" bend as we were obliged to fall back 2 miles.

May 25, 1804

Camped at the mouth of a creek called River a Chouritte [Riviere La Charrette], above a small French village of seven houses and as many families, settled at this place to be convenient to hunt, and trade with the Indians. The people at this village is poor, houses small; they sent us milk and eggs to eat.

The Expedition had at last settled into something of a routine, and it became possible to think of fine tuning some of its arrangements and procedures. On **May 26**, a new set of "detachment orders" was recorded in the Orderly Book, in response to the realities the Corps had found in its journey upriver:

Opposite: The Missouri River rolls majestically along past the foot of Tavern Bluff, where the Corps of Discovery pitched camp on the evening of May 23, 1804. Below: A fur-trading post from 1762, Fort Charrette, near Washington, Missouri, was abandoned in the 1840s after flooding, but has now been painstakingly restored as a Historic Village.

The commanding officers direct that the three squads under the command of Sergeants Floyd, Ordway and Pryor, heretofore forming two messes each, shall until further orders constitute three messes only, the same being altered and organized as follows....

Sergeant Charles Floyd

PRIVATES
Hugh McNeal
Patric Gass
Reubin Fields
John B. Thompson
John Newman
Richard Winsor
Francis Rivet
Joseph Fields

Sergeant John Ordway

PRIVATES
William Bratton
John Colter
Moses B. Reed
Alexander Willard
William Warner
Silas Goodrich
John Potts, and
Hugh Hall

Sergeant Nathaniel Pryor

PRIVATES
George Gibson
George Shannon
John Shields
John Collins
Joseph Whitehouse
Peter Wiser
Peter Crusat, and
Francis Labuche

The commanding officers further direct that the remainder of the detachment shall form two messes; and that the same be constituted as follows....

Patron, Baptist Dechamps

ENGAGÉS
Etienne Mabbauf
Paul Primaut
Charles Hébert
Baptist La Jeunesse
Peter Pinaut
Peter Roi, and
Joseph Collin

Corporal Richard Warvington

PRIVATES
Robert Frasier
John Boleye
John Dame
Beinezer Tuttle, and
Isaac White

Sergeant John Ordway will continue to issue the provisions and make the details for guard or other duty. The day after tomorrow lyed corn and grease will be issued to the party; the next day pork and flour; and the day following Indian meal and pork; and in conformity to that routine provisions will continue to be issued to the party until further orders. Should any of the messes prefer Indian meal to flour they may receive it accordingly—no pork is to be issued when we have fresh meat on hand.

Labuche and Crusat will man the larboard bow oar alternately, and the one not engaged at the oar will attend as the Bowsman, and when the attention of both these persons is necessary at the bow, their oar is to be manned by any idle hand on board.

MERIWETHER LEWIS, Captain

WM CLARK, Captain

June 5, 1804

Passed a projecting rock on which was painted a figure and a creek at 2 miles above called Little Manitou Creek, from the painted rock. This creek 20 yards wide on the larboard side. Passed a small creek on larboard side opposite a very bad sand bar of several miles in extent…here my servant York swam to the sand bar to gather greens for our dinner, and returned with a sufficient quantity [of] wild cresses or tongue grass. We passed up for 2 miles on the larboard side of this sand and was obliged to return, the water uncertain, the quicksand moving. We had a fine wind, but could not make use of it, our mast being broke.

Our scout discovered the fresh sign of about 10 Indians. I expect that those Indians are on their way to war, against the Osage nation. Probably they are the Saukees.

June 7, 1804

Set out early. Passed the head of the island opposite which we camped last night, and [took] breakfast at the mouth of a large creek on the south shore of 30 yards wide called Big Manitou.

Above: Fog swathes the waters and wooded banks of the Missouri, not far from Jefferson City. The Expedition stopped near here on the night of June 4, 1804. **Opposite:** *May 27 found the explorers at the point where the Gasconade joined the Missouri.*

A short distance above the mouth of this creek is several curious paintings and carving on the projecting rock of limestone inlaid with white, red and blue flint, of a very good quality. The Indians have taken of this flint great quantities. We landed at this inscription and found it a den of rattlesnakes: we

---

MASTERS OF ALL THEY SURVEYED

Though officially a detachment of the army, and organized accordingly, the Corps of Discovery was never regarded as being on a mission of military conquest. Yet it was an act of possession-taking, nevertheless—however peaceful its apparent intent, and however scientific the preoccupations of its leaders. The White Man of the early nineteenth century made the earth his own by taking its measure—literally: by measuring its dimensions, charting its positions, mapping it out, and reducing the "unruly wilderness" to "rational order." Hence Jefferson's original instructions to Lewis and Clark that "Beginning at the mouth of the Missouri, you will take observations of latitude and longitude, at all remarkable points …that they may with certainty be recognized hereafter."

From a navigational point of view, unmapped as it was, the landscape they were entering was as featureless as any open ocean—so Lewis and Clark used the seafarer's tools: the sextant and the chronometer (basically a sophisticated clock that could be relied upon to keep correct time). These enabled them to plot latitude (distance north of the equator) by measuring the angle the sun made with the horizon at the hour of noon, and to calculate longitude (east–west position) by recording the angles between the moon and certain stars at night or by measuring the difference between chronometer and local noon. By taking sightings on distant landmarks from different points, they could plot their positions with some accuracy, building up a basic map of the territories through which they traveled.

had not landed 3 minutes before three very large snakes was observed in the crevices of the rocks and killed. At the mouth of the last-mentioned creek, Captain Lewis took four or five men and went to some licks, or springs of salt water, from two to four miles up the creek, on [the] right side. The water of those springs are not strong—say from 4 to 600 gallons of water for a bushel of salt. Passed some small willow islands and camped at the mouth of a small river called Good Woman's River [Bonne Femme Creek, Boonville, Missouri]. This river is about 35 yards wide and said to be navigable for pirogues several leagues. Captain Lewis with 2 men went up the creek a short distance. Our hunters brought in three bear this evening, and informs that the country through which they passed from the last creek is fine, rich land, and well watered.

Above: Sunrise over the Missouri at the explorers' campsite on June 9, 1804. *Opposite:* The Corps celebrated July 4, 1804, in what is now the Lewis and Clark State Park, near Rushville, Missouri: Clark commented then on the river's richness in waterfowl.

AN UNEXPECTED THREAT

On **June 24**, just below Little Blue River, in Jackson County, Missouri, **Clark** had to intervene when the explorers' meat supply came under threat from an unexpected quarter:

"The current of this river comes with great velocity, rolling its sands into the Missouri...."

I joined the boat this morning at eight o'clock. I will only remark that during the time I lay on the sand waiting for the boat, a large snake swam to the bank immediately under the deer which was hanging over the water, and no great distance from it. I threw chunks and drove this snake off several times. I found that he was so determined on getting to the meat, I was compelled to kill him, the part of the deer which attracted this snake I think was the milk from the bag of the doe.

I observed great quantities of bear signs, where they had passed in all directions through the bottoms in search of mulberries, which were in great numbers in all the bottoms through which our party passed.

SALT LICK CITY

The salt springs the Expedition discovered would become the basis for a significant industry in the years that followed, after Nathan and Daniel Morgan Boone (sons of the more famous Daniel) went into partnership with James and Jesse Morrison in 1805. They boiled up brine in vast iron kettles, collecting the salt that encrusted the bottoms as the water evaporated off, and shipping it down river to St. Louis. There it was eagerly bought by the city's up-and-coming meat and tanning industries. A settlement grew up around the springs—though, within a generation, the Boones had lost their commercial advantage and been eclipsed by competitors. Today, "Boone's Lick" is a much-visited historic site.

A Frugal Feast

July 4 found the Expedition near what is now the all-American city of Atchison, Kansas, but which then seemed a very long way indeed from the territory of the United States, and without the wherewithal to celebrate with style. Instead, the men ate simply, and commemorated the occasion in a place name, as **Clark** explains:

We passed a creek twelve yards wide, on the larboard side, coming out of an extensive prairie reaching within two hundred yards of the river. As this creek has no name, and this being the Fourth of July, the day of the Independence of the United States, we called it "Fourth of July 1804 Creek." We dined on corn. Captain Lewis walked on shore above this creek and discovered a high mound from the top of which he had an extensive view. Three paths came together at the mound. We saw great numbers of goslings today which were nearly grown. The lake is clear and contains great quantities of fish and geese and goslings. This induced me to call it Gosling Lake. A small creek and several springs run into the lake on the east side from the hills. The land on that side is very good.

Rough Waters

July 21, 1804

At seven o'clock the wind lulled and it commenced raining; arrived at the lower mouth of the Great River Platt at ten o'clock.

This great river being much more rapid than the Missouri forces its current against the opposite shore. The current of this river comes with great velocity, rolling its sands into the Missouri, filling up its bed and compelling it to encroach on the starboard shore. We found great difficulty in passing around the sand at the mouth of this river. Captain Lewis and myself with six men in a pirogue went up this Great River Platt about two miles. Found the current very rapid, rolling over sands, passing through different channels, none of them more than five or six feet deep, about 900 yards wide at the mouth. I am told by one of our party who wintered two winters on this river that "it is much wider above, and does not rise more than five or six feet." [It] spreads very wide and from its rapidity and rolling sands cannot be navigated with boats or pirogues. The Indians pass this river with skin boats which is flat and will not turn over. The Otos, a small nation, reside on the south side ten leagues higher up.

July 22, 1804

Set out very early with a view of getting some situation above in time to take equal altitudes and take observations, as well as one calculated to make our party comfortable in a situation where they could receive the benefit of a shade.

This being a good situation and much nearer the Oto's town than the mouth of the Platt, we concluded to delay at this place a few days and send for some of the chiefs of that nation, to let them know of the change of government, the wishes of our government to cultivate friendship with them, the objects of our journey, and to present them with a flag and some small presents.

Some of our provisions in the French pirogue being wet, it became necessary to dry them a few days. Wind hard from northwest. Five deer killed today.

Nobody Home

July 25, 1804

Several hunters out today; at two o'clock Drewyer and Peter returned from the Oto village, and informed that no Indians were at their towns. They saw some fresh signs of a small party, but could not find them. In their route to the towns (which is about 18 miles west), they passed through an open prairie, passed Papillon or Butterfly Creek and a small, beautiful river which runs into the Platt a little below the town called "Corne de Cerf" or Elkhorn River.

July 28, 1804

Drewyer brought in a Missouri Indian which he met with hunting in the prairie. This Indian is one of the few remaining of that nation, and lives with the Otos, his camp about four miles from the river. He informs that the "great gang" of the nation were hunting the buffalo in the plains. His party was small, consisting only of about 20 lodges.

"…they put their wives and children to death with a view of their all going together to some better country."

On **August 2**, a party of Oto at last appeared, with M. Fairfong—a Frenchman who had lived among them for several years and now acted as their interpreter. They were made welcome, and a meeting arranged for the following day. As **Clark** notes in his journal, the U.S. emissaries went to some trouble to put on an impressive show for them, parading in full-dress uniform—a display not just of friendship but of strength, and a certain severity:

Made up a small present for those people in proportion to their consequence, also a package with a medal to accompany a speech for the grand chief. After breakfast we collected those Indians under an awning of our mainsail; in presence of our party paraded and delivered a long speech to them expressive of our journey, the wishes of our government, some advice to them and directions how they were to conduct themselves.…

Those chiefs all delivered a speech, acknowledging their approbation to the speech and promising to pursue the advice and directions given them; that they were happy to find that they had fathers which might be depended on etc.

We gave them a canister of powder and delivered a few presents to the whole.… After Captain Lewis's shooting the air gun a few shots (which astonished those natives), we set out and proceeded on five miles on a direct line, passed a point on the starboard shore and around a large sand bar on the larboard shore and camped on the upper point. The mosquitoes excessively troublesome this evening. Great appearance of wind and rain to the northwest; we prepare to receive it.

Below: "At 7 o'clock" on July 7, the Expedition's craft were caught by "a violent gust of wind," with rain to follow, here at French Bottom, near today's town of St. Joseph, Missouri.

A PROSPECT OF PELICANS

While little of **Lewis's** journal survives for the first ten months of the Expedition, one passage that does is his **August 8** account of the Missouri's pelicans:

This day after we had passed the River Souix [sic], as called by Mr. Mackary (or as is more properly called the Stone River) I saw a great number of feathers floating down the river. Those feathers had a very extraordinary appearance, as they appeared in such quantities as to cover pretty generally sixty or seventy yards of the breadth of the river. For three miles after I saw those feathers continue to run in that manner: we did not perceive from whence they came. At length we were surprised by the appearance of a flock of pelican at rest on a large sand bar attached to a small island, the number of which would if estimated appear almost incredible.

A BADGER

"Joseph Fields killed and brought in an animal called by the French 'Brarowe,'" reports Clark in his journal for July 30. "This animal burrows in the ground and feeds on flesh (prairie dogs), bugs and vegetables. His shape and size is that of a beaver; his head, mouth, etc., is like a dog's with short ears; his tail and hair like that of a groundhog, and longer, and lighter.... His legs are short and, when he moves, just sufficient to raise his body above the ground. He is of the bear species." He is not really, of course, for all Clark's confidence: A member of the mustelid family, the badger is actually a relative of the polecat and the mink.

IN SEARCH OF THE OMAHA

Like the Oto, Captain **Clark** reports, the Omaha were out on the plains when the Corps came calling—but there was more to their wandering ways, he suggests, than the call of the buffalo:

August 14, 1804

The men sent to the Mahar [Omaha] town last evening has not returned. We conclude to send a spy to know the cause of their delay. At about twelve o'clock the party returned and informed us that they could not find the Indians, nor any fresh sign: those people have not returned from their buffalo hunt. Those people having no houses, no corn or anything more than the graves of their ancestors to attach them to the old village, continue in pursuit of the buffalo longer than others who has greater attachments to their native village. The ravages of the smallpox (which swept off 400 men, and women and children in proportion) has reduced this nation not exceeding 300 men and left them to the insults of their weaker neighbors, which before was glad to be on friendly terms with them. I am told when this fatal malady was among them they carried their frenzy to very extraordinary length, not only of burning their village, but they put their wives and children to death with a view of their all going together to some better country. They bury their dead on the top of high hills and raise mounds on top of them. The cause or way those people took the smallpox is uncertain; the most probable, from some other nation by means of a war party.

SUMMIT CONFERENCE

At last, on **August 18**, Lewis and **Clark** met some members of the Oto and Missouri peoples—decimated by smallpox, the two depleted nations had effectively merged. For the first time, but by no means the last, the Americans found themselves being asked to mediate local enmities. While, to the white men, the message they brought the Indians from their "great father" (President Jefferson) was a clear assertion of American authority, their welcome was clearly not as conquerors but as arbitrators:

We had some talk with the chiefs about the origin of the war between them and the Omahas etc., etc. It commenced in this way…two of the Missouri tribe residing with the Otos went to the Omahas to steal horses. They killed them both, which was a cause of revenge on the part of the Missouris and Otos. They also brought war on themselves nearly in the same way with the Pania [Pawnee] Loups, and they are greatly in fear of a just revenge from the Panias for taking their corn from the Pania towns in

A SCIENTIST'S EYE

If Lewis's delight in nature is clear, he never let his enthusiasm impede his pursuit of scientific exactitude. Having marveled at the pelicans' number and beauty, he promptly shot one, measured it meticulously, and recorded his description:

The beak is a whiteish yellow, the underpart connected to a bladder-like pouch. This pouch is connected to both sides of the lower beak and extends down on the underside of the neck and terminates in the stomach. This pouch is uncovered with feathers, and is formed of two skins, the one on the inner and the other on the outer side, a small quantity of flesh and strings of which the animal has at pleasure the power of moving or drawing in such manner as to contract it at pleasure. In the present subject, I measured this pouch and found its contents five gallons of water. The feet are webbed large and of a yellow color. It has four toes; the hinder toe is longer than in most aquatic fowls, the nails are black, not sharp, and an inch in length. The plumage generally is white; the feathers are thin compared with the swan, goose or most aquatic fowls and has but little or no down on the body.

SMALLPOX

The experience of the Omaha, Oto, and Missouri peoples was unfortunately by no means unusual—several tribes were swept away completely by smallpox epidemics. Epidemiologists estimate, indeed, that in every region of the Americas, 90 percent of the native population was carried off by disease within a century of the white man's arrival. Claims of genocide are surely misplaced (though there were examples of infected blankets and clothing being given to Indians as a matter of deliberate policy), yet the effects were no less devastating for being unintended.

Native Americans were uniquely vulnerable, having lived in isolation for so long—and from having been descended from a comparatively small number of common ancestors. Millennia of migration, trade, and war had made Eurasia a vigorous melting pot for disease—thus strengthening immune systems—whilst generations of intermarriage had assured the existence of a much larger gene pool. It was, therefore, unusual for even the most virulent outbreaks to afflict such a large proportion of the European population: The Black Death of the fourteenth century killed "only" a third of Europe's people.

Smallpox was feared even so; its fevers, headaches, and joint pains being nothing compared to the maddening irritation of the pustular blisters (the actual "pox") that spread across the skin—and which disfigured the faces of survivors for the rest of their lives. In parts of Europe, it claimed the sort of death rates not seen since the plagues of medieval times. Native Americans were powerless against it.

their absence hunting this summer. Captain Lewis's birthday: the evening was closed with an extra gill of whiskey and a dance until eleven o'clock.

August 19, 1804

Prepared a small present for the chiefs and warriors present. The main chief breakfast[ed] with us and begged for a sun glass. Those people are all naked, covered only with breech clouts, blankets or buffalo robes, the flesh side painted of different colors and figures. At ten o'clock we assembled the chiefs and warriors, nine in number, under an awning, and Captain Lewis explained the speech sent to the nation.… The three chiefs and all the men or warriors made short speeches approving the advice and counsel their great father

"Those people are all naked, covered only with breech clouts, blankets or buffalo robes…"

had sent them, and concluded by giving themselves some credit for their acts.

We then brought out the presents…and gave all some small articles and 8 carats of tobacco. We gave one small medal to one of the chiefs, and a certificate to the others of their good intentions.…

We gave them a dram and broke up the council. The chiefs requested we would not leave them this evening. We determined to set out early in the morning. We showed them many curiosities, and the airgun, which they were most astonished at. Those people begged much for whiskey. Sergeant Floyd is taken very bad all at once with a bilious colic. We attempt to relieve him without success as yet; he gets worse, and we are much alarmed at his situation.

August 20, 1804

Sergeant Floyd much weaker and no better. Made Mr. Fairfong the interpreter a few presents, and the Indians a canister of whiskey. We set out under a

Opposite, above: The site of an Omaha burial ground after the smallpox epidemic that had ravaged the area before the explorers' arrival in August 1804.

gentle breeze from the southeast and proceeded on very well. Sergeant Floyd as bad as he can be—no pulse, and nothing will stay a moment on his stomach or bowels. Passed two islands on the starboard side and at the first bluff on the starboard side sergeant Floyd died with a great deal of composure. Before his death he said to me, "I am going away. I want you to write me a letter." We buried him on the top of the bluff ½ mile below a small river to which we gave his name. He was buried with the Honors of War, much lamented. A cedar post with the name "Sergeant C. Floyd died here 20th of August 1804" was fixed at the head of his greave. This man at all times gave us proofs of his firmness and determined resolution to do service to his country and honor to himself. After paying all the honor to our deceased brother we camped in the mouth of Floyd's River, about 30 yards wide. A beautiful evening.

AN ABUNDANT HAUL

Some sense of the sheer bounty of the wilderness in which the expedition now found itself can be had from Clark's records of two fishing trips made from their Camp "three miles northeast of the Omaha village" on August 15 and 16:

I went with ten men to a creek dammed by the beavers about halfway to the village. With some small willows and bark we made a drag and hauled up the creek, and caught 318 fish of different kind, i.e. Pike, Bass, Salmon, Perch, Red Horse, Small Cat….Captain Lewis took 12 men and went to the pond and creek between camp and the old village and caught upwards of 800 fine fish: 79 Pike; 8 Salmon resembling Trout; 1 Rock; 1 Flatback; 127 Buffalo and Red Horse; 4 Bass and 490 Cats, with many small Silverfish.

THE HILL OF DEMONS

The Corps of Discovery represented a nation which, while it had broken free from its European masters, had been founded upon the principles of the European Enlightenment of the eighteenth century. So scornful had the Founding Fathers been of any sort of "superstition" that they had refused to recognize the authority even of the longest-established Christian churches. It was only logical, therefore—graceless though it may seem from the perspective of the present day—that Lewis and Clark should wish to demonstrate their disdain for what they saw as primitive native beliefs. In a plain beside the White Stone (Vermillion) River, says **Clark**, in his journal for **August 24**,

A high hill is situated, and appears of a conic form, and by the different nations of Indians in this quarter is supposed to be the residence of devils. That they are in human form with remarkable large

heads, and about 18 inches high; that they are very watchful, and are armed with sharp arrows with which they can kill at a great distance. They are said to kill all persons who are so hardy as to attempt to approach the hill. They state that tradition informs them that many Indians have suffered by those little people, and among others three Omaha men fell a sacrifice to their merciless fury not many years since. So much do the Omaha, Sioux, Oto and other neighboring nations believe this fable that no consideration is sufficient to induce them to approach the hill.

August 25, 1804

A cloudy morning. Captain Lewis and myself concluded to go and see the mound which was viewed with such terror by all the different nations in this quarter.... The regular form of this hill would in some measure justify a belief that it owed its origin to the hand of man; but as the earth and loose pebbles and other substances of which it was composed bore an exact resemblance to the steep ground which border on the creek in its neighborhood we concluded it was most probably the production of nature.

The only remarkable characteristic of this hill, admitting it to be a natural production, is that it is insulated or separated a considerable distance from any other, which is very unusual in the natural order or disposition of the hills.

The surrounding plains is open, void of timber, and level to a great extent, hence the wind, from whatever quarter it may blow, drives with unusual force over the naked plains and against this hill.

*Opposite: The "Spirit Mound," near Vermillion, South Dakota, scaled by a skeptical Lewis and Clark on August 25, 1804. **Left:** Atop his grave near Sioux City, Iowa, a modern monument commemorates the work of War Eagle (c.1785–1851) for peace between Native Americans and white newcomers to the region.*

The insects of various kinds are thus involuntarily driven to the mound by the force of the wind, or fly to its leeward side for shelter. The small birds whose food they are consequently resort in great numbers to this place in search of them....

One evidence which the Indians give for believing this place to be the residence of some unusual spirits is that they frequently discover a large assemblage of birds about this mound. [That] is in my opinion a sufficient proof to produce in the savage mind a confident belief of all the properties which they ascribe it.

FLOYD'S BLUFF

Sergeant Floyd was to be a traveler even in death; by the late 1850s, the bluff on which he was buried was slowly being eroded by Missouri floods, and it began to be feared that his remains might be lost forever. They were therefore carefully exhumed and moved about 200 yards to the east for reburial in the base of a purpose-built memorial. The stately stone obelisk rising 100 feet tall still stands atop Floyd's Bluff, overlooking what is now a part of South Sioux City.

THE YANKTON SIOUX

The Expedition's arrival at the mouth of the James River on August 25 marked their entrance into the territory of the Yankton Sioux. A tribe of the larger Lakota group (itself, as Clark points out, a subdivision of the Dakota nation), the Yankton conformed to what has now become a conventional stereotype of the Native American. Their appearance certainly impressed their visitors, as **Clark** confided in his journal entry for **August 29**:

The Sioux's camps are handsome, of a conic form, covered with buffalo robes painted different colors, and all compact and handsomely arranged. Covered all round, an open part in the center for the fire.... Each lodge has a place for cooking detached. The lodges contain from ten to fifteen persons.

August 30, 1804

The Sioux is a stout, bold-looking people, the young men handsome and well-made. The greater part of them make use of bows and arrows; some few fusils [muskets] I observe among them. Notwithstanding they live by the bow and arrow, they do not shoot so well as the northern Indians. The warriors are very much decorated with paint, porcupine quills

and feathers; large leggings and moccasins; all with buffalo robes of different colors. The squaws wore petticoats and a white buffalo robe with the black hair turned back over their necks and shoulders.

August 31, 1804

I took a vocabulary of the Sioux language, and the answer to a few queries such as referred to their situation, trade, number, war, etc., etc. This nation is divided into 20 tribes, possessing separate interests. Collectively, they are numerous—say, from 2 to 3,000 men. Their interests are so unconnected that some bands are at war with nations with which other bands are on the most friendly terms. This great nation who the French has given the nickname of "Sioux" call themselves "Dakota."

Above, main picture: A dog hovers while Dakota Sioux cut meat and hang it up on poles to dry. **Inset:** *"Invocation, Sioux"—a spiritual scene recorded by Curtis in 1907.* **Opposite:** *The War Dance of the Sioux, as depicted in an 1890 illustration. White America admired and distrusted the Dakota in equal measure.*

WHO WERE THE SIOUX?

The name Sioux was, as Clark was aware 200 years ago, a foreign imposition for a people more accurately referred to as the Dakota. Even this, however, oversimplifies the reality. The word "Dakota" itself means "ally"—which implies an association of different peoples rather than a single nation as such. Clark himself noted that the "Sioux" comprised twenty different tribes, each of which, he pointed out, possessed "separate interests." (So separate were those interests, indeed, that those he met could name no more than twelve groups of the supposed twenty: the Dakota themselves seemed to him to have been hazy about the exact composition of their nation.) There are, in fact, three main groups: the Dakota proper, the Lakota, and the Nakota. To make matters more confusing for outsiders, the word Lakota is also sometimes used as a blanket term for the grouping as a whole.

Hence the continuing appeal—for outsiders at least—of the handy catch-all title, "the Sioux"; but the name is understandably rejected by the people themselves. The French term takes its origin from the word "Nadowe-is-iw," which means "snake" or "enemy" in the tongue of the Anishinabe. That these longstanding foes of the Dakota should have used such language is natural enough, of course—but it is unfortunate that so hostile a name should have stuck so doggedly.

The Corps of Discovery came across two main groups in the course of their travels. The Yankton Sioux, whom they found by the James River, belonged to the Nakota group, and they would meet the Teton Lakota a few weeks later, when they ventured westward onto the Great Plains.

THE GREAT PLAINS

✸ ❖ ✸

*"This scenery, already rich, pleasing
and beautiful, was still farther
heightened by immense herds of buffalo,
deer, elk and antelope, which we saw
in every direction…"*

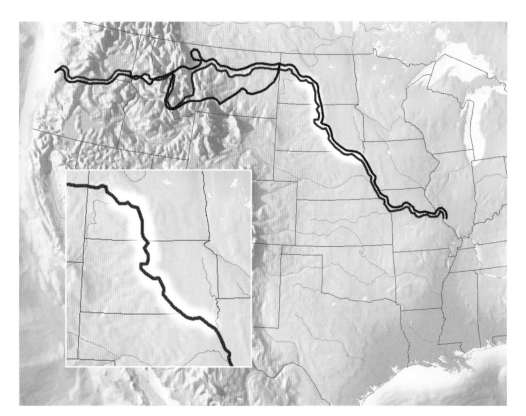

Opposite: *The Missouri River, the Expedition's highway to the unknown, stretches away above Fort Mandan, North Dakota. More rugged than the name implies, the terrain of the Great Plains made for difficult traveling: with all its hazards, the river offered by far the quicker and the safer route.*

U p to this point the Corps of Discovery had been following the twists and turns of the river through predominantly wooded country. Now it was striking out across the open grasslands of the Great Plains. Running the length of the North American continent from Saskatchewan south to Texas, this high plateau slopes imperceptibly westward to the foothills of the Rocky Mountains. Today, this territory has apparently been tamed, its rolling vastness fenced and plowed, its soils the basis for one of the richest agricultural regions of the modern world. Yet, even now, the Great Plains could hardly be described as a hospitable landscape; an unmistakable hint of the old wildness still remains. The sheer scale of the scene is awesome, for one thing: that endless sea of grass, that overarching sky, are enough to send an agoraphobic thrill through the most experienced outdoor traveler. Raw winds rush unimpeded across these empty spaces, bringing cruel blizzards in winter, and lacerating dust storms in the aridity of the summer months. Historical memory, meanwhile, lends a note of bleakness all of its own, for it was on this stage that the tragedy of the Plains Indians was enacted.

Old stereotypes die hard, perhaps especially those that have been painstakingly established with the best of motives. While today's attitudes toward the Plains Indians of this era are infinitely more benign than those that prevailed among the white settlers of the time, they arguably come no nearer to acknowledging the full complexity of those societies, which were swept away by the remorseless expansion of the white man's culture. If the supposed "state of nature" in which they once lived saw the Native Americans virtually dismissed as subhuman "savages," many now elevate them as inspired possessors of a kind of mystic wisdom. The second perception may be far more flattering than the first, but ultimately perhaps does no greater justice to the realities experienced by a group of peoples who had lives and histories all their own. The destructive role of white civilization—though undeniable—is often oversimplified, too: the story of the West is far less clear-cut, and far more interesting, than we tend to imagine.

One could go as far as saying that what seems to us to be the iconic image of the Native American—the nomadic buffalo hunter—could never have existed had it not been for the intervention of the white man. For while Indians had always ventured out onto the open prairies from the cultivated areas or wooded slopes of the Missouri valley, they had never been able to kill buffalo in sufficient numbers for the animal to form the basis of their lifeways. The buffalo may have been the apex of many tribes' economic existence, but buffalo hunting on foot could not constitute a mode of existence in itself. The white man's part in constructing the culture of

Below: Three Sioux make their way on horseback across the Badlands of South Dakota, photographed by Curtis around 1910.

the Plains was crucial, even if it was indirect, for that culture could never have developed without the additional speed, range, and endurance provided by the horse. A native of Eurasia, where it seems to have been domesticated around 4,000 years ago, this animal had been entirely absent from the Americas before the arrival of the Spanish. Its use among Native Americans did not become widespread until the middle of the seventeenth century—and even then it was mainly employed as a pack animal. Only by slow degrees did the practice of riding become well established and extend into the continent's interior, reaching northern areas of the Great Plains by around 1750. The superlative horsemanship of the Plains Indians is certainly no myth, yet neither was it rooted in what we might see as a longstanding "tradition." By the time of Lewis and Clark, the practice was only two to three generations old, as indeed was the whole way of life that had been made possible by the coming of the horse.

The westward stride of the white man's empire had been anticipated by the expansion of native peoples onto the Great Plains—for all the now-legendary "Plains Indians" were, in fact, comparative newcomers. The Cheyenne, for example, had hunted, trapped, and gathered nuts and berries in the deep woods of Minnesota before moving west around the end of the seventeenth century. For a time they took up farming, subsisting on the usual trinity of corn, beans, and squashes, with annual forays out onto the prairie after the migrating buffalo. Only gradually in the generations that followed did they abandon their settled existence for that of the nomadic buffalo hunter on the high plains. Key to their success in this new venture, their steadily improving horsemanship also equipped them well as warriors; and the adoption of the gun, obtained from European traders, made them even more formidable. In time, they would strike an alliance with the Teton Lakota, perhaps the most celebrated "Plains Indians" of all—though they, too, were recent arrivals from the woods to the east of the Missouri.

The large-scale movement of peoples cannot but have a destabilizing effect: the Great Plains themselves still had the feel of a region "up for grabs," while the repercussions of this migration were felt indirectly in intertribal tensions farther

Above: *Built for the Cheyenne Sun Dance—and photographed by Curtis, around 1910—this lodge is the typical tepee in everything but scale.*

Above: *Circular mounds are all that remains of the old Mandan village at Double Dutch, near Bismarck, North Dakota, abandoned a century before the Corps of Discovery came this way.*

afield to the north and east. Sharply exacerbating the instability, there had been the impact of smallpox epidemics—another indirect consequence of the coming of the Europeans. But the chosen lifestyle of the Plains Indians also had a bearing on the situation. Romantically carefree as it may seem, the life of the nomad has always been precarious: Open country never quite seems to give human communities all the things that they require. The warlike reputations of so many nomadic peoples—from the Cheyenne and Sioux to the fearsome Huns and Mongols of Eurasia—have stemmed from precisely this persistent pressure to make up the deficiencies of their lifestyles. When nomads have a surplus they may trade, but failing that they must take what they need by force. Aggression is thus part and parcel of the nomadic life: There was room for very few such societies, even in an arena as vast as the Great Plains.

Life on the Great Plains was thus a great deal more complicated than the cliché would have it; the regional economy a great deal more sophisticated than we may assume. Trade between farmers and nomads had quickly become a major activity for both communities, while both were quick to respond to the overtures of a new breed of independent traders representing European companies. The notion that Lewis and Clark were stepping into a beautiful virgin land, untouched by human evil, unsullied by commerce, could hardly have been farther from the truth. At every stage of their journey across the Great Plains they found themselves asked to arbitrate in acrimonious disputes between neighboring groups, to bear messages of peace or warnings of war from one community to the next. The old fantasy of European culture, that of the white explorer being welcomed as a god, never showed the slightest sign of being realized in the case of Lewis and Clark. It remains striking, though, how often and eagerly their coming was seized upon by peoples caught in seemingly irresolvable enmities; their status as outsiders making them revered, if not as deities then as "honest brokers." Despite their first-hand experience of all this confusion and conflict, they seem to some extent to have held on to their idealizing sense of the Great Plains as a land of natural purity and timeless innocence.

After two months traversing the open plains and encountering its inhabitants, animal as well as human, the explorers found that ice was beginning to impede their progress upriver, so they looked for suitable winter quarters. They set up camp north of present-day Bismarck, North Dakota, near a number of Mandan and Hidatsa villages, naming their temporary home "Fort Mandan."

Left: Around an empty hearth, the everyday artifacts of a vanished domesticity are poignantly displayed at the Knife River Indian Villages National Historic Site at Stanton, North Dakota.

Below: Expedition members may have seen just this sort of South Dakota sunset when they camped here September 16–18, 1804. Today, though, the Missouri forms a lake here—Francis Case—held back by the Fort Randall Dam.

A FORAY ASHORE

"Having for many days past confined myself to the boat," wrote **Lewis** in his journal for **September 17**,

"This scenery, already rich, pleasing and beautiful, was still farther heightened by immense herds of buffalo, deer, elk and antelope, which we saw in every direction feeding on the hills and plains."

I determined to devote this day to amuse myself on shore with my gun and view the interior of the country between the river and Corvus [Crow] Creek. Accordingly, before sunrise I set out with six of my best hunters, two of whom I dispatched to the lower side of Corvus Creek, two with orders to hunt the bottoms and woodland on the river, while I retained two others to accompany me in the intermediate country. One quarter of a mile in rear of our camp which was situated in a fine open grove of cotton wood past a grove of plum trees loaded with fruit and now ripe. [I] observed but little difference between this fruit and that of a similar kind common to the Atlantic states. The trees are smaller and more thickly set. This forest of plum trees garnish a plain about 20 feet more elevated than that on which we were encamped; this plain extends back about a mile to the foot of the hills one mile distant and to which it is gradually ascending. This plain extends with the same breadth from the creek below to the distance of near three miles above parallel with the river, and it is entirely occupied by the burrows of the barking squirrel; this animal appears here in infinite numbers and the shortness and verdure of grass gave the plain the appearance throughout its whole extent of beautiful bowling-green in fine order.... A great number of wolves of the small kind, hawks and some polecats were to be seen. I presume that those animals feed on this squirrel.

[We] found the country in every direction for about three miles intersected with deep ravines and steep irregular hills of 100 to 200 feet high; at the tops of these hills the country breaks off as usual into a fine level plain extending as far as the eye can

Above: A red-tailed hawk of the type that Lewis may have seen, September 17. Right: Crow Creek, South Dakota, where the Expedition camped September 18–20, 1804, has now been flooded by the waters of the Big Bend Dam.

reach. From this plain I had an extensive view of the river below, and the irregular hills which border the opposite sides of the river and creek. The surrounding country had been burnt about a month before and young grass had now sprung up to height of 4 inches presenting the live green of the spring; to the west a high range of hills stretched across the country from north to south and appeared distant about 20 miles; they are not very extensive as I could plainly observe their rise and termination. No rock appeared on them and the sides were covered with verdure similar to that of the plains. This scenery, already rich, pleasing and beautiful, was still farther heightened by immense herds of buffalo, deer, elk and antelope, which we saw in every direction feeding on the hills and plains. I do not think I exaggerate when I estimate the number of buffalo which could be comprehended at one view to amount to 3,000.

DOG, RAT, OR SQUIRREL?

"Ground Rat," "Prairie Dog," "Barking Squirrel": Lewis and Clark use all these names for a creature that is, admittedly, difficult to categorize. Naturalists have settled for the title of "black-tailed prairie dog" for *Cynomys ludovicianus*, a ground-dwelling rodent that lives in often extensive colonies across the Great Plains. Lewis several times notes complexes of burrows that

sprawl across the open grassland like small cities. "We poured into one of the holes five barrels of water without filling it," he reports at one point, going on to describe the unfortunate occupant in more detail:

Those animals are about the size of a small squirrel; shorter and thicker, the head much resembling a squirrel in every respect, except the ears which is shorter, his tail like a ground squirrel which they shake and whistle when alarmed, the toe nails long. They have fine fur and the longer hairs is gray.

THE BISON ECONOMY

We have no reason to think that Lewis was exaggerating when he claimed to see 3,000 bison "at one view": With an overall population of around 60 million, a herd this size would have been entirely unexceptional. There is an unmistakable air of Eden about the South Dakota scene he encounters on his excursion: the bounty of nature is to be seen in everything from plums to polecats, from prairie dogs to deer. And all untouched by human presence—or so, at least, it must have seemed at first sight, though Lewis would come to learn how far such "natural" richness underpinned an important human economy.

No species was more vital in this regard than the buffalo or bison: For the native peoples of the Plains, it was the most vital of resources. Not only could its meat be cooked and eaten fresh, or preserved with fat and berries as "pemmican," but its hides could be used (with or without fur) for clothing, bedding or for making tepees. Its bones were invaluable in making tools, its hair and sinews in sewing or making bowstrings; its hooves were boiled down to make glue, and even its dung could be burned as fuel.

The bison thus provided the basis for a stable economy on which, in turn, rested a rich and enduring Indian culture: Only with white settlement would this balance be disturbed. If the advent of the gun made only a marginal difference, the enclosure of vast tracts for ranching and farming did far more damage, barring the natural highways the herds had followed in their migrations for untold centuries. In white men's eyes not a resource but a pest, the bison was hunted down in vast numbers; countless more were killed to feed the builders of the western railroads. It has been suggested that the slaughter was actually part of a policy of "cultural genocide"—with the buffalo gone, a whole way of life was destroyed. By the turn of the twentieth century, the great bison herds were history, and the species neared extinction. However, thanks to the National Parks and protection programs, today there are sustainable managed herds, numbering some 350,000 head of buffalo.

AN UNEQUAL STRUGGLE

Both as sportsman and scientist, **Lewis** saw the antelope as a challenge: "my object was if possible to kill a female antelope, having already procured a male." To this end, he and his companions had "various windings in pursuit of several herds" they had sighted, but, as things were to turn out, to no avail (**September 17**).

We found the antelope extremely shy and watchful insomuch that we had been unable to get a shot at them; when at rest they generally select the most elevated point in the neighborhood, and as they are watchful and extremely quick of sight and their sense of smelling very acute it is almost impossible to approach them within gunshot; in short they will frequently discover and flee from you at the distance of three miles.

I had this day an opportunity of witnessing the agility and the superior fleetness of this animal which was to me really astonishing. I had pursued and twice surprised a small herd of seven. In the first instance they did not discover me distinctly and therefore did not run at full speed, though they took care before they rested to gain an elevated point where it was impossible to approach them under cover, except in one direction, and that happened to be in the direction from which the wind blew towards them. Bad as the chance to approach them was, I made the best of my way toward them, frequently peeping over the ridge with which I took care to conceal myself from their view, the male, of which there was but one, frequently circled the summit of the hill on which the females stood in a group, as if to look out for the approach of danger. I got within about 200 paces of them when they smelled me and fled; I gained the top of the eminence on which they stood as soon as possible, from whence I had an extensive view of the country: the antelopes which had disappeared in a steep ravine now appeared at the distance of about three miles on the side of a ridge…. So soon had these antelopes gained the distance at which they had again appeared to my view I doubted at first that they were the same that I had just surprised, but my doubts soon vanished when I beheld the rapidity of their flight along the ridge before me. It appeared rather the rapid flight of birds than the motion of quadrupeds. I think I can safely venture the assertion that the speed of this animal is equal if not superior to that of the finest blooded courser.

"It appeared rather the rapid flight of birds than the motion of quadrupeds."

Above: The pronghorn antelope, whose "agility and … superior fleetness" so astonished Captain Lewis. The animal is believed to have evolved this extraordinary ability to run at high speed so as to be able to escape the now-extinct American cheetah.

THE TETON SIOUX

"At half past one o'clock this morning," recorded **Clark** in his journal for **September 21**,

The sandbar on which we camped began to undermine and give way, which alarmed the sergeant on guard; the motion of the boat awakened me. I got up and by the light of the moon observed that the sand had given away both above and below our camp and was falling in fast. I ordered all hands on as quick as possible and pushed off. We had pushed off but a few minutes before the bank under which the boat and pirogues lay gave way, which would certainly have sunk both pirogues. By the time we made the opposite shore our camp fell in. We made a second camp for the remainder of the night and at daylight proceeded on to the gouge of this great bend.

We saw some camps and tracks of the Sioux which appear to be old—three or four weeks.

September 23, 1804

The river is nearly straight for a great distance … past a creek on the south shore 16 yards wide we call Reuben Creek as Reuben Fields found it…. Three Sioux boys came to us, swam the river and informed us that the band of Sioux called the Tetons of 80 lodges were camped at the next creek above, and 60 lodges more a short distance above. We gave those boys two carats of tobacco to carry to their chiefs, with directions to tell them that we would speak to them tomorrow.

September 24, 1804

We prepared some clothes and a few medals for the chiefs of the Teton's bands of Sioux which we expect to see today at the next river; observe a great deal of stone on the sides of the hills on the south shore. We saw one hare today. Prepared all things for action in case of necessity. Our pirogue went to the island for the meet. Soon after the man on shore ran up the bank and reported that the Indians had stolen the horse. We soon after met 5 Indians, and anchored out some distance and spoke to them; informed them we were friends,

and wished to continue so but were not afraid of any Indians. Some of their young men had taken the horse sent by their great father for their chief and we would not speak to them until the horse was returned to us again.

September 25, 1804

A fair morning, the wind from the southeast. All well, raised a flagstaff and made an awning or shade on a sandbar in the mouth of Teton River, for the purpose of speaking with the Indians under. The boat crew on board at 70 yards' distance from the bar. The five Indians which we met last night continued; about 11 o'clock the first and second chiefs came. We gave them some of our provisions to eat; they gave us great quantities of meat, some of which was spoiled. We feel much at a loss for the want of an interpreter: the one we have can speak but little.

Met in council at 12 o'clock, and after smoking, agreeable to the usual custom, Captain Lewis proceeded to deliver a speech which we were obliged to curtail for want of a good interpreter. All our party paraded; gave a medal to the Grand Chief ....

Invited those Chiefs on board to show them our boat and such curiosities as was strange to them. We gave them ¼ a glass of whiskey which they appeared to be very fond of. [They] sucked the bottle after it was out and soon began to be troublesome—one, the second chief, assuming drunkenness as a cloak for his rascally intentions. I went with those chiefs (which left the boat with great reluctance) to shore with a view of reconciling those men to us. As soon as I landed the pirogue, three of their

Opposite, below: A Teton Sioux performing the "Vision Cry," a chanting and fasting ceremony, photographed by Curtis, 1907. Below and opposite, above: "The Offering": A Teton Sioux with pipe and bison skull (opposite) and Slow Bull (below, with two companions) perform the rituals of the Hu Kalawa Pi *ceremony, as recorded by Curtis in 1907.*

men seized the cable of the pirogue, the chief's soldier hugged the mast, and the second chief was very insolent both in words and gestures … declaring I should not go on, stating he had not received presents sufficient from us. His gestures were of such a personal nature I felt myself compelled to draw my sword. At this motion Captain Lewis ordered all under arms in the boat, those with me also showed a disposition to defend themselves and me; the Grand Chief then took hold of the rope and ordered the young warriors away. I felt myself warm and spoke in very positive terms.

FIRST IMPRESSIONS

The explorers had got off on the wrong foot with the Teton Sioux on their first meeting. Within a couple of days, though, everyone was in a much better mood. Even so, the ever-wary Clark was not impressed by the manner and appearance of the Teton Sioux. They struck him as suspicious of strangers, and Clark did not feel comfortable. They were, he recorded,

Generally ill-looking and not well made, their legs small generally. They grease and black themselves when they dress, make use of a hawk's feathers about their heads… The squaws are cheerful, fine-looking women — not handsome. High cheeks; dressed in skins, a petticoat and robe which folds back over their shoulder, with long wool. They do all their laborious work and are I may say perfect slaves to the men, as are all squaws of nations much at war, or where the women are more numerous than the men.

Above, right: The Missouri River looked quite different when the Expedition camped here September 29 to October 1, 1804. Lake Oahe is now a reservoir, and this view is at present-day Gettysburg, South Dakota.

Though all-out conflict was avoided, the jostling and name-calling continued for some hours. Clark's attempts at peacemaking were rejected by the chiefs, who refused to shake his hand. Nervous and a little irritable after the day's events, the Expedition members limped away to camp near Pierre, South Dakota, a mile or so upstream. With a certain bleak irony, Clark named the spot "Bad-Humoured Island."

Affairs of State

Matters had soon improved to such an extent that Lewis and Clark were invited to attend a meeting of Teton elders, who had made no secret of their desire to win the white man's assistance in their ongoing feuds with other neighboring tribes. **Clark** was treated with every ceremony when he went ashore on the evening of **September 26:**

I was met by about ten well-dressed young men who took me up in a robe highly decorated and set me down by the side of their chief on a dressed robe in a large council house. This house formed a three-quarter circle of skins well dressed and sewn together. Under this shelter about 70 men sat, forming a circle. In front of the chiefs a place of six feet diameter was clear and the pipe of peace raised on sticks under which there was swan's down scattered…. Soon after they set me down, the men went for Captain Lewis, brought him the same way, and placed him also by the chief. In a few minutes an old man rose and spoke, approving what we had done, and informing us of their situation requesting us to take pity on them…. The great chief then rose with great state, speaking to the same purpose, as far as we could learn, and then with great solemnity took up the pipe of peace and, after pointing it to the heavens, the four corners of the globe and the earth, he made some dissertation, lit it, and presented the stem to us to smoke….

We smoked for an hour until dark and all was cleared away. A large fire was made in the center, about ten musicians playing on tambourines, long

Below: An impassioned Indian orator strikes a Roman pose before his council in this stirring scene of traditional Dakota democracy in action, as depicted by a nineteenth-century artist.

sticks with deer and goat's hoofs tied so as to make a jingling noise and many others of a similar kind. Those men began to sing and beat on their tambourines; the women came forward highly deco-

THE NATIVE AMERICAN WAY OF WAR

As the "cheerfulness" Clark noticed in the Teton war dance suggests, there was a ritualized quality to conflict among some of America's native peoples: It was nothing like the sort of "total war" we have seen in more modern times. War was still a serious business, though: Clark's notes here hint at the human tragedies involved in small-scale campaigns that flared up constantly down generations without ever entering the historical record.

In this tribe I saw 25 squaws and boys taken thirteen days ago in a battle with the Mahas. In this battle they destroyed 40 lodges, killed 75 men, and some boys and children, and took 48 prisoners, women and boys.

rated in their way, with the scalps and trophies of war of their fathers, husbands, brothers or near connections, and proceeded to dance the war dance, which they did with great cheerfulness until about 12 o'clock, when we informed the chiefs that they were fatigued. They then retired, and we, accompanied by four chiefs, returned to our boat. They stayed with us all night.

By September 28, the Teton chiefs were warning that the Mahas were planning to attack, rob, and massacre the expedition—though Lewis and Clark suspected that this might merely be the cover for an ambush the Teton were envisaging themselves. Despite all the shows of friendship, relations with the Teton remained strained to the end. The explorers' anxieties were only increased by the loss of an anchor, which meant they had to tie up their boat rather closer than was comfortable to the river shore.

THE TABLES TURNED

For most societies in human history, mice have been regarded as, at best, a nuisance and, at worst, a downright menace—stealing or spoiling the food supplies of communities who may have had all too little in reserve. The Arikara had, it seems, however, found a way of turning the tables. Among the other delicacies they offered expedition members was a "rich and very nourishing" bread made of corn and beans, the latter apparently "robbed" from the mice of the prairie, which gather and collect them in their nests.

Farming Folk

It was with relief that the Expedition headed upriver, leaving Teton territory on October 2 as they passed Plum Island, which they themselves named "Caution Island" after the state of high alert for ambush in which they steered clear. By October 8 they were sailing past the settlements of a very different people, the Arikara, or (as the explorers called them) "Rickerree."

THE "THREE SISTERS"

That the Arikara's farming regime should have centered on corn, beans, and squashes is no surprise: This trinity was central to Native American agriculture from the very first. What the Iroquois would call the "three sisters... those on whom our life depends" had been grown in prehistoric times by the first known farming peoples of Mexico's Oaxaca Valley. A true trinity, the crops were inseparable, for while maize might be very much the staple, it was not in itself sufficient to sustain human life. What anthropologists long suspected, modern nutritionists have confirmed: Beans and squashes were not there merely to provide variety, but a vital complement to the corn. High though it is in starch, maize is very low in protein and completely lacking in certain crucial amino acids. This deficit could be made up with beans and squash. A fourth ingredient was required, however, to make such a diet complete: the addition of a pinch of wood ash to cooking maize. A universal ritual among indigenous farmers, this custom has only in recent times been understood in scientific terms: It releases the niacin that otherwise remains locked up in the corn.

Two of our men discovered the Rickerree village, about the center of the island on the left side on the main shore. This island is about 3 miles long, separated from the left shore by a channel of about 60 yards wide, very deep. The island is covered with fields, where those people raise their corn, tobacco, beans. Great numbers of those people came on the island to see us pass.

"Those people express an inclination to be at peace with all nations."

October 12, 1804

I rose early. After breakfast we joined the Indians who were waiting on the bank for us to come out and go and council; we accordingly joined them and went to the house of the second Chief Lassel where there was many chiefs and warriors and we set some time before the council commenced. This man spoke at some length declaring his disposition to believe and pursue our councils, his intention of going to visit his great father, acknowledged the satisfaction in receiving the presents etc, raising a doubt as to the safety in passing the nations below, particularly the Sioux. [He] requested us to take a Chief of their nation and make a good

peace with Mandans and [the] nations above. After answering those parts of the second chief's speech which required it, which appeared to give general satisfaction, we went to the village of the third chief and as usual some ceremony took place before he could speak to us on the great subject…. He presented us with about 10 bushels of corn, some beans and squashes, all of which we accepted with much pleasure.

Above: An earth lodge in modern replica form, as seen in the Arikara Village in the Whitlock Recreational Area, Gettysburg, South Dakota. Right: An earth-lodge interior on display at the Knife River Indian Villages National Historic Site at Stanton, North Dakota.

DISPOSED TO DIPLOMACY

The generosity of the Arikara was no more disinterested than that of the Teton (or, of course, the explorers' own), though unlike the Sioux they sought security in peace rather than an edge in war, their great chief asking the white men to make peace on his people's behalf with their Mandan enemies farther upriver. The peacefulness of their everyday existence, if **Clark's** account of the Arikara is to be believed (**October 12**), seems to stem directly from the violence of their origins as a people:

This nation is made up of ten different tribes… who had formerly been separate, but by commotion and war with their neighbours have come reduced and compelled to come together for protection. The corruption of the language of those different tribes has so reduced the language that the different villages do not understand all the words of the others. Those people are dirty, kind, poor and extravagant, possessing national pride, not beggarly, receive what is given with great pleasure. [They] live in warm houses, large and built in an octagon form forming a cone at top which is left open for the smoke to pass. Those houses are generally 30 or 40 foot diameter, covered with earth on poles, willows and grass to prevent the earth passing through. Those people express an inclination to be at peace with all nations. The Sioux who trade the goods which they get of the British traders for their corn, and have great influence over the Rickerrees, poison their minds and keep them in perpetual dread.

Left: A young Arikara woman clad in buckskin, late nineteenth century, North Dakota. Below: Attempts by incredulous Arikara to rub the black pigment from York's skin are enshrined in (white) tradition, though Lewis and Clark make no mention of it in the Journals. *The supposed scene is depicted here in a painting by Charles Russell.*

AFRICAN…BUT AMERICAN?

"Those Indians," writes Clark of the Arikara, "were much astonished at my servant. They never saw a black man before. All flocked around him and examined him from top to toe. He carried on the joke and made himself more terrible than we wished him to do." Clark's "servant," York, was in fact his slave: He had been given to Clark as his attendant when both were boys, and so fell uncomfortably between the status of childhood companion and mere possession. Yet out here in the wilderness, beyond the constraining bounds of "civilization," an entirely different set of social rules seemed to apply. Rather than being dis-

criminated against for his color or despised for his servile status, he was valued for his contribution, just like any other Expedition member. Tragically, this enlightened treatment would end abruptly with the Expedition's conclusion: An embittered York would spend years in a frantic struggle to secure his freedom. Back in the world in which he had been raised, Clark returned to type as southern slave owner, whilst York was left haunted by the loss of the equality and respect he had so briefly enjoyed.

A COURT MARTIAL

A long way from St. Louis now, the Expedition was far removed from the country it represented; all institutional authority was invested in the persons of Lewis and Clark themselves. Out here in the wilderness, any breakdown in discipline could have fatal consequences for all; any lack of firmness in the leadership might result in problems farther down the line. Hence the seriousness with which they took any sign of insubordinate muttering among the Expedition members. As **Lewis** records, **October 13:**

"His nation never whipped even their children, from their birth."

The Court martial convened this day for the trial of John Newman, charged with "having uttered repeated expressions of a highly criminal and mutinous nature; the same having a tendency not only to destroy every principle of military discipline, but also to alienate the affections of the individuals composing this detachment to their officers, and disaffect them to the service for which they have been so sacredly and solemnly engaged." The prisoner pled not guilty to the charge exhibited against him. The court, after having duly considered the evidence adduced, as well as the defense of the said prisoner, are unanimously of opinion that the prisoner John Newman is guilty of every part of the charge exhibited against him, and do sentence him agreeably to the rules and articles of war, to receive seventy-five lashes on his bare back, and to be henceforth discarded from the permanent party engaged for North Western discovery; two thirds of the court concurring in the sum and nature

Below: *"A beautiful country on both sides of the river,"* according to Captain Clark. On October 24, 1804, the Expedition stopped to camp near present-day Washburn, North Dakota.

of the punishment awarded. The commanding officers further direct that John Newman in future be attached to the mess and crew of the red pirogue as a laboring hand on board the same, and that he be deprived of his arms and accoutrements, and not be permitted the honor of mounting guard until further orders; the commanding officers further direct that in lieu of guard duty from which Newman has been exempted by virtue of this order, that he shall be exposed to such drudgeries as they may think proper to direct from time to time with a view to the general relief of the detachment.

Clark, October 14, 1804

At 1 o'clock we halted on a sand bar and after dinner executed the sentence of the Court Martial so far as giving the corporal punishment.

The punishment of this day alarmed the Indian chief very much. He cried aloud (or affected to cry). I explained the cause of the punishment and the necessity…. His nation never whipped even their children, from their birth.

Below: In this traditional Arikara medicine ceremony, photographed c.1908, six men chant over the accompaniment of rattles.

ACHES AND PAINS

By late October, well upriver, the Expedition had left the lands of the Arikara far behind. Also behind them, though, were the balmy days of summer. "Last night at 1 o'clock," records Clark on October 22, "I was violently and suddenly attacked with the rheumatism in the neck which was so violent I could not move. Captain Lewis applied a hot stone wrapped in flannel, which gave me some temporary ease." Notwithstanding his discomfort, Clark had no choice but to push on with his companions. "My neck is yet very painful," he notes at the end of his day's journeying. They may have been involved in an epic undertaking, but Lewis and Clark and their companions were prey to all the petty discomforts associated with long-distance travel out of doors: the blisters, the sweats, the chills, the sheer exhaustion.

THE MERCANTILE MANDAN

Homebodies though they may have been, the Mandan could hardly be said to have a narrow existence, for they had contacts with other peoples the length and breadth of the Great Plains. Though the Mandan grew the same crops in the same ways as other indigenous farmers did, they seem to have put special effort into producing specifically for what we would call the "export trade." Parties of Cree, Cheyenne, Assiniboin, Crow, and Sioux would come to their villages to buy corn and tobacco, bringing horses, meat, and other items in exchange. More recently, these natives had been joined by European "free traders"—mainly French. Though ultimately under contract to British and French companies, which provided them with luxury and metal goods to trade for furs and tobacco, these men were extraordinarily independent, and would "go native" for years at a time. One, Toussaint Charbonneau, met Lewis and Clark in the Mandan village and signed up as their interpreter. He brought with him one of his Indian wives, the Shoshone Sacagawea, who was three months pregnant. Their knowledge of the languages and the territories of the peoples in the uplands rising to the west would stand the expedition in good stead as it pushed its way farther upstream.

MEETING THE MANDAN

"Several parties of Mandans rode to the river on the southern shore to view us," records **Clark** in his journal for **October 24**; "indeed they are continually in sight satisfying their curiosity as to our appearance, etc." Within a few days they had reached the Mandan village:

This village is situated on an eminence of about 50 feet above the water in a handsome plain. It contains houses in a kind of picket work. The houses are round and very large, containing several families, as also their horses, which is tied on one side of the entrance.... The Mandans graze their horses in the day on grass, and at night give them a stick of cottonwood to eat. Horses, dogs and people all pass the night in the same lodge or round house, covered with earth with a fire in the middle.

November 12, 1804

A very cold night. Early this morning the Big White principal Chief of the lower village of the Mandans came down. He packed about 100 lb. of fine meat on his squaw for us. We made some small presents to the squaw and child; gave a small ax with which she was much pleased ... The interpreter says that the Mandan nation as they (old men) say came out of a small lake where they had gardens; many years ago they lived in several villages on the Missouri low down. The smallpox destroyed the greater part of the nation and reduced them to one village and some small ones. All the nations before this malady were afraid of them; after they were reduced, the Sioux and other Indians waged war and killed a great many, and they moved up the Missouri. Those Indians still continued to wage war, and they moved still higher.... The Mandans are at war with all who make war only, and wish to be at peace with all nations. Seldom the aggressors.

If the peaceful ways of the Mandan made them the perfect hosts, their contacts with other native peoples made them well worth getting to know. With the nights getting longer and weather conditions deteriorating by the day, Lewis and Clark decided to set up camp here and make "Fort Mandan" their winter quarters. Once again, Lewis and Clark found themselves admitted to the most solemn councils of the Indian elders; once again, their influence was sought in the resolution of tensions between the tribes. This time, though, there were indications that they were themselves being manipulated by Mandan guile as a means of gaining the upper hand over their neighbors and rival traders, the Hidatsa.

*Above: Between around 1575 and 1781, there were no fewer than eighty lodges like this one in Mandan, North Dakota. **Opposite, above:** The interior of a Mandan chief's hut, depicted by Karl Bodmer. **Opposite, below:** The Mandan Village, as envisioned by a nineteenth-century artist.*

WINTER TAKES HOLD

On **December 7**, **Clark** described how a chief came to the camp to tell the explorers that:

A large drove of buffalo was near, and his people were waiting for us to join them in a chase. Captain Lewis took 15 men and went out and joined the Indians, who were, at the time he got up, killing the buffalo on horseback with arrows which they done with great dexterity. His party killed 10 buffalo, five of which we got to the fort by the assistance of a horse in addition to what the men packed on their backs. One cow was killed on the ice after drawing her out of a vacancy in the ice in which she had fallen, and butchered at the fort. Those we did not get in was taken by the Indians under a custom which is established amongst them—i.e., any person seeing a buffalo lying without an arrow sticking in him, or some particular mark, takes possession.

THE HIDATSA

The Mandan's neighbors to the northwest, the Hidatsa lived along the Knife River in North Dakota. They, too, were an important farming and trading people. Yet, while their relations with the Mandan had always been friendly, the Hidatsa had a warlike streak that their fellow traders

lacked: They regularly sent out parties of warriors to raid Shoshone and Blackfeet villages to westward. War was not only an economic and political activity for them, bringing in booty and establishing power, but a vital part of their ritual lives—the means by which their youths came fully into manhood. Yet, warlike as they were, the Hidatsa would be no match for those Mandan schemers who succeeded in souring relations between their rival traders and the expedition.

By now, the cold weather was beginning to dominate the winter days. "The thermometer stood this morning at 1 degree below 0," lamented **Clark**. "Three men frost bit badly today." The following day, **December 8**,

In the evening on my return to the fort I saw great numbers of buffalo coming into the bottom on both sides of the river. This day being cold, several men returned a little frost bit, one of the men with his feet badly frost bit.

December 11, 1804

A very cold morning wind from the north. The thermometer at 4 o'clock at 21 degrees below 0 which is 53 degrees below the freezing point and getting colder. The sun shows and reflects two images, the ice floating in the atmosphere being so thick that the appearance is like a fog dispersing.

Above: The Mandan performing a bison dance, as sketched by Karl Bodmer. **Opposite, below:** *Winter takes hold on a Great Plains landscape.* **Opposite, inset:** *A Hidatsa warrior performs the Dog Dance.*

Christmas Day was celebrated with (carefully rationed) cannon fire; likewise New Year's 1805. Expedition members organized music and dancing for the local people, "I found them much pleased at the dancing of our men," says Clark; "I ordered my black servant to dance, which amused the crowd very much, and somewhat astonished them, that so large a man should be active."

More dancing followed, with what **Clark** described on **January 5, 1805**, as "a curious custom":

The old men arrange themselves in a circle and after smoking a pipe, which is handed them by a young man, dressed up for the purpose, the young men—who have their wives back of the circle—each go to one of the old men with a whining tone and request the old man to take his wife (who presents herself naked except a robe) and sleep with her. The girl then takes the old man (who very often can scarcely walk) and leads him to a convenient place for the business, after which they return to the lodge. If the old man returns to the lodge without gratifying the man and his wife, he offers her again and again… All this is to cause the buffalo to come near so they may kill them.

A "curious custom" it may have been, but as Clark himself would scrupulously record, the year's first buffalo were indeed sighted two days later.

There was work to be done as well: on January 5, according to Clark, "several Indians visit us with their axes to get them mended." There was frostbite to be treated, and, on January 15, an eclipse of the moon to be observed. By the beginning of February the condition of the expedition's boats was causing concern. "The situation of our boat and pirogues is now alarming," wrote **Lewis, February 3**:

Previous pages: The Expedition's winter camp at Fort Mandan, North Dakota, in modern reconstruction. Right: Mato-tope, a Mandan Chief. Below: An interior view at Fort Mandan: Lewis and Clark's own quarters must have looked much like these.

They are firmly enclosed in the ice and almost covered with snow. The ice which encloses them lies in several strata of unequal thicknesses which are separated by streams of water. This is peculiarly unfortunate because so soon as we cut through the first strata of ice the water rushes up and rises as high as the upper surface of the ice and thus creates such a depth of water as renders it impracticable to cut away the lower strata, which appears attached to and confining the bottom of the vessels. The instruments we have hitherto used have been the ax only…. We then determined to attempt freeing them from the ice by means of boiling water which we purposed heating in the vessels by means of hot stones, but this expedient also proved fruitless, [because the stones] burst into

Main photograph: *Mandan women gather berries in an early twentieth-century photograph by Edward Curtis.* **Inset photograph:** *A Mandan medicine man offers up the buffalo skull during a traditional ceremony (Curtis, 1908).*

small particles on being exposed to the heat of the fire. We now determined as the dernier resort to prepare a parcel of iron spikes and attach them to the end of small poles of convenient length and endeavour by means of them to free the vessels from the ice. We have already prepared a large rope of elk skin and a windlass by means of which we have no doubt of being able to draw the boat on the bank provided we can free it from the ice.

Meanwhile, the specialist blacksmiths among the visitors were helping to earn the Expedition's keep: "The blacksmiths take a considerable quantity of corn today in payment for their labor," notes **Lewis** on **February 6**. These craftsmen have, he says,

Proved a happy resource to us in our present situation as I believe it would have been difficult to have devised any other method to have procured corn from the natives. The Indians are extravagantly fond of sheet iron, of which they form arrow-points and manufacture into instruments for scraping and dressing their buffalo robes.

But there was rejoicing when, on **February 7, 1805**, the Expedition gained a new member, Sacagawea being "delivered of a fine boy. It is worthy of remark," adds **Lewis**,

That this was the first child which this woman had born, and as is common in such cases her labor was tedious and the pain violent. Mr. Jessaume informed me that he had frequently administered a small portion of the rattle of the rattlesnake, which he assured me had never failed to produce the desired effect, that of hastening the birth of the child. Having the rattle of a snake by me, I gave it to him and he administered two rings of it to the woman broken in small pieces with his fingers and added to a small quantity of water. Whether this medicine was truly the cause or not I shall not undertake to determine, but I was informed that she had not taken it more than ten minutes before she brought forth.

By late February the weather began to improve. "A delightful day, [we] put out our clothes to the sun," wrote Lewis. The Mandan told the explorers that they had sent

several men on their annual early-spring mission to consult a "medicine stone" to help them predict details of events destined to affect them during the coming year.

On February 23, Clark noted that "all hands employed in cutting the pirogues loose from the ice, which was nearly even with their top." One boat was freed that day, and progress was made loosening the second. By the beginning of March, the Expedition members were making preparations for the next stage of their adventure. On March 18, Toussaint Charbonneau was enlisted to join the Corps as an interpreter, and a few days later, the canoes were carried to the river in readiness for departure.

*Opposite: By mid-March the ice was starting to melt, the river just beginning to run freely. **Below**: No American woman has been commemorated in so many statues as Sacagawea.*

SACAGAWEA AND SON

The younger of Charbonneau's two wives, Sacagawea had been born into the Shoshone people—also known as the Snake Indians—but was captured in childhood by raiders from the Hidatsa. They had sold her to Charbonneau as a slave and, having brought her up, he then married her. He appears to have acquired two to three wives this way. Sacagawea was to prove a great asset to the Expedition, not only as interpreter, but as intermediary: she was, it turned out, the sister of one of the Shoshone chiefs they encountered in the Rockies.

Jean-Baptiste, the boy born at Fort Mandan, would set out strapped on to his mother's back. He would see the Pacific, and return, a triumphant toddler. After his mother died in 1812, he was brought up by Clark at his St. Louis home. At eighteen, still a celebrity, he was taken to Germany by the aristocrat-adventurer Duke Paul of Württemberg, to be shown off as an exotic semisavage round the courts of Europe. In the end, though, the West reclaimed him: From 1829 he worked as a trapper and mountain guide. He died in 1866, while on his way to join the Montana Gold Rush.

HIGHER
GROUND

---✦---✦---

*"Hearing a tremendous roaring above me
I continued my route across the point of a
hill...and was again presented by one of the
most beautiful objects in nature, a cascade."*

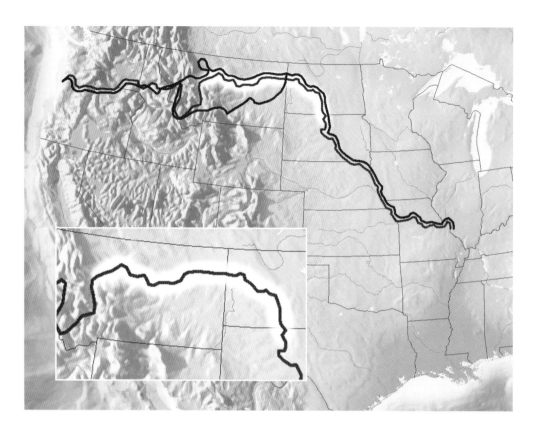

Opposite: *Much of the terrain Lewis and Clark traversed during their epic journey must have been in a similar pristine state to this "preserved wilderness" in Glacier National Park, Montana.*

I n his Second Annual Message to the Nation delivered in 1830, President Andrew Jackson had a question for the American people. "What good man," he asked,

"would prefer a country covered with forests and ranged by a few thousand savages to our extensive Republic, studded with cities, towns, and prosperous farms embellished with all the improvements which art can devise or industry execute, occupied by more than 12,000,000 happy people, and filled with all the blessings of liberty, civilization and religion?"

It was a rhetorical question, of course—he could safely assume his audience of electors would share his vision of an America in which any area not brought to full productiveness in industrial or agricultural use was seen as,

quite literally, a "wasteland." In the name of that great project of improvement, Native Americans would be expelled from their home territories *en masse* and herded onto reservations in remoter areas, whole peoples displaced to make way for European settlers. Much of modern Georgia and Tennessee were opened up for development in this way under Jackson's own administration; his successors would extend his "civilizing" mission ever farther westward. The economic benefits of such a strategy have been enduring, the human costs long hidden to all except the Native Americans themselves. Only very belatedly did white America come to acknowledge that there might have been any such costs at all, that one man's "removal policy" might have been another's "trail of tears." When Lewis and Clark were making their epic journey, Jackson's speech was still a quarter-

Above: *"Savages" in need of "civilizing," or the spirit of America personified? Crow warriors look out from an outcrop in Montana in this late nineteenth-century photograph.*

century off, yet the Corps of Discovery can clearly be seen as the very vanguard of that same "civilizing" venture. To the Expedition members had fallen the task of laying claim to the western wilderness, those lands brought to the United States under the terms of the Louisiana Purchase. Their preliminary work in exploring and mapping out the new territories would represent the first decisive step toward their future domestication and development.

Up until now, the Corps of Discovery had been making its way through territories that, while not as yet settled by Europeans, had to some extent been explored by trappers and traders (for the most part French). Beyond Fort Mandan, however, the real wilderness began: "We were now," wrote Lewis, "about to penetrate a country at least two thousand miles in width on which the foot of civi-

lized man had never trodden." We might question, once again, the unselfconscious certainty that "civilization" was the white man's monopoly. Indeed, by today's standards, white America's dealings with the native peoples over subsequent decades would not necessarily seem "civilized" at all, given the unedifying mix of greed, treachery, ruthlessness—and even wanton bloodlust—shown. Civilization has always been a problematic notion: Throughout human history, those who have believed they possessed it have committed acts of cruelty against those "lesser" nations they considered not to. This was true in classical Greece and in the empire of the ancient Romans, and has sadly remained the way into modern times. Despite courageous and sustained resistance, the Indian Wars of the nineteenth century were an overwhelmingly one-sided conflict.

Yet, if in their unselfconscious arrogance Lewis's words suggest all that was deplorable in the prevailing outlook of the time, there are hints as well of something more admirable and uplifting. The sheer anticipation he clearly feels, his obvious excitement at striking out into unknown country, proclaim the sincerity and strength of his attachment to the land. Often in his journals Lewis's regard for the great outdoors is expressed with such awed solemnity that his attitude can only be described as reverence. Many Americans since have shared this all-but-religious devotion to the great outdoors. For them, the soul of America is to be found not in its great cities, splendid as they are, but in its mountains, its forests, its lakes, its rivers, and its running streams. Those influenced by such feelings range from famous writers like Ralph Waldo Emerson and Thoreau and artists like Frederick Edwin Church to those countless ordinary men and women down the generations who have found their own fulfillment in outdoor pursuits and recreation. Lewis will hardly have been the first American to respond to nature in this way (his reaction puts him very much in tune with the poets and artists of European Romanticism and its adherents in the United States)—yet he was very early in giving the feeling expression. And he expressed it in what would turn out to be a terribly important document: The *Journals* of Lewis and Clark have, as we have seen, a real claim to be the founding epic of the United States of America, and it gives the love of nature a central place in the national life.

"Do I contradict myself? Very well then, I contradict myself. (I am large; I contain multitudes.)" So wrote the poet Walt Whitman, another who found inspiration

Below: *The American vetch (*Vicia americana*), seen here growing wild in Montana, epitomizes both the beauty and the fragility of the Western landscape.*

in America's wide open spaces. That Americans should set such store both by their country's economic development and by the unspoiled innocence of its wilderness does, on the face of it, appear to be a contradiction. Yet if it is so, it is a contradiction that goes to the very heart of American life, a key component of that enormously complex—often bewildering—thing we call the American character. Since the days of Lewis and Clark, the United States has become the leading economic and political force in the world, very much at the cutting edge in the area of technological progress. Yet even today, even for Americans who spend practically their entire lives in our great cities, the wilderness has retained an immense significance. Thanks to Theodore Roosevelt, that significance has been honored in the establishment of a system of great National Parks, their existence a matter of pride to many millions of Americans, some of whom may never even visit them. In short, an advanced, industrialized, and largely urban America still feels a strong, almost spiritual, connection with its wilderness: the one, it seems, psychologically underwritten by the other.

Not, of course, that there is so much genuine wilderness to be found these days. The territories traversed by the Corps of Discovery in the spring of 1805 are a case in point. These western plains may have no great cities, yet few landscapes in the world have been more successfully set to work: Andrew Jackson's vision triumphantly realized. Open country this may be, but it is assuredly no wilderness: North Dakota is one of America's leading

Right: Edible cow parsnip grows in abundance among the aspens on the floor of a Montana forest. The "wilderness" was a source of sustenance for native peoples.

grain-producing states. Montana too, in its eastern parts, is a major grower of wheat, while both states have successful and long-established oil industries. Only farther westward, where the plains of Montana rise up into the Rocky Mountain foothills, do we find anything like the sort of scene that greeted Lewis and Clark—and even here, in fact, appearances are deceptive. These "wild" forests have, for generations now, been carefully managed by commercial loggers or, with the backing of government, by a growing body of conservationists. Even here there has been a human cost: The "removals" farther east had their parallels here. In some cases, by a bitter irony, native communities were moved to make way for wildlife, just as in Georgia and Tennessee they had been displaced to clear space for farms. Their presence now was deemed to detract from what it was felt ought to be a purely "natural"—and thus unpeopled—wilderness.

Today, for better or for worse, no part of America has remained untouched by civilization: Even the great Missouri River itself has been taken in hand. Six great dams in the Dakotas and Montana have made much of the upper river into a series of spreading lakes. These have brought great gains—for navigation, for power generation, for flood control, and for leisure and recreation—but there have been losses too, in terms of ecological impoverishment. Gone are the shifting sandbanks, the shallows and swamps, the countless little creeks and inlets of a river rationalized too drastically, perhaps, to provide a safe and speedy interstate for barges. Today, pressure is mounting for the river flow to be managed more imaginatively, to restore an approximation of that environmental variety and those dramatic seasonal fluctuations that once made the Missouri River's ecosystem so dynamic and diverse.

Above: *When Lewis and Clark came through in April 1805, Lake Sakakawea, North Dakota, did not exist. Even the mighty Missouri has been tamed and set to work.*

THE BIG THAW

Spring may have been a long time coming, but its eventual arrival was dramatic—releasing the full force of a river that had for months been running only sluggishly, largely icebound. And, as Captain **Clark** would witness, the torrent came bearing gifts—unwary bison that had found themselves marooned on floes of ice:

March 29, 1805

Few Indians visit us today. They are now attending on the river bank to catch the floating buffalo.

March 30, 1805

The ice came down in great quantities. The river rose 13 inches the last 24 hours. I observed the extraordinary dexterity of the Indians in jumping from one cake of ice to another, for the purpose of catching the buffalo as they float down. Many of the cakes of ice which they pass over are not two feet square. The plains are on fire in view of the fort on both sides of the river. It is said to be common for the Indians to burn the plains near their villages every spring, for the benefit of their horses, and to induce the buffalo to come near to them.

Above: Buffalo graze the Plains in a painting by Karl Bodmer (c.1833). Above, right: A black-billed magpie of the type sent home by Lewis and Clark. Opposite: "A Canoe Striking on a Tree" in distress, as on April 8, 1805: a sketch by Expedition member Patrick Gass.

A MESSAGE HOME

At this, the point of no return, with the Expedition about to push on into unknown country and less navigable waters, Lewis and Clark took the chance to send the barge back to St. Louis laden with items for the interest of President Jefferson. Among very many others, these included:

The bones and skeleton of a small burrowing wolf of the prairies, the skin being lost by accident.

1 robe representing a battle between the Sioux and Ricarees [Arikara] against the Minnetarees and Mandans.

No. 4 Box. Specimens of plants numbered from 1 to 60.

A specimen of the fur of the antelope.

A specimen of a plant, and a parcel of its roots highly prized by the natives as an efficacious remedy in cases of the bite of the rattlesnake or mad dog.

1 earthen pot such as the Mandans manufacture and use for culinary purposes.

1 tin box containing insects, mice, etc.

Cage no. 6 contains a living burrowing squirrel of the prairies.

Cage no. 7 contains 4 living magpies.

CAPTAIN LEWIS TAKES LEAVE

April 7, 1805 (Lewis)

Having on this day at 4 p.m. completed every arrangement necessary for our departure, we dismissed the barge and crew with orders to return without loss of time to St. Louis. A small canoe with two French hunters accompanied the barge; these men had ascended the Missouri with us the last year.

Our vessels consisted of six small canoes, and two large pirogues. This little fleet, although not quite so respectable as those of Columbus or Captain Cook, were still viewed with as much pleasure as those deservedly famed adventurers ever beheld theirs; and I dare say with quite as much anxiety for their safety and preservation. We were now about to penetrate a country at least two thousand miles in width, on which the foot of civilized man had never trodden; the good or evil it had in store for us was for experiment yet to determine, and these little vessels contained every article by which we were to subsist or defend ourselves. However, as the state of mind in which we are generally gives the coloring to events, when the imagination is suffered to wander into futurity, the picture which now presented itself to me was a most pleasing one. Entertaining as I do the most confident hope of succeeding in a voyage which had formed a darling project of mine for the last

> *"I could but esteem this moment of my departure as among the most happy of my life. The party are in excellent health and spirits."*

ten years, I could but esteem this moment of my departure as among the most happy of my life. The party are in excellent health and spirits, zealously attached to the enterprise, and anxious to proceed; not a whisper or murmur of discontent to be heard among them, but all act in unison, and with the most perfect harmony. I took an early supper this evening and went to bed. Captain Clark, myself, the two interpreters and the woman and child sleep in a tent of dressed skins.

April 8, 1805

Set out early this morning. The wind blew hard against us, from the north-west. We therefore traveled very slowly. I walked on shore, and visited the Black Cat, took leave of him after smoking a pipe as is their custom and then proceeded on slowly by land about four miles, where I awaited the arrival of the party. At 12 o'clock they came up and informed me that one of the small canoes was behind in distress. Captain Clark returned, found she had filled with water and all her loading wet. We lost half a bag of biscuit, and about thirty pounds of powder by this accident. The powder we regard as a serious loss, but we spread it to dry immediately and hope we shall still be able to restore the greater part of it.

THE BURNING BLUFFS

April 9, 1805

The bluffs of the river which we passed today were upwards of a hundred feet high, formed of a mixture of yellow clay and sand—many horizontal stratas of carbonated wood, having every appearance of pitcoal at a distance [actually semi-formed "brown" coal or lignite], were seen in the face of these bluffs. These stratas are of unequal thickness from 1 to 5 feet, and appear at different elevations above the water, some of them as much as eighty feet. Considerable quantities of pumice stone and lava appear in many parts of these hills where they are broken and washed down by the rain and melting snow. When we halted for dinner the squaw busied herself in searching for the wild artichokes, which the mice collect and deposit in large hoards. This operation she performed by penetrating the earth with a sharp stick about some small collections of driftwood. Her labor soon proved successful, and she procured a good quantity of these roots. The flavor of this root resembles that of the Jerusalem artichoke.

April 10, 1805

The country on both sides of the Missouri from the tops of the river hills is one continued level plain as far as the eye can reach, in which there is not even a solitary tree or shrub to be seen, except such as from their moist situations or the steep declivities of hills are sheltered from the ravages of the fire. About 1½ miles down this bluff from this point the bluff is now on fire and throws out considerable quantities of smoke which has a strong sulphurous smell. The appearance of the coal in the bluffs continues as yesterday.

Above: Crow Flies High Butte dominates the river valley not far from Newtown, North Dakota. The Corps of Discovery camped here April 8, 1805.

A FORMIDABLE FOE

April 13, 1805

We found a number of carcasses of the Buffalo lying along shore, which had been drowned by falling through the ice in winter and lodged on shore by the high water when the river broke up about the first of this month. We saw also many tracks of the white bear of enormous size, along the river shore and about the carcasses of the Buffalo, on which I presume they feed. We have not as yet seen one of these animals, though their tracks are so abundant and recent. The men as well as ourselves are anxious to meet with some of these bear. The Indians give a very formidable account of the strength and ferocity of this animal, which they never dare to attack but in parties of six, eight or ten persons; and are even then frequently defeated with the loss of one or more of their party. The savages attack this animal with their bows and arrows and the indifferent guns with which the traders furnish them. With these they shoot with such uncertainty, and at so short a distance, that they frequently miss their aim and fall a sacrifice to the bear. Two Minnetarees were killed during the last winter in an attack on a white bear. This animal is said more frequently to attack a man on meeting with him, than to flee from him. When the Indians are about to go in quest of the white bear, previous to their departure, they paint themselves and perform all those superstitious rites commonly observed when they are about to make war upon a neighboring nation.

Below, inset: "Furious and formidable": two grizzlies spar. *Below:* North Dakota Indians perform a ritual with bison hides and skull.

TEEMING WITH LIFE

Within a week of its departure from Fort Mandan, the Expedition was well and truly in unknown country—but the wilderness, as **Lewis** would find, was anything but empty.

April 15, 1805

In a little pond formed by this rivulet where it entered the bottom, I heard the frogs crying for the first time this season; their note was the same with that of the small frogs which are common to the lagoons and swamps of the United States. I saw great quantities of geese feeding in the bottoms, of which I shot one. Saw some deer and elk, but they were remarkably shy. I also met with great numbers of grouse or prairie hens, as they are called by the English traders of the Northwest.

April 17, 1805

We saw immense quantities of game in every direction around us as we passed up the river, consisting of herds of buffalo, elk and antelopes with some deer and wolves. Though we continue to see many tracks of the bear we have seen but very few of them, and those are at a great distance generally running from us. I therefore presume that they are extremely wary and shy; the Indian account of them does not correspond with our experience so

Below: *A raging grizzly looks around, surveying a scene of devastation. The fury of this beast, it was claimed, could hardly be overstated.*

URSUS HORRIBILIS

The names given to the different animal species in Lewis and Clark's journals often have a certain vagueness, even a fluidity. Confusing as it is, this can be readily understood. The Corps of Discovery was, after all, traveling through unknown country zoologically as well as geographically: Only later would the various different plants and animals be clearly and definitively categorized. It is still a bit of a shock, however, to hear so much mention of a White Bear—clearly not the Arctic polar bear but a denizen of the western plains and forests. To make matters still more puzzling, the same creature is also identified as the Brown Bear and the Yellow Bear—just about any color, it seems, as long as it isn't black. That distinction is crucial: As Lewis notes on April 29, what we now call the Grizzly Bear is a more intimidating beast entirely.

The legs of this bear are somewhat longer than those of the black, as are its talons and tusks incomparably larger and longer…its color is yellowish brown, the eyes small, black and piercing. These are all the particulars in which this animal appeared to me to differ from the black bear. It is a much more furious and formidable animal, and will frequently pursue the hunter when wounded. It is astonishing to see the wounds they will bear before they can be put to death.

far. Captain Clark saw a curlew today. There were three beaver taken this morning by the party. The men prefer the flesh of this animal to that of any other which we have or are able to procure at this moment. I eat very heartily of the beaver myself, and think it excellent, particularly the tail and liver.

April 22, 1805

I ascended to the top of the cut bluff this morning, from whence I had a most delightful view of the country, the whole of which except the valley formed by the Missouri is void of timber or underbrush, exposing to the first glance of the spectator immense herds of buffalo, elk, deer and antelopes feeding in one common and boundless pasture. We saw a number of beaver feeding on the bark of the trees along the verge of the river, several of which we shot, found them large and fat. Walking on shore this evening I met with a buffalo calf which attached itself to me and continued to follow close at my heels until I embarked and left it. It appeared alarmed at my dog, which was probably the cause of its so readily attaching itself to me. Captain Clark informed me that he saw a large drove of buffalo pursued by wolves today; that they at length caught a calf which was unable to keep up with the herd. The cows only defend their young so long as they are able to keep up with the herd, and seldom return any distance in search of them.

Top: Lewis saw "immense herds of buffalo, elk, deer and antelopes feeding in one boundless pasture" on the plains above the Little Missouri near what is now Watford City, North Dakota. *Above, inset:* A bull elk. *Above:* A prairie chicken.

A Sandstorm

DAKOTA DEATH RITES

Writing in his journal for April 20, Lewis described a particularly macabre discovery the Corps had made that day:

Saw the remains of some Indian hunting camps, near which stood a small scaffold of about 7 feet high on which were deposited two dog sleighs with their harness. Underneath this scaffold a human body was lying, well rolled in several dressed buffalo skins and near it a bag of the same materials containing sundry articles belonging to the deceased, consisting of a pair of moccasins, some red and blue earth, beaver's nails, instruments for dressing the buffalo skin, some dried roots, several plaits of the sweet grass, and a small quantity of Mandan tobacco. I presume that the body, as well as the bag containing these articles, had formerly been placed on the scaffold as is the custom of these people, but had fallen down by accident.

His presumption is surely correct: All the Dakotan peoples seem to have followed this tradition of exposing their dead on platforms until decomposition of the flesh was completed. Only then would the bones be buried in earthen mounds.

April 24, 1805

The wind blew so hard during the whole of this day that we were unable to move, notwithstanding that we were sheltered by high timber from the effects of the wind, such was its violence that it caused the waves to rise in such a manner as to wet many articles in the small canoes before they could be unloaded. Sore eyes is a common complaint among the party. I believe it originates from the immense quantities of sand which is driven by the wind from the sandbars of the river in such clouds that you are unable to discover the opposite bank of the river in many instances. The particles of this sand are so fine and light that they are easily supported by the air, and are carried by the wind for many miles, and at a distance exhibiting every appearance of a column of thick smoke. So penetrating is this sand that we cannot keep any article free from it; in short, we are compelled to eat, drink, and breathe it very freely. My pocket watch is out of order; she will run only a few minutes without stopping. I can discover no radical defect in her works, and must therefore attribute it to the sand, with which she seems plentifully charged, notwithstanding her cases are double and tight.

"A Most Pleasing View"

Captain **Lewis**, ever lyrical, was plainly moved by what he saw when traveling through the deep woods around the confluence of the Yellowstone and Missouri rivers, on **April 25**:

I ascended the hills from whence I had a most pleasing view of the country, particularly of the wide and fertile valleys formed by the Missouri and the Yellowstone Rivers, which occasionally

unmasked by the wood on their borders disclose their meanderings for many miles in their passage through these delightful tracts of country.

The whole face of the country was covered with herds of buffalo, elk and antelopes; deer are also abundant, but keep themselves more concealed in the woodland. The buffalo, elk and antelope are so

gentle that we pass near them while feeding without appearing to excite any alarm among them, and when we attract their attention they frequently approach us more nearly to discover what we are, and in some instances pursue us a considerable distance apparently with that view.

But (**April 29**) the experience seems to have left his friend and comrade in characteristically prosaic mood:

Captain Clark measured these rivers just above their confluence: found the bed of the Missouri 520 yards wide, the water occupying 330, its channel deep. The Yellowstone River, including its sandbar, 858 yards, of which the water occupied 297 yards, the deepest part 12 feet.

Opposite: One of those "tracts of country" that so pleased Lewis, near Trenton, North Dakota. Top: Another scene along the river, near Williston, North Dakota. Above: Mule deer bucks, to Lewis a sign that he is "approaching a hilly or mountainous country."

HIGH PLAINS HAUTE CUISINE

May 9, 1805

Captain Clark killed 2 bucks and 2 buffalo. I also killed one buffalo, which proved to be the best meat. It was in tolerable order. We saved the best of the meat, and from the cow I killed we saved the necessary materials for making what our wrighthand cook Charbonneau calls the *boudin blanc*, and immediately set him about preparing them for supper. This "white pudding" we all esteem one of the greatest delicacies of the forest; it may not be amiss therefore to give it a place. About 6 feet of the lower extremity of the large gut of the buffalo is the first morsel that the cook makes love to: this he holds fast at one end with the right hand, while with the forefinger and thumb of the left he gently compresses it, and discharges what he says *is not good to eat*, but of which in the sequel we get a moderate portion. The muscle lying underneath the shoulder blade next to the back, and fillets are next sought. These are kneaded up very fine with a good portion of kidney suet. To this composition is then added a just proportion of pepper and salt and a small quantity of flour. Thus far advanced, our skillful operator Charbonneau seizes his receptacle, which has never once touched the water, for that would entirely destroy the regular order of the whole procedure—you will not forget that the side you now see is that covered with a good coat of fat provided the animal be in good order; the operator seizes the receptacle, I say, and tying it fast at one end turns it inward and begins now with repeated evolutions of the hand and arm, and a brisk motion of the finger and thumb, to put in what he says is *bon pour manger*; thus, by stuffing and compressing

Above, right: A "faithful shepherd": the gray wolf. Opposite: "An American having struck a bear but not killed him, escapes into a tree": sketch by Patrick Gass of the Discovery Corps.

NOT SUCH A BIG BAD WOLF

Lewis appears to have been distinctly underwhelmed by the gray wolf of the western woodlands and plains: "[It] is not as large as those of the Atlantic states," he observes. "They are lower and thicker made, shorter legged," he adds, unflatteringly. "Their color, which is not affected by the seasons, is a gray or blackish brown and every intermediate shade from that to a cream-colored white." He even permits himself a rare moment of ironic humor as he concludes with an account of the gray wolves' way of hunting: "We scarcely see a gang of buffalo without observing a parcel of those faithful shepherds on their skirts in readiness to take care of the maimed wounded."

he soon distends the receptacle to the utmost limits of its power of expansion. Thus when the sides of the receptacle are skillfully exchanged, the outer for the inner, and all is completely filled with something good to eat, it is tied at the other end. It is then baptised in the Missouri with two dips and a flirt, and bobbed into the kettle from whence, after it be well boiled, it is taken and fried with bear's oil until it becomes brown, when it is ready to assuage the pangs of a keen appetite such as travelers in the wilderness are seldom at a loss for.

BESET BY PERILS

May 11, 1805

The banks are falling in very fast. I sometimes wonder that some of our canoes or pirogues are not swallowed up by means of these immense masses of earth which are eternally precipitating themselves into the river. We have had many hairbreadth escapes from them, but providence seems so to have ordered it that we have as yet sustained no loss in consequence of them.

About 5 p.m. my attention was struck by one of the party running at a distance towards us and making signs and hallooing as if in distress. I ordered the pirogues put to, and waited until he arrived. I now found that it was Bratton, the man with the sore hand, whom I had permitted to walk on shore. He arrived so much out of breath that it was several minutes before he could tell me what had happened. At length he informed me that he had shot a brown bear which immediately turned on him and pursued him a considerable distance, but he had wounded it so badly that it could not quite overtake him. I immediately turned out with seven of the party in quest of this monster. We at length found his trail and pursued him about a mile by the blood through very thick brush. We finally found him concealed in some very thick brush and shot him through the skull with two balls. We proceeded to dress him as soon as possible. We found him in good order. It was a monstrous beast. The hair is remarkably long, fine and rich though he appears partially to have discharged his winter coat. We now found that Bratton had

shot him through the center of the lungs, notwithstanding which he had pursued him near half a mile and had returned more than double that distance and with his talons had prepared himself a bed in the earth of about 2 feet deep and five long and was perfectly alive when we found him which could not have been less than 2 hours after he received the wound. These bears being so hard to die rather intimidates us all: I must confess that I do not like the gentleman, and had rather fight two Indians than one bear.

May 14, 1805

It was after the sun had set we had been halted by an occurrence, which I have now to recapitulate, and which although happily passed without ruinous injury, I cannot recollect but with the utmost trepidation and horror: this is the upsetting and narrow escape of the white pirogue. It happened unfortunately for us this evening that Charbonneau was at the helm of this pirogue, instead of Drewyer, who had previously steered her. Charbonneau cannot swim and is perhaps the most timid waterman in the world. In this pirogue were embarked our papers, instruments, books, medicine, a great part of our merchandise and in short almost every article indispensably necessary to further the views, or ensure the success of the enterprise in which we are now launched to the distance of 2,200 miles.

Suffice it to say that the pirogue was under sail when a sudden squall of wind struck her obliquely, and turned her considerably. The steersman, alarmed, instead of putting her before the wind, luffed her up into it. The wind was so violent that it drew the brace of the squaresail out of the hand of the man who was attending it, and instantly upset the pirogue—and would have turned her completely topsy-turvy had it not been for the resistance made by the awning against the water. In this situation Captain Clark and myself both fired our guns to attract the attention if possible of the crew and ordered the halyards to be cut and the sail hauled in, but they did not hear us. Such was their confusion and consternation at this moment that they suffered the pirogue to lie on her side for half a minute before they took the sail in. The pirogue then righted, but had filled within an inch of the gunwales. Charbonneau, still crying to his God for mercy, had not yet recollected the rudder, nor could the repeated orders of the bowsman, Cruzat, bring him to his recollection until he threatened to shoot him instantly if he did not take hold of the rudder and do his duty. The waves by this time were running very high, but the fortitude, resolution and good conduct of Cruzat saved her. He ordered 2 of the men to throw out the water with some kettles that fortunately were convenient, while himself and two others rowed her ashore, where she arrived scarcely above the water.

THE BIGHORN

One of the glories of the western wilderness, the bighorn made a big impression on Captain Lewis, as is clear from the entry in his journal for May 25.

As we ascended the river today I saw several gangs of the bighorned animals on the face of the steep bluffs and cliffs on the starboard side, and sent Drewyer to kill one, which he accomplished. Captain Clark and Bratton, who were on shore, each killed one of these animals this evening. The head and horns of the male which Drewyer killed weighted 27 lbs. It was somewhat larger than the head of the common deer, the body rather thicker, deeper and not so long in proportion to its height as the common deer. The head and horns are remarkably large compared with the other part of the animal. The whole form is much more delicate than that of the common goat.

The horns are largest at their base, and occupy the crown of the head almost entirely. They are compressed, bent backwards and lunated, the surface swelling into wavy rings which, encircling the horn, continue to succeed each other from the base to the extremity and become less elevated and more distant as they recede from the head. This horn is used by the natives in constructing their bows. I have no doubt but it would make elegant and useful hair combs, and might probably answer as many valuable purposes to civilized man as it does to the savages, who form their water-cups, spoons and platters of it.

They feed on grass, but principally on the aromatic herbs which grow on the cliffs and inaccessible heights which they usually frequent. The places they generally select to lodge is the crannies or crevices of the rocks in the faces of inaccessible precipices, where the wolf nor bear can reach them and where indeed man himself would in many instances find a similar deficiency. Yet these animals bound from rock to rock and stand apparently in the most careless manner on the sides of precipices of many hundred feet.

Above: Female "bighorns," if truth be told, hardly warrant the name at all. Only in the male, **left,** do we see the Ovis canadensis headgear in all its glory.

"SLAUGHTER RIVER"

Approaching Arrow Creek, Montana, members of the Corps were shocked to come upon a hideous scene of carnage, as **Lewis** reports in his journal for **May 29**:

Today we passed on the starboard side the remains of a vast many mangled carcasses of buffalo which had been driven over a precipice of 120 feet by the Indians and perished. The water appeared to have washed away a part of this immense pile of slaughter and still there remained the fragments of at least a hundred carcasses. They created a most horrid stench. In this manner the Indians of the Missouri destroy vast herds of buffalo at a stroke. For this purpose one of the most active and fleet young men is selected and disguised in a robe of buffalo skin, having also the skin of the buffalo's head with the ears and horns fastened on his head in form of a cap. Thus caparisoned, he places himself at a convenient distance between a herd of buffalo and a precipice proper for the purpose, which happens in many places on this river for miles together. The

"...the whole are precipitated down the precipice forming one common mass of dead and mangled carcasses."

*Above: An Indian buffalo hunt on the Plains, as depicted by a nineteenth-century artist. **Opposite:** The Madison Buffalo Jump, west of Bozeman, Montana, over which many buffalo would be driven to their deaths in a simple, but wasteful, method of hunting practiced during prehistoric times.*

other Indians now surround the herd on the back and flanks and at a signal agreed on all show themselves at the same time moving forward towards the buffalo. The disguised Indian or decoy has taken care to place himself sufficiently nigh the buffalo to be noticed by them when they take to flight, and running before them they follow him in full speed to the precipice, the cattle behind driving those in front over and seeing them go do not look or hesitate about following until the whole are precipitated down the precipice forming one common mass of dead and mangled carcasses.

THE BUFFALO JUMP

The method of hunting described by Lewis is believed to have been practiced by Native Americans from the earliest times. One site in Alberta, Canada, has been shown to have been in use 7,000 years ago. The bison is a big, strong beast—and a swift runner—by no means easy for the stone-age hunter to bring down: A system like this tilted the advantage dramatically in his favor. The obvious drawback of the method was the indiscriminate destruction it caused, and the appalling waste: Far more animals were killed than could possibly be eaten—or even preserved. Only the very topmost of a heap of heavy victims could conceivably be reached; those caught lower down in the unmovable mass of bodies would be left to rot. The "green" credentials of pre-historic hunters tend to be taken for granted (and it is true that they would never wreak the sort of havoc their successors would, mounted on horseback and armed with rifles; still less the terrible destruction caused by those white hunters who finally brought about the buffalo's near-extinction). Yet they did not always live in perfect equilibrium with their environment. Paleo-Indian hunters are held by some archeologists to have had their share of responsibility for the wave of extinctions that followed the last Ice Age.

AN AWESOME SIGHT

Lewis was struck by the sublime strangeness of the scene that greeted the expedition at White Cliffs, Montana, on **May 31**, but he was characteristically concerned to offer a scientific explanation:

The hills and river cliffs which we passed today exhibit a most romantic appearance. The bluffs of the river rise to the height of from 2 to 300 feet and in most places nearly perpendicular: they are formed of remarkable white sandstone which is sufficiently soft to give way readily to the impression of water. Two or three thin horizontal stratas of white free-stone, on which the rains or water make no impression, lie imbedded in these cliffs of soft stone near the upper part of them. The earth on the top of these cliffs is a dark rich loam which, forming a gradually ascending plain, extends back from ½ a mile to a mile where the hills commence and rise abruptly to a height of 300 feet more. The water in the course of time in descending from those hills and plains on either side of the river has trickled down the soft sand cliffs and worn it into a thousand grotesque figures, which with the help of a little imagination and an oblique view, at a distance are made to represent elegant ranges of lofty freestone buildings, having their parapets well stocked with statuary. So perfect indeed are those walls that I should have thought that nature had attempted here to rival the human art of masonry, had I not recollected that she had first begun her work.

A Cache

By early June the Expedition was climbing steadily through the Rocky Mountain foothills, the channel narrowing and the current running swifter against them. On **June 9**, finding themselves beside what they had named the Marias River, **Lewis** realized that steps would have to be taken to respond to the changing conditions:

We determined to deposit at this place the large red pirogue, all the heavy baggage which we could possibly do without and some provision, salt, tools, powder and lead etc. with a view to lighten our vessels and at the same time to strengthen their crews by means of the seven hands who have been heretofore employed in navigating the red pirogue. Accordingly, we set some hands to digging a hole or cellar for the reception of our stores. These holes in the ground or deposits are called by the *engagés* *"caches."* On enquiry I found that Cruzat was well acquainted with this business and therefore left the management of it entirely to him.

The cache being completed, I walked to it and examined its construction. The situation a dry one, which is always necessary. A place being fixed on for a cache, a circle about 20 inches in diameter is first described. The turf or sod of this circle is carefully removed, being taken out as entire as possible in order that it may be replaced in the same situation when the cache is filled and secured. This circular hole is then sunk perpendicularly to the

depth of one foot—if the ground be not firm somewhat deeper. They then begin to work it out wider as they proceed downwards until they get it about six or seven feet deep, giving it nearly the shape of the kettle or lower part of a large still. As the earth is dug it is handed up in a vessel and carefully laid on a skin or cloth and then carried to a place where it can be thrown in such manner as to conceal it, usually into some running stream where it is washed away and leaves no traces which might lead to the discovery of the cache. A parcel of small dry sticks are then collected and with them a floor is made of three or four inches thick which is then covered with some dry hay or a raw hide well dried. On this the articles are deposited, taking care to keep them from touching the walls by putting other dry sticks between as you stow away the merchandise. When nearly full the goods are covered with a skin and earth thrown in and well rammed until with the addition of the turf first removed the whole is on a level with the surface of the ground. In this manner dried skins or merchandise will keep perfectly sound for several years. The traders of the Missouri, particularly those engaged in trade with the Sioux, are obliged to have frequent recourse to this method in order to avoid being robbed.

THE GREAT FALLS

Splendor succeeded splendor as the expedition climbed steadily through western Montana. On **June 13**, **Lewis** would encounter the Great Falls:

I had proceeded about two miles when my ears were saluted with the agreeable sound of a fall of water and advancing a little further I saw the spray arise above the plain like a column of smoke which would frequently disappear again in an instant, caused I presume by the wind, which blew pretty hard from the southwest. I did not, however, lose my direction to this point, which soon began to make a roaring too tremendous to be mistaken for any cause short of the great falls of the Missouri.

I hurried down the hill which was about 200 feet high and difficult of access, to gaze on this sublimely grand spectacle.

Opposite: Decision Point Junction, not far from Loma, Montana: the Corps camped here, June 2–10, 1805. Above: The sun comes up on the river at the Rainbow Falls, Great Falls, Montana. Below: Ryan Falls, one magnificent part of that cataract-complex the Great Falls—for Lewis (as for so many since) "the grandest sight I ever beheld."

Immediately at the cascade the river is about 300 yards wide. About ninety or a hundred yards of this next the larboard [port-side] bluff is a smooth, even sheet of water falling over a precipice of at least eighty feet. The remaining part of about 200 yards on my right forms the grandest sight I ever beheld. The height of the fall is the same as the other but the irregular and somewhat projecting rocks below receive the water in its passage down and break it into a perfect white foam which assumes a thousand forms in a moment, sometimes flying up in jets of sparkling foam to the height of fifteen or twenty feet and scarcely formed before large rolling bodies of the same beaten and foaming water is thrown over and conceals them. In short, the rocks seem to be most happily fixed to present a sheet of the whitest beaten froth for 200 yards in length and about 80 feet perpendicular. The water after descending strikes against the abutment before mentioned or that on which I stand and seems to reverberate and being met by the more impetuous current they roll and swell into half-formed billows of great height which rise and again disappear in an instant.

From the reflection of the sun on the spray or mist which arises from these falls there is a beautiful rainbow produced which adds not a little to the beauty of this majestically grand scenery. After writing this imperfect description I again viewed the falls and was so much disgusted with the imperfect idea which it conveyed of the scene that I determined to draw my pen across it and begin again, but then reflected that I could not perhaps succeed better than penning the first impressions of the mind.

More delights were to follow, as **Lewis's** journal for **June 14** would record:

Hearing a tremendous roaring above me I continued my route across the point of a hill a few hundred yards further and was again presented by one of the most beautiful objects in nature, a cascade of about fifty feet perpendicular stretching at right angles across the river from side to side to the distance of at least a quarter of a mile. Here the river pitches over a shelving rock, with an edge as regular and as straight as if formed by art, without a niche or break in it. The water descends in one even and uninterrupted sheet to the bottom, where dashing against the rocky bottom it rises into foaming billows of great height and rapidly glides away, hissing, flashing and sparkling as it departs. The spray rises from one extremity to the other to 50 feet. I now thought that, if a skillful painter had been asked to make a beautiful cascade, that he would most probably have presented the precise image of this one.

THE PORTAGE

His romantic raptures over, Lewis had to attend to more practical matters: Beautiful as they were, these waterfalls and rapids represented a severe logistical challenge to the explorers. By **June 15** Clark had concluded that an overland portage would be necessary; two days later **Lewis** was making arrangements for the Expedition's boats to be carried overland, up precariously steep and rocky trails, around these barriers:

Captain Clark set out early this morning with five men to examine the country and survey the river and portage as had been concerted last evening. I set six men at work to prepare four sets of truck wheels with couplings, tongues and bodies, that they might either be used without the bodies for transporting our canoes, or with them in transporting our baggage.

A week later, the portage was still only getting under way, as **Clark** makes clear:

Had the remaining canoe hauled out of the water to dry, and divided the baggage into 3 parcels, one of which the party took on their backs and one wagon with truck wheels to the canoes 3 miles in advance. After getting up their loads they divided men and load and proceeded on with 2 canoes on truck wheels as before. I accompanied them 4 miles and then returned, my feet being very sore from the walk over ruts, stones and hills.

There was one moment of respite for the party, as **Lewis** noted on **June 25**:

It is worthy of remark that the winds are sometimes so strong in these plains that the men informed me that they hoisted a sail in the canoe and it had driven her along on the truck wheels. This is really sailing on dry land.

On the whole, though, it was backbreaking work which proceeded with agonizing slowness. The portage would not be completed until the second week of July.

Above, left: "From the reflection of the sun on the spray or mist ... there is a beautiful rainbow produced": the Rainbow Falls. *Above, right:* "Explorers at the Portage": Lewis, Clark, York, and the dog Seaman in a sculpture by Bob Scriver at the Broadwater Overlook Park.

WATER WHITEOUT

At times, the dangers of the roaring river were compounded by further torrents of water that came cascading from the skies, as Captain **Clark** notes in his log for Saturday, **June 29**:

I took my servant and one man, Charbonneau our interpreter, and his squaw accompanied him. Soon after I arrived at the falls, I perceived a cloud which appeared black and to threaten immediate rain.

Left and below: *The Missouri River drops 512 feet over the course of several waterfalls in a 10-mile stretch near Great Falls, Montana. The water can be deceptively calm in places, but the Expedition members encountered terrible conditions here.*

torrent of water which was pouring down the hill into the river with immense force, tearing everything before it, taking with it large rocks and mud. I took my gun and shot pouch in my left hand, and with the right scrambled up the hill pushing the interpreter's wife (who had her child in her arms) before me, the interpreter himself making attempts to pull up his wife by the hand, much scared and nearly without motion. We at length reached the top of the hill safe, where I found my servant in search of us, greatly agitated for our welfare. Before I got out of the bottom of the ravine, which was a flat dry rock when I entered it, the water was up to my waist and wet my watch. I scarcely got out before it raised 10 feet deep, with a torrent which was terrible to behold, and by the time I reached the top of the hill at least 15 feet of water. On arrival at the camp on the willow run met the party who had returned in great confusion to the run leaving their loads in the plain, the hail and wind being so large and violent in the plains, and them naked, they were much bruised, and some nearly killed; one knocked down three times and others, without hats or anything on their heads, bloody, and complained very much. I refreshed them with a little grog. Soon after the run began to rise and rose 6 feet in a few minutes. I lost at the river in the torrent the large compass…a serious loss, as we have no other large one.

The first shower was moderate, accompanied with a violent wind, the effects of which we did not feel. Soon after, a torrent of rain and hail fell more violent than ever I saw before. The rain fell like one volley of water falling from the heavens and gave us time only to get out of the way of a

OVER THE
ROCKIES

---✳---✳---

"This evening we entered much the most remarkable cliffs that we have yet seen... Every object here wears a dark and gloomy aspect. The towering and projecting rocks in many places seem ready to tumble on us."

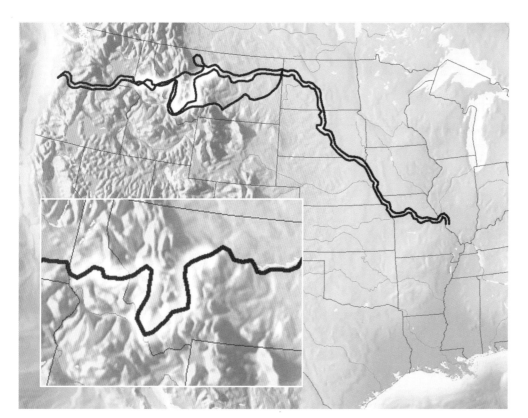

The grueling portage had been completed, and the canoes were afloat again, yet the worst of the westward journey was by no means over. For the moment, indeed, the Expedition was still climbing steadily day by day. The Missouri's source, and the high Rocky Mountains, lay some way ahead. Despite the difficulties of making progress against so fast-flowing a river current, and despite the all but crushing rigors of the recent portage, Lewis was well aware that things might have been much harder still. Paradoxically, he might have been more heartened if they had been. A few weeks later, on August 10, we find him reflecting ruefully on the relative gentleness of their climb this far, and what it must imply for their journey beyond the continental divide:

I do not believe that the world can furnish an example of a river running to the extent which the Missouri and Jefferson Rivers do through such a mountainous country and at the same time so navigable as they are. If the Columbia furnishes us such another example, a communication across the continent by water will be practicable and safe. But this I can scarcely hope from a knowledge of its having in its comparatively short course to the ocean the same number of feet to descend which the Missouri and Mississippi have from this point to the Gulf of Mexico.

Though acknowledged here for the first time, this realization must have been growing on him gradually over several weeks as the Corps of Discovery pushed farther and farther westward with no sign of their ascent approaching an end. Lewis and Clark had been plotting their longitude at regular intervals en route; that of the Pacific coastline was well known. The two figures were getting far too close for comfort. The dream of a convenient commercial route to the Pacific was thus fading away, quite literally by degrees, yet Lewis will have found compensations in the grandeur all around him. His journals speak so vividly to us precisely because he shares our sense of the sublime—and there are few things so sublime as America's Western mountains.

The Western Cordillera, as geographers call it, is a complex system of mountain ranges running the entire length of the Americas, from Alaska to Tierra del Fuego. The Andes of South America are part of the same chain—as, technically, are the mountains of western Antarctica. North America's most important range, the Rockies, rise to their highest point at Mt. Elbert, Colorado (14,431 feet), several hundred miles to the south of where the Corps of Discovery was making its crossing. Concerned not with mountaineering but with waterborne exploration, the Corps aimed to avoid the peaks and traverse the least challenging passes—even so, its members would find themselves faced with a good deal of arduous climbing. The name of the Rockies is often used loosely to denote an entire region of western North America—but the mountains comprise just one of a number of ranges, as Lewis and Clark would discover to their cost. Between these jagged rows of peaks are lower, though still emphatically rugged, areas—deep valleys, basins, and plateaus—like the Columbia Plateau, across which the Expedition would have to make its way.

"The mountains do not appear very high in any direction, though the tops of some of them are partially covered with snow. This convinces me that we have ascended to a great height since we have entered the rocky mountains."

Conscious though they undoubtedly were of their historic role in opening up new country, Expedition members will have had little sense of just how true that really was. Though their formation some 50 million years ago makes these mountains unimaginably antique in any human-historical terms, in the geological scheme of things they might have been created yesterday. It was not until the beginning of the Cenozoic Era that the inexorable expansion of the Pacific Ocean forced cataclysmic change all along the western edge of the

American landmass. Or rather, the Laurasian landmass, for at that time America and Eurasia were still a single continent, the latter just on the point of being split apart and driven steadily eastward as what would become the Atlantic Ocean inched ever wider year by year. Both oceans began as deep yet narrow fissures, through which magma—molten rock—welled slowly up through the earth's crust from its core, cooling and solidifying to create new rock. As this accumulated in mid-ocean, existing plates of crust were forced apart, pushing the continents farther away from one another, infinitesimally slowly but relentlessly. The mountains of the Western Cordillera can be seen as the solid record of that slow-

motion collision in which, over innumerable millennia, the oceanic plates of the Pacific ran up against the continental crust of the Americas. A sculpted shockwave, frozen in stone, they reveal the awe-inspiring violence of the earth's creation: hard rock strata tortured, twisted this way and that by incalculable forces.

The actual construction of the mountains took place over millions of years and in a number of different ways, the most important of which, perhaps, was the process of "subduction." Comprising denser rock, formed deep in the earth, the oceanic plate was heavier than the continental crust, so its natural tendency when the two collided was to push firmly downward. This forced the landmass to ride up,

Above: *"I ... did not despair of shortly finding a passage over the mountains." The Lemhi Pass, on the border between Montana and Idaho, the point at which—on August 12, 1805—the Expedition reached the Continental Divide.*

creating an upland region above the area of collision, whose contours were thrown into further confusion by that process known as "folding," when layers of rock are concertinaed and buckled by unbear-

Above: A shimmering mist of purple camas flowers cloaks the floor of the Lolo Pass. The camas is as useful as it is attractive, its ground-up roots yielding a nutritious flour, which saw native communities through those lengthy periods when other sustenance was scarce.

able forces so that a level plain may become a mountain range. Add in the secondary seismic consequences of these two processes—the earthquakes and volcanoes that result when the continental crust is put under such pressure—and we begin to appreciate why the Cordillera is so complex a landscape as well as such a spectacular one. Not that the story ends there: The role of the great glaciations has also to be recognized, though the last one

occurred less than 20,000 years ago, the merest blink of an eye in the geological chronology. Miles thick in places, the ice sheets gouged out deep valleys and mountain hollows, setting their own unique signature on the mountain scene. Such titanic struggles dwarf any human drama, of course; no amount of geological knowledge can give us any meaningful sense of the incredible violence of these events. Yet the mountain landscape in its breathtaking beauty still seems to carry the imprint of its origins: Its jagged peaks, its plunging abysses hint at the unthinkable tumults that first brought them into being. But the mountains have a very different side, too: Nowhere in America can greater peace and tranquility be found than among their echoing heights, their wooded slopes, their secluded valleys. They are by no means an empty space, though. This landscape is miraculously rich in wildlife; the cougar haunts its crags, the eagle scuds across its skies. Below, along babbling streams, birds fill the air with song; every spring the valleys erupt in a multicolored symphony of flowers. And in any case, at the time when Lewis and Clark were passing this way, the region might have seemed less wild and forbidding than it does now, because so many native communities had found ways of living in these uplands. It was here, indeed, that—as though in a fairytale— Charbonneau's wife Sacagawea found her long-lost brother, a Shoshone chief. The mountains could be both a fearful wilderness and a place of homecoming.

UNDER WAY

"We arose very early this morning," wrote **Lewis** in his log for Monday, **July 15**, 1805.

[We] assigned the vessels their loads and had it put on board. We now found our vessels eight in number all heavily laden, notwithstanding our several deposits; though it is true we have now a considerable stock of dried meat and grease. We find it extremely difficult to keep the baggage of many of our men within reasonable bounds; they will be adding bulky articles of but little use or value to them. At 10 a.m. we once more saw ourselves fairly under way, much to my joy, and I believe that of every individual who compose the party.

Early this morning we passed about 40 little booths formed of willow bushes to shelter them from the sun; they appeared to have been deserted about 10 days. We supposed they were Snake Indians. They appeared to have a number of horses with them. This appearance gives me much hope of meeting with these people shortly.

Drewyer killed a buffalo this morning near the river and we halted and breakfasted on it. Here for the first time I ate of the small guts of the buffalo cooked over a blazing fire in the Indian style without any preparation of washing or other cleansing and found them very good.

THE PRICKLY PEAR

"The prickly pear is now in full bloom," records Lewis, "and forms one of the beauties as well as the greatest pests of the plains." Countless hikers since then have known exactly what he meant. With its delicate yellow flower, *Opuntia fragilis* lends a lovely beauty to apparently barren slopes, while its engorged stem—the "pear" itself—is good to eat. But it is formidably protected by a bristling array of spines, as members of the Corps would be reminded over and over again as they picked their way painfully across these Rocky Mountain slopes. On July 20, for instance, Clark would note that the feet of his men were "so stuck with prickly pear and cut with the stones that they were scarcely able to march at a slow gait this afternoon."

Above: "We pursued our route through a high rolling plain." Montana's Big Belt Mountains stand out against the sky, an intimidating backdrop to the section of the Missouri up which the Expedition continued its way on July 16, 1805. Left: A pretty flower—but its spines are vicious: the prickly pear.

July 17, 1805

The sunflower is in bloom and abundant in the river bottoms. The Indians of the Missouri, particularly those who do not cultivate maize, make great use of the seed of this plant for bread, or use it in thickening their soup. They most commonly first parch the seeds and then pound them between two smooth stones until they reduce it to a fine meal. To this they sometimes merely add a portion of water and drink it in that state, or add a sufficient quantity of marrow grease to reduce it to the consistency of common dough and eat it in that manner. The last composition I think much best, and have eaten it in that state heartily and think it a palatable dish. There is but little of the broad-leafed cottonwood above the Falls, much the greater portion being of the narrow-leafed kind. There are a great abundance of red, yellow, purple and blackcurrants and serviceberries now ripe and in great perfection. I find these fruits very pleasant, particularly the yellow currant which I think vastly preferable to those of our gardens.

July 18, 1805

Saw a large herd of the bighorned animals on the immensely high and nearly perpendicular cliff opposite to us. On the face of this cliff they walked about and bounded from rock to rock with apparent unconcern where it appeared to me that no quadruped could have stood, and from which had they made one false step they must have been precipitated at least 500 feet. This animal appears to frequent such precipices and cliffs, where in fact they are perfectly secure from the pursuit of wolf, bear or even man himself.

We passed the entrance of a considerable river on the starboard side, about 80 yards wide, being nearly as wide as the Missouri at that place. This handsome, bold and clear stream we named in honor of the Secretary of War, calling it Dearborn's River.

"Whenever we get a view of the lofty summits of the mountains the snow presents itself, although we are almost suffocated in this confined valley with heat."

As we were anxious now to meet with the Shoshones or Snake Indians as soon as possible in order to obtain information relative to the geography of the country and also, if necessary, some horses, we thought it better for one of us—either Captain Clark or myself—to take a small party and proceed on up the river some distance before the canoes. [We wanted] to discover them, should they be on the river, before the daily discharge of our guns, which was necessary in procuring subsistence for the party, should alarm and cause them to retreat to the mountains and conceal themselves, supposing us to be their enemies, who visit them usually by the way of this river. Accordingly, Captain Clark set out this morning after breakfast with Joseph Fields, Potts, and his servant York.

THE GATES OF THE MOUNTAINS

July 19, 1805

The mosquitoes are very troublesome to us as usual. This morning we set out early and proceeded on very well, though the water appears to increase in velocity as we advance. The current has been strong all day and obstructed with some rapids, though these are but little broken by rocks and are perfectly safe. The river deep, from 100 to 150 yards wide. I walked along shore today and killed an antelope. Whenever we get a view of the lofty summits of the mountains the snow presents

Above: "From the singular appearance of this place, I called it the Gates of the Rocky Mountains," *wrote Lewis in his journal, July 19, 1805. But upon what perils did this awesome portal open? Expedition members must have wondered.*

itself, although we are almost suffocated in this confined valley with heat. The pine cedar and balsam fir grow on the mountains in irregular assemblages or spots mostly high up on their sides and summits. This evening we entered much the most remarkable cliffs that we have yet seen. These cliffs rise from the water's edge on either side perpendicularly to the height of 1,200 feet. Every object here wears a dark and gloomy aspect. The towering and projecting rocks in many places seem ready to tumble on us. The river appears to have forced its way through this immense body of solid rock for the distance of 5¾ miles, and where it makes its exit below has thrown on either side vast columns of rocks, mountains high. The river appears to have worn a passage just the width of its channel, or 150 yards. It is deep from side to side, nor is there in the first 3 miles of this distance a spot except one of a few yards in extent on which a man could rest the sole of his foot. Several fine springs burst out at the water's edge from the interstices of the rocks. It happens, fortunately, that, although the current is strong, it is not so but what it may be overcome with the oars, for it was late in the evening before I entered this place and was obliged to continue my route until sometime after dark before I found a place sufficiently large to encamp my small party.... From the singular appearance of this place, I called it the *Gates of the Rocky Mountains*.

LEWIS'S WOODPECKER

"I saw a black woodpecker (or crow) today, about the size of the lark woodpecker, as black as a crow. I endeavored to get a shot at it but could not. It is a distinct species of woodpecker. It has a long tail and flies a good deal like the jaybird." So wrote Lewis confidently in his journal for July 20; later ornithologists would concur with his view that a new species had been identified. In honor of its discoverer, this beautiful black-and-russet bird was named after him: Lewis's Woodpecker or, in Latin, *Melanerpes lewis*.

EARLY WARNING

Both Lewis and Clark confessed themselves puzzled as to why the Indians should have set fire to large areas alongside the trail ahead of them as they made their way upward across the Rockies. "I observe a Smoke rise to our right about 12 miles distant," wrote Clark on July 20,

The causes of this smoke I can't account for certainly, though think it probable that the Indians have heard the shooting of the party below and set the prairies or valley on fire to alarm their camps, supposing our party to be a war party coming against them. I left signs to show the Indians if they should come on our trail that we were not their enemies.

July 22, 1805

The Indian woman recognizes this country and assures us that this is the river on which her relations live, and that the Three Forks are at no great distance. This piece of information has cheered the spirits of the party, who now begin to console themselves with the anticipation of shortly seeing the head of the Missouri, yet unknown to the civilized world.

Too Easy?

On **July 24**, **Lewis** expressed his bemusement that a river running through such apparently precipitous terrain should, for now at least, be affording such plain sailing:

I fear every day that we shall meet with some considerable falls or obstruction in the river, notwithstanding the information of the Indian woman to the contrary, who assures us that the river continues much as we see it. I can scarcely form an idea of a river running to great extent through such a rough, mountainous country without having its stream intercepted by some difficult and dangerous rapids or falls.

Opposite: "Much the most remarkable cliffs that we have yet seen." The Gates of the Mountains, Montana.
Above: "The men complain of being much fatigued; their labor is excessively great." Today, ironically, the Missouri at Canyon Ferry Reservoir, near Townsend, Montana, is a center for relaxation and water sports.

Not that the explorers had everything their own way:

Our trio of pests still invade and obstruct us on all occasions. These are the mosquitoes, eye gnats and prickly pear, equal to any three curses that ever poor Egypt labored under except the *Mahometan yoke.* The men complain of being much fatigued. Their labor is excessively great. I occasionally encourage them by assisting in the labor of navigating their canoes, and have learned to "push a tolerable good pole," in their phrase.

THE THREE FORKS

On **July 25**, **Clark**'s advance party reached the parting of the ways:

We proceeded on a few miles to the Three Forks of the Missouri. Those three forks are nearly of a

*Above: The Madison and Jefferson Rivers merge at Three Forks, Montana. The Corps of Discovery came this way on July 26–9, 1805. **Opposite:** A Flathead group outside a tepee in a wooded area of what is now the Glacier National Park, northwestern Montana, in this photograph taken by Edward Curtis.*

size. The North Fork appears to have the most water and must be considered as the one best calculated for us to ascend.

After breakfast (which we made on the ribs of a buck killed yesterday), I wrote a note informing Captain Lewis the route I intended to take, and proceeded on up the main North Fork through a valley, the day very hot.

Charbonneau, our interpreter, nearly tired out, one of his ankles failing him. The bottoms are extensive and tolerable land covered with tall grass and prickly pears. The hills and mountains are high, steep and rocky.

ELUSIVE INDIANS

Clark's increasingly anxious search for the Shoshone was beginning to take a toll on his health, as **Lewis** reports in his journal for **July 27**. There was, however, no question of his search being abandoned: failure to find the Indians—and their horses—might threaten the success of the entire enterprise.

Captain Clark arrived very sick, with a high fever on him, and much fatigued and exhausted. He informed me that he was very sick all last night, had a high fever and frequent chills and constant aching pains in all his muscles. This morning, notwithstanding his indisposition, he pursued his

"We are now several hundred miles from the bosom of this wild and mountainous country, where game may be expected shortly to become scarce."

intended route to the middle fork about 8 miles and, finding no recent sign of Indians, rested about an hour and came down the middle fork to this place. Captain Clark thought himself somewhat bilious and had not had a passage for several days. I prevailed on him to take a dose of Rush's pills, which I have always found sovereign in such cases, and to bathe his feet in warm water and rest himself.... We begin to feel considerable anxiety with respect to the Snake Indians. If we do not find them, or some other nation who have horses, I fear the successful issue of our voyage will be very doubtful, or at all events much more difficult in its accomplishment. We are now several hundred miles from the bosom of this wild and mountainous country, where game may rationally be expected shortly to become scarce, and subsistence precarious, without any information with respect to the country, not knowing how far these mountains continue, or where to direct our course to pass them to advantage or intercept a navigable branch of the Columbia. Or, even were we on such a one, the probability is that we would not find any timber within these mountains large enough for canoes, if we judge from the portion of them through which we have passed. However, I still hope for the best.... My two principal consolations are that, from our present position, it is impossible that the southwest fork can head with the waters of any other river but the Columbia, and that if any Indians can subsist in the form of a nation in these mountains with the means they have of acquiring food, we can also subsist.

MAKING HISTORY

The need having arisen to find fitting names for the three forks—or, more strictly speaking, the three tines of the one fork!—**Lewis** was clearly conscious of the historic importance of the moment:

July 28, 1805

Both Captain Clark and myself corresponded in opinion with respect to the impropriety of calling either of these streams the Missouri, and accordingly agreed to name them after the President of the United States and the Secretaries of the Treasury and State, having previously named one river in honor of the Secretaries of War and Navy. In pursuance of this resolution we called the southwest fork, that which we meant to ascend, Jefferson's River, in honor of that illustrious personage Thomas Jefferson. The middle fork we called Madison's River, in honor of James Madison, and the southeast fork we called Gallitin's River in honor of Albert Gallitin.

A historic moment for the United States, then, but there was another history to be found here too, as becomes apparent a little later in this same entry:

Our present camp is precisely on the spot that the Snake Indians were encamped at the time the Minnetarees of the Knife River first came in sight of them five years since. From hence they retreated about three miles up Jefferson's River and concealed themselves in the woods. The Minnetarees pursued, attacked them, killed 4 men, 4 women, a number of boys, and made prisoners of all the females and four boys. Sacagawea, our Indian woman, was one of the female prisoners taken at that time, though I cannot discover that she shows any emotion of sorrow in recollecting this event, or of joy in being restored to her native country. If she has enough to eat, and a few trinkets to wear, I believe she would be perfectly content anywhere.

Lewis seems to have been a decent, humane individual and he no doubt reported the truth as he perceived it—yet it was clearly convenient for him to see Sacagawea in this way. This same air of impassiveness would of course tell badly against Native Americans in the decades to come, allowing their white rulers to rationalize their policies of displacement.

Below: The Scalp Dance of the Minnetaree, as depicted by a nineteenth-century artist. **Opposite:** The South Boulder River, outside of Cardwell, Montana. Lewis led a party up here on August 1, 1805, in search of the Shoshone.

BEAVER DAMS

NATURE'S ENGINEER

Rising from a firm foundation of mud and stones, its branch and brushwood structure meticulously caulked with mud and vegetation, the beaver dam is a miracle of instinctive engineering. Added to year by year, and generation by generation, a dam may reach an aston- ishing extent: examples have been found up to 300 yards in length. And the dam is just the beginning: in the deep pond that forms behind it, the beaver builds its mud-and- stick lodge, its walls thick enough to withstand the most determined attacks from wolves and other predators. Its underwater entrances remain ice-free even in the depths of the severest winter, allowing the beaver to swim back and forth as it will between the lodge and the stack of logs and branches that serves it as a foodstore. Though it will eat more delicate water plants when it can get them, the beaver's staple fare is bark and twigs, so its con- struction materials are a by-product of its daily diet. A large rodent, weighing up to 55 pounds, the beaver is equipped with enormous and exceptionally strong incisors, just the thing for gnawing down and stripping riverside trees.

Today much of the upper Missouri is controlled by a series of vast concrete dams, constructed by the Army Corps of Engineers. Yet even when Lewis and Clark first came this way, these waters did not run completely free, as **Lewis** noted:

July 30, 1805
Saw a vast number of beaver in many large dams which they had made in various bayous of the river which are distributed to the distance of three or four miles on this side of the river, over an extensive bottom of tim- bered and meadow lands intermixed.

August 2, 1805
We saw some very large beaver dams today in the bottoms of the river, several of which were five feet high and overflowed several acres of land. These dams are formed of willow brush, mud and gravel, and are so closely interwoven that they resist the water perfectly. The base of this work is thick and rises nearly perpendicularly on the lower side, while the upper side, or that within the dam, is gently sloped. The brush appears to be laid in no regular order, yet acquires a strength by the irregularity with which they are placed by the beaver that it would puzzle the ingenuity of man to give them.

MOUNTING CONCERN

As the days went by, with no sign of the Shoshone—or of any end to what was coming to seem an interminable climb—**Lewis**'s concern was becoming clear, as in his journal for Thursday, **August 8**:

The Indian woman recognized the point of a high plain to our right which she informed us was not very distant from the summer retreat of her nation, on a river beyond the mountains which runs to the west. This hill, she says, her nation calls the Beaver's Head, from a conceived resemblance of its figure to the head of that animal. She assures us that we shall either find her people on this river or on the river immediately west of its source, which from its present size cannot be very distant. As it is now all-important for us to meet with those people as soon as possible, I determined to proceed tomorrow with a small party to the source of the principal stream of this river and pass the mountains to the Columbia, and down that river until I found the Indians. In short, it is my resolution to find them, or some others who have horses, if it should cause me a trip of one month. For without horses we shall be obliged to leave a great part of our stores, of which it appears to me that we have a stock already sufficiently small for the length of the voyage before us.

August 10, 1805

The mountains do not appear very high in any direction, though the tops of some of them are partially covered with snow. This convinces me that we have ascended to a great height since we have entered the Rocky Mountains, yet the ascent has been so gradual along the valleys that it was scarcely perceptible by land. I do not believe that the world can furnish an example of a river running to the extent which the Missouri and Jefferson Rivers do through such a mountainous country and at the same time so navigable as they are. If the Columbia furnishes us such another example, a communication across the continent by water will be practicable and safe. But this I can scarcely hope from a knowledge of its having in its comparatively short course to the ocean the same number of feet to descend which the Missouri and Mississippi have from this point to the Gulf of Mexico.

Right: Beside what is now Clark Canyon Reservoir, the Corps established a base camp, sinking their canoes for safe storage and making a cache of provisions for the return journey. In forays from here over the mountains, the explorers would make contact with the Shoshone and find them led by a relative of Sacagawea, hence the name of this site: "Camp Fortunate."

An Unsatisfactory Encounter

On **August 11**, at long last, **Lewis** could report,

I discovered an Indian on horseback, about two miles distant, coming down the plain towards us. With my glass I discovered from his dress that he was of a different nation from any that we had yet seen, and was satisfied of his being a Shoshone. His arms were a bow and quiver of arrows, and he was mounted on an elegant horse without a saddle, and a small string which was attached to the under-jaw of the horse which answered as a bridle. I was overjoyed at the sight of this stranger, and had no doubt of obtaining a friendly introduction to his nation, provided I could get near enough to him to convince him of our being white men. I therefore proceeded towards him at my usual pace. When I had arrived within about a mile, he made a halt, which I did also and, unloosing my blanket from my pack, I made him the signal of friendship known to the Indians of the Rocky Mountains and those of the Missouri, which is by holding the mantle or robe in your hands at two corners and then throwing it up in the air higher than the head, bringing it to the earth as if in the act of spreading it, thus repeating three times. This signal of the robe has arisen from a custom among all those nations of spreading a robe or skin for their guests to sit on when they are visited. This signal had not the desired effect. He still kept his position, and seemed to view Drewyer and Shields—who were now coming in sight on either hand—with an air of suspicion. I would willingly

have made them halt, but they were too far distant to hear me, and I feared to make any signal to them lest it should increase the suspicion in the mind of the Indian of our having some unfriendly design upon him. I therefore hastened to take out of my sack some beads, a looking glass and a few trinkets, which I had brought with me for this purpose, and, leaving my gun and pouch with McNeal, advanced unarmed towards him.

He remained in the same steadfast posture until I arrived in about 200 paces of him, when he turned his horse about and began to move off slowly from me. I now called to him in as loud a voice as I could command, repeating the word *tab-ba-bone*, which in their language signifies *white man*. But, looking over his shoulder, he still kept

"I repeated the word tab-ba-bone and held up the trinkets in my hands, and stripped up my shirt-sleeve to give him an opportunity of seeing the color of my skin…"

his eye on Drewyer and Shields, who were still advancing, neither of them having sagacity enough to recollect the impropriety of advancing when they saw me thus in parley with the Indian. I now made a signal to these men to halt. Drewyer obeyed, but Shields—who afterwards told me he did not observe the signal—still kept on. The Indian halted again and turned his horse about, as if to wait for me, and I believe he would have remained until I came up with him had it not been for Shields, who still pressed forward. When I arrived within about 150 paces I again repeated the word *tab-ba-bone* and held up the trinkets in my hands, and stripped up my shirt-sleeve to give him an opportunity of seeing the color of my skin, and advanced leisurely towards him. But he did not remain until I got nearer than about 100 paces, when he suddenly turned his horse about, gave him the whip, leaped the creek and disappeared in the willow brush in an instant, and with him vanished all my hopes of obtaining horses for the present.

Below: A Flathead camp on the Jacko River, recorded by Curtis in 1910. The Salish-speaking Flathead were the easternmost of the Plateau peoples.

An Objective Achieved; An Objective Postponed

Lewis's bitter disappointment was much alleviated the next day when the Expedition found itself at what was (mistakenly) assumed to be the source of the Missouri. In fact, that great river originates in the various little streams flowing into Upper Red Rock Lake in western Montana, but who would begrudge him this long-awaited and hard-earned moment of triumph?

At the distance of 4 miles further, the road took us to the most distant fountain of the waters of the Mighty Missouri, in search of which we had spent so many toilsome days and restless nights. Thus far I had accomplished one of those great objects on which my mind has been unalterably fixed for many years. Judge then of the pleasure I felt in allaying my thirst with this pure and ice-cold water which issues from the base of a low mountain or hill of a gentle ascent for ½ a mile. The mountains are high on either hand, leave this gap at the head of this rivulet through which the road passes. Here I halted a few minutes and rested myself. Two miles below, McNeal had exultingly stood with a foot on each side of this little rivulet, and thanked his God that he had lived to bestride the mighty and heretofore deemed endless Missouri.

Yet in the very moment of glory, reaching the Great Divide 7,373 feet (2,247m) up on the Lemhi Pass, Lewis would find himself confronting a sobering prospect—no easy descent to the Pacific, but more high mountains.

After refreshing ourselves, we proceeded on to the top of the dividing ridge, from which I discovered immense ranges of high mountains still to the West of us, with their tops partially covered with snow.

Still, to have crossed the Continental Divide—the line demarcating the watersheds of those rivers that flowed westward into the Pacific from those that flowed eastward toward the Atlantic—was a major achievement, and Lewis would not be downcast for long.

I now descended the mountain about ¾ of a mile, which I found much steeper than the opposite side, to a handsome, bold, running creek of cold, clear water. Here I first tasted the water of the great Columbia River.

Above: There are more trees here than when Lewis and Clark came this way in August 1805, but otherwise the Lemhi Pass looks much the same. Stands of Douglas fir and Lodgepole pine punctuate open expanses of sagebrush and grass (inset). All looks serene, but at 7,373 feet above sea level appearances can be deceptive: conditions can deteriorate rapidly.

MEETING THE SHOSHONE

On **August 13** the Expedition came into contact with more Shoshone—a man and two women, with their dogs. Initially, at least, the Indians remained extremely wary:

When we had arrived within half a mile of them, I directed the party to halt and, leaving my pack and rifle, I took the flag, which I unfurled and advanced singly towards them. The women soon disappeared behind the hill; the man continued until I arrived within a hundred yards of him, and then likewise absconded, though I frequently repeated the word *tab-ba-bone* sufficiently loud for him to have heard it. I now hastened to the top of the hill where they had stood, but could see nothing of them. The dogs were less shy than their masters. They came about me pretty close. I therefore thought of tying a handkerchief about one of their necks with some beads and other trinkets and then let them loose to search their fugitive owners, thinking by this means to convince them of our pacific disposition towards them, but the dogs would not suffer me to take hold of them. They also soon disappeared....

We had not continued our route more than a mile when we were so fortunate as to meet with three female savages. The short and steep ravines which we passed concealed us from each other until we arrived within 30 paces. A young woman immediately took to flight; an elderly woman and a girl of about 12 years old remained. I instantly laid by my gun and advanced towards them. They appeared much alarmed but saw that we were too near for them to escape by flight. They therefore seated themselves on the ground, holding down their heads as if reconciled to die, which they expected no doubt would be their fate. I took the elderly woman by the hand and raised her up, repeated the word *tab-ba-bone* and stripped up my shirt-sleeve to show her my skin, to prove to her the truth of the assertion that I was a white man, for my face and hands, which have been constantly exposed to the sun, were quite as dark as their own. They appeared instantly reconciled, and the men coming up I gave these women some beads, a few moccasin awls, some pewter looking-glasses and a little paint.... I now painted their tawny cheeks with some vermilion, which with this

nation is emblematic of peace. After they had become composed, I informed them by signs that I wished them to conduct us to their camp, that we were anxious to become acquainted with the chiefs and warriors of their nation. They readily obeyed, and we set out, still pursuing the road down the river.

We had marched about 2 miles when we met a party of about 60 warriors mounted on excellent horses, who came in nearly full speed. When they arrived I advanced towards them with the flag, leaving my gun with the party about 50 paces behind me. The chief and two others, who were a little in advance of the main body, spoke to the women, and they informed them who we were and exultingly showed the presents which had been given them. These men then advanced and embraced me very affectionately in their way, which is by putting their left arm over your right shoulder, clasping your back, while they apply their left cheek to yours and frequently vociferate the word *âh-hí-e, âh-hí-e*—that is, I am much pleased, I am much rejoiced. Both parties now advanced and we were all caressed and besmeared with their grease and paint till I was

> *"Both parties now advanced and we were all caressed and besmeared with their grease and paint till I was heartily tired of the national hug."*

heartily tired of the national hug. I now had the pipe lit and gave them smoke; they seated themselves in a circle around us and pulled off their moccasins before they would receive or smoke the pipe. This is a custom among them, as I afterwards learned, indicative of a sacred obligation of sincerity in their profession of friendship, given by the act of receiving and smoking the pipe of a stranger. Or which is as much as to say that they wish they may always go barefoot if they are not sincere—a pretty heavy penalty if they are to march through the plains of their country. After smoking a few pipes with them I distributed some trifles among them, with which they seemed much pleased, particularly with the blue beads and vermilion.

I now informed the chief that the object of our visit was a friendly one, that after we should reach his camp I would undertake to explain to him fully those objects, who we were, from whence we had come and whither we were going; that in the meantime I did not care how soon we were in motion, as the sun was very warm and no water at hand. They now put on their moccasins, and the principal chief Cameahwait made a short speech to the warriors. I gave him the flag, which I informed him was an emblem of peace among white men, and now that it had been received by him it was to be respected as the bond of union between us.

Back at the camp, Lewis and his men were invited to participate in a second, more formal, pipe ceremony:

Here we were seated on green boughs and the skins of antelopes. One of the warriors then pulled up the grass in the center of the lodge, forming a small circle of about 2 feet in diameter. The chief next produced his pipe and native tobacco and began a long ceremony of the pipe when we were requested to take off our moccasins, the chief having previously taken off his as well as all the warriors present. This we complied with. The chief then lit his pipe at the fire kindled in this little magic circle and, standing on the opposite side of the circle, uttered a speech of several minutes in length, at the conclusion of which he pointed the stem to the four cardinal points of the heavens, first beginning at the east and ending with the north. He now presented the pipe to me as if desirous that I should smoke, but when I reached my hand to receive it he drew it back and repeated the same ceremony three times, after which he pointed the stem first to the heavens, then to the center of the magic circle, smoked himself with three whiffs, and held the pipe until I took as many as I thought proper. He then held it to each of the white persons and then gave it to be consumed by his warriors.

This pipe was made of a dense, semitransparent green stone, very highly polished, about 2½ inches long and of an oval figure, the bowl being in the same direction with the stem. A small piece of burned clay is placed in the bottom of the bowl to separate the tobacco from the end of the stem and is of an irregularly rounded figure not fitting the tube perfectly close in order that the smoke may pass.

THE "PEACE PIPE"

The pipe was a central feature of ceremonial life for many native North American peoples. Its heaven-seeking smoke suggesting piety (like Old World incense), the sense of bonding as it was passed from man to man. The pipe was the perfect way of sealing an agreement, or rounding off some important ritual. It would thus be used before a hunt, after successful business dealings, as part of a healing ceremony or for that matter in preparation for war—and also to cement a friendship or political alliance. So while the pipe may be a Native American institution, the narrow notion of the "peace pipe" belongs to the white man—for it was in this particular context that he encountered the tradition. One such encounter is depicted in this illustration by Patrick Gass.

A Family Reunion

their curiosity very much, and they seemed quite as anxious to see this monster as they were the merchandise which we had to barter for their horses.

August 17, 1805

An Indian who had straggled some little distance down the river returned and reported that the white men were coming, that he had seen them just below. They all appeared transported with joy, and the chief repeated his fraternal hug. I felt quite as much gratified at this information as the Indians appeared to be. Shortly after, Captain Clark arrived with the interpreter Charbonneau and the Indian woman, who proved to be a sister of Chief Cameahwait. The meeting of those people was really affecting, particularly between Sacagawea and an Indian woman who had been taken prisoner at the same time with her and who had afterwards escaped from the Minnetarees and rejoined her nation.

Sacagawea was still with the main party, yet to meet up with her people again. But as **Lewis** noted, on **August 16**:

I had mentioned to the chief several times that we had with us a woman of his nation who had been taken prisoner by the Minnetarees, and that by means of her I hoped to explain myself more fully than I could do signs. Some of the party had also told the Indians that we had a man with us who was black and had short curling hair. This had excited

Top: "Janey," as Sacagawea was known, was treated with kindness but also a great deal of condescension by Lewis and Clark, who could hardly have guessed how her story would stir the imagination of a later age. This statue is to be seen at the Lewis and Clark State College, Lewiston, Idaho. Right: The Lemhi River valley, near the site of Sacagawea's reunion with her brother, Chief Cameahwait.

THE SHOSHONE REPUBLIC

Lewis was shocked by the Shoshone's poverty, but impressed both by their happy stoicism and their democratic ease, as he observed in his notes for **August 19**:

They are not only cheerful but even gay, fond of gaudy dress and amusements. Like most other Indians they are great egotists and frequently boast of heroic acts which they never performed. They are also fond of games of risk. They are frank, communicative, fair in dealing, generous with the little they possess, extremely honest and by no means beggarly. Each individual is his own sovereign master, and acts from the dictates of his own mind, the authority of the chief being nothing more than mere admonition, supported by the influence which the propriety of his own exemplary conduct may have acquired him in the minds of the individuals who compose the band. The title of chief is not hereditary, nor can I learn that there is any ceremony of installment…. In fact every man is a chief, but all have not an equal influence on the minds of the other members of the community, and he who happens to enjoy the greatest share of confidence is the principal chief.

"Like most other Indians they are great egotists and frequently boast of heroic acts which they never performed."

Lewis was less impressed with what might be called the Shoshone's domestic politics:

The Shoshones may be estimated at about 100 warriors, and about three times that number of women and children. They have more children among them than I expected to have seen among a people who procure subsistence with such difficulty. There are very few old persons, nor did they appear to treat those with much tenderness or respect. The man is the sole proprietor of his wives and daughters, and can barter or dispose of either as he thinks proper. A plurality of wives is common among them…. They seldom correct their children, particularly the boys, who soon become masters of their own acts. They give as a reason that it cows and breaks the spirit of the boy to whip him, and that he never recovers his independence of mind after he is grown. They treat their women but with little respect, and compel them to perform every species of drudgery. They collect the wild fruits and roots, attend to the horses or assist in that duty, cook, dress the skins and make all their apparel, collect wood and make their fires, arrange and form their lodges, and when they travel pack the horses and take charge of all the baggage. In short, the man does little else except attend his horses, hunt and fish.

He was even less complimentary about their physical appearance:

These people are diminutive in stature, thick ankles, crooked legs, thick, flat feet, and in short but illy formed, at least much more so in general

"MOST ELEGANT"

"The tippet of the Snake Indians is the most elegant piece of Indian dress I ever saw," says Lewis in his journal for August 20. "The neck or collar of this is formed of a strip of dressed otter skin with the fur. It is about four or five inches wide and is cut out of the back of the skin, the nose and eyes forming one extremity and the tail the other." The "tippet," a sort of ornamental shawl, was worn over a robe of deer or antelope, bighorn—or, where possible, buffalo. The Shoshone may have been poor—and in Lewis's eyes ill-favored—but they took the greatest pains with their self-presentation.

than any nation of Indians I ever saw. Their complexion is much that of the Sioux, or darker than the Minnetarees, Mandans or Shawnees. Generally, both men and women wear their hair in a loose, lank flow over the shoulders and face…. The dress of the men consists of a robe, long leggings, shirt, tippet, and moccasins; that of the women is also a robe, chemise and moccasins. Sometimes they make use of short leggings. The ornaments of both men and women are very similar, and consist of several species of seashells, blue and white beads, brass and iron armbands, plaited cords of the sweet grass, and collars of leather ornamented with the quills of the porcupine dyed of various colors, among which I observed the red, yellow, blue, and black. The ear is perforated in the lower part to receive various ornaments, but the nose is not, nor is the ear lacerated or disfigured for this purpose as among many nations. The men never mark their skins by burning, cutting, nor puncturing and introducing a coloring matter as many nations do. Their women sometimes puncture a small circle on their forehead, nose or cheeks and thus introduce a black matter—usually soot and grease—which leaves an indelible stain, though this even is by no means common. Their arms offensive and defensive consist in the bow and arrows, shield, some lances….

From the middle of May to the first of September these people reside on the waters of the Columbia, where they consider themselves in perfect security from their enemies as they have not as yet ever found their way to this retreat. During this season the salmon furnish the principal part of their subsistence, and as this fish either perishes or returns about the 1st of September they are compelled at this season in search of subsistence to resort to the Missouri, in the valleys of which there is more game, even within the mountains. Here they move slowly down the river in order to collect and join other bands either of their own nation or the Flatheads, and having become sufficiently strong, as they conceive, venture on the eastern side of the Rocky Mountains into the plains, where the buffalo abound. But they never leave the interior of the mountains while they can obtain a scanty subsistence, and always return as soon as they have acquired a good stock of dried meat in the plains, thus alternately obtaining their food at the risk of their lives and retiring to the mountains while they consume it.

Above: On August 21, 1805, having followed the Lemhi River down to its confluence with the Salmon River, the Corps set up camp before this bluff, at the mouth of Tower Creek, just north of Salmon, Idaho.

MOUNTAIN DIPLOMACY

A few days later, on **August 20**, **Lewis** spent a day smoking and chatting with the Shoshone, gaining further insights into an existence characterized above all by chronic insecurity:

They informed me that they could pass to the Spaniards by the way of the Yellowstone River in 10 days. I can discover that these people are by no means friendly to the Spaniards. Their complaint is that the Spaniards will not let them have firearms and ammunition, that they put them off by telling them that if they suffer them to have guns they will kill each other, thus leaving them defenseless and an easy prey to their bloodthirsty neighbors to the east of them, who, being in possession of firearms, hunt them up and murder them without respect to sex or age and plunder them of their horses on all occasions. They told me that, to avoid their enemies who were eternally harassing them, they were obliged to remain in the interior of these mountains at least two thirds of the year, where they suffered, as we then saw, great hardships for the want of food, sometimes living for weeks without meat and only a little fish, roots and berries. But this, added Cameahwait, with his fierce eyes and lank jaws grown meager for the want of food, would not be the case if we had guns. We could then live in the country of buffalo and eat as our enemies do…. We do not fear our enemies when placed on an equal footing with them.

"We do not fear our enemies when placed on an equal footing with them."

I told them that the Minnetarees, Mandans and Ricarees of the Missouri had promised us to desist from making war on them, and that … after our finally returning to our homes towards the rising sun, white men would come to them with an abundance of guns and every other article necessary to their defense and comfort, and that they would be enabled to supply themselves with these articles on reasonable terms in exchange for the skins of the beaver, otter and ermine so abundant in their country.

Above: The explorers found a small Shoshone camp when they reached the North Fork of the Salmon River on August 22, 1805. Its inhabitants were poor and hungry—and so nervous that many fled on the Expedition's arrival. Opposite: The Salmon River at North Fork, Idaho: the "dreadful narrows" explored by Clark's reconnaissance party on August 24, 1805.

IN THE NAME OF HONOR

"These people have many names in the course of their lives," observed **Lewis** of the Shoshone on **August 24**:

For it seems that every important event by which they happen to distinguish themselves entitles them to claim another name, which is generally selected by themselves and confirmed by the nation. Those distinguishing acts are the killing and scalping an enemy, the killing [of] a white bear, leading a party to war who happen to be successful, either in destroying their enemies or robbing them of their horses, or individually stealing the horses of an enemy. These are considered acts of equal heroism among them, and that of killing an enemy without scalping him is considered of no importance. In fact, the whole honor seems to be founded in the act of scalping, for if a man happens to slay a dozen of his enemies in action and others get the scalps or first lay their hand on the dead person, the honor is lost to him who killed them and devolves on those who scalp or first touch them. Among the Shoshones, as well as all the Indians of America, bravery is esteemed the primary virtue, nor can anyone become eminent among them who has not at some period of his life given proofs of his possessing this virtue, and so completely inter-woven is this principle with the earliest elements of thought that it will in my opinion prove a serious obstruction to the restoration of a general peace among the nations of the Missouri.

A FISH TRAP

At one Shoshone village, Expedition members saw a weir specially designed for catching salmon. As Lewis reports:

It extended across four channels of the river, which was here divided by three small islands. Three of these channels were narrow, and were stopped by means of trees fallen across, supported by which stakes of willow were driven down sufficiently near each other to prevent the salmon from passing. About the center of each a cylindric basket of eighteen or 20 feet in length, terminating in a conic shape at its lower extremity, formed of willows, was opposed to a small aperture in the weir, with its mouth upstream to receive the fish…. The weir in the main channel was somewhat differently contrived. There were two distinct weirs formed of poles and willow sticks, quite across the river, at no great distance from each other. Each of these were furnished with two baskets, the one weir to take them ascending and the other in descending.

THE DESCENT BEGINS

After talking to the Shoshone about the way ahead, **Lewis** decided to leave the canoes behind and buy horses, with a view to building new boats once conditions allowed it farther downstream. As he wrote on **August 29**,

Our wish is to get a horse for each man to carry our baggage, and for some of the men to ride occasionally. The horses are handsome, and much accustomed to be changed as to their pasture. We cannot calculate on their carrying large loads and feed on the grass which we may calculate on finding in the mountains through which we may expect to pass on our route.

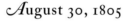

August 30, 1805

Finding that we could purchase no more horses than we had for our goods etc. (and those not a sufficient number for each of our party to have one, which is our wish), I gave my fusil to one of the men and sold his musket for a horse, which completed us to 29 total horses. We purchased pack cords, made saddles and set out on our route down the river by land.

Above: "Passed remarkable rocks resembling pyramids," noted Lewis on August 31, 1805. The formation is still to be seen, standing ten miles north of Salmon, Idaho. Below: The Salmon River, commented Clark, "is almost one continued rapid." This section is at North Fork, Idaho.

SCALPING

Little is really known of the origins of scalping, though it is believed to have begun in far-off prehistoric times, and is assumed in some way to represent the victor's taking possession of the life-force of his vanquished enemy. A French soldier, known only as "J.C.B.," who fought the Indians near what is now the U.S.-Canada border, south of Quebec, left a memorable description of how the scalp was actually taken:

"The savage quickly seizes his knife, and makes an incision around the hair from the upper part of the forehead to the back of the neck. Then he puts his foot on the shoulder of the victim, whom he has turned over face down, and pulls the hair off with both hands, from back to front.

Afterwards, once he was at leisure, the Indian brave would scrape the skin clean of flesh and dry it in the sun, before painting it red and carefully combing out the hair. He would then hang his macabre trophy—perhaps with others—on a stick as a banner for battle, or display it proudly round the door of his lodge or tepee."

The descent, it soon became clear, would be arduous:

September 2, 1805

Proceeded on through thickets in which we were obliged to cut a road; over rocky hillsides where our horses were in perpetual danger of slipping to their certain destruction, and up and down steep hills where several horses fell. Some turned over, and others slipped down steep hillsides. One horse crippled and two gave out.

September 3, 1805

Hills high and rocky on each side. In the after part of the day, the high mountains closed the creek on each side and obliged us to take on the steep sides of those mountains—so steep that the horses could scarcely keep from slipping down…but little to eat.

September 9, 1805

We continued our route down the valley about four miles and crossed the river. It is here a handsome stream about 100 yards wide and affords a considerable quantity of very clear water. The banks are low, and its bed entirely gravel. The stream appears navigable, but from the circumstance of there being no salmon in it I believe that there must be a considerable fall below.

September 12, 1805

The road through this hilly country is very bad, passing over hills and through steep hollows, over falling timber, etc., etc. Continued on and passed some most intolerable road on the sides of the steep, stony mountains.

September 15, 1805

Several horses slipped and rolled down steep hills which hurt them very much. The one which carried my desk and small trunk turned over and rolled down the mountain for 40 yards and lodged against a tree. Broke the desk—the horse escaped and appeared but little hurt....

After two hours delay we proceeded on up the mountain...I could observe high, rugged mountains in every direction as far as I could see.

Above: "The road through this hilly country is very bad, passing over hills and through steep hollows, over falling timber, etc, etc." Idaho's Lolo Pass, at Crooked Forks.
Opposite: Clark ventured up this valley with a small party in the early days of September 1805 to see whether it offered a shortcut through the mountains to the Columbia River. The resulting frustrations have been immortalized in its modern title, "Lost Trail Pass." Below: The Expedition found an easier route along the Bitterroot River valley to the Creek they called, with relief and gratitude, "Traveler's Rest."

September 16, 1805

Began to snow about 3 hours before day and continued all day.... I have been wet and as cold in every part as I ever was in my life, indeed I was at one time fearful my feet would freeze.

September 19, 1805

Frazier's horse fell from this road in the evening, and rolled with his load near a hundred yards into the creek. We all expected that the horse was killed, but to our astonishment, when the load was taken off him he arose to his feet and appeared to be but little injured. In 20 minutes he proceeded with his load. This was the most wonderful escape I ever witnessed. The hill down which he rolled was almost perpendicular, and broken by large irregular and broken rocks.

September 21, 1805

I find myself growing weak for the want of food and most of the men complain of a similar deficiency, and have fallen off very much.

So September went by in an apparently endless round of hardship, those few Native Americans they met being too hard pressed themselves to have much in the way of provisions they could trade. By October, overtaxed bodies were starting to register the stresses and strains. As **Clark** reports on **October 5**:

At least they were back afloat now, having successfully built themselves canoes. From here on, their progress would be easier—and, with the current carrying them, a great deal swifter. Supplies of food were still short, and many fell sick in the days that followed, but they could sense that the worst of their hardships would soon be at an end. Within a few days, indeed, they had reached the villages of the Chopunnish (Nez Percé). They proved friendly, by and large, and had ample food.

Nothing to eat except dried fish and roots. Captain Lewis and myself ate a supper of roots boiled, which swelled us in such a manner that we were scarcely able to breathe for several hours.… Our hunters with every diligence could kill nothing. The hills high and rugged and woods too dry to hunt the deer which is the only game in the neighborhood. Several squaws came with fish and roots which we purchased of them for beads, which they were fond of. Captain Lewis not so well today as yesterday.

Opposite: Lewis and Clark converse with the Nez Percé, as depicted in a statue at Lewis and Clark State College, Lewiston, Idaho. Above: The Clearwater River winds before a line of tepees at the Nez Percé reservation near Orofino, Idaho, just as it must have done when Lewis and Clark stopped here 200 years ago. Right: A Nez Percé scout on horseback, captured by the camera of Curtis early in the twentieth century. Below: "Proceeded on through a beautiful country for three miles to a small plain in which I found many Indian lodges." Weippe Prairie, Idaho, where the Expedition met the Nez Percé, September 20, 1805.

DOWN TO THE SEA

"Great joy in camp. We are in view of the ocean, this great Pacific Ocean which we have been so long anxious to see, and the roaring...made by the waves breaking on the rocky shores may be heard distinctly."

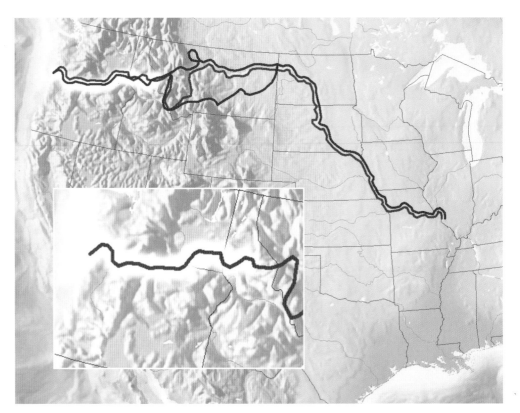

Opposite: *Ocean spray and the never-ending thunder of the ocean breakers: The Pacific Coast was a new experience for men who thought they had seen the most magnificent sights and faced every challenge the Western wilderness could confront them with. The Corps of Discovery spent four months through the winter of 1805–06 near this bay at Indian Point, Cannon Beach, Oregon.*

Lewis and Clark could be forgiven for feeling quite relieved as they reached the relatively open-running waters of the Snake River. The preceding weeks had marked not just the hardest but the most frightening phase of their journey to date. Predictable though they might have been in theory (indeed, Lewis had admitted having feared rather worse), in practice nothing could have prepared them for the physical and mental rigors of the Rocky Mountain portage. That done, there had been the arduous and apparently endless ascent to the Lemhi Pass—the culmination, they had promised themselves, of their climb. Yet they had finally reached the heights of the Great Divide only to find that there was no finality about it. They were met with the panoramic prospect not of the Pacific, but of yet more mountains. Even when their long-delayed descent had begun, they had found themselves cheated of their tri-umph, as hunger—and anxiety—gnawed away at them from the inside. That they should have come this far only to die of hunger had never been in the script, yet must suddenly have seemed only too real a possibility to the exhausted men. Their journals for late September show an expedition in danger of spinning out of control, its leaders alert to the dangers yet helpless, drained by hunger and fatigue, and laid low with illness. Only weeks before, on July 27, Lewis had—perhaps arrogantly—consoled himself:

If any Indians can subsist in the form of a nation in these mountains with the means they have of acquiring food, we can also subsist.

Yet this confidence must have been severely shaken by the fact that those native communities they had encountered in the early days of their descent had plainly been all but prostrated by hunger and want themselves. With no corn or squash to be had, no vegetable food at all, indeed, beyond the most meager roots and berries—and certainly no sign of their own hunters finding game in significant amounts—the explorers were in a very dangerous situation.

Now, however, it looked as though the Expedition was back on course at last— even if Lewis was already fretting at the thought that they were behind schedule! And while he had already worked out that the Columbia River must descend very steeply, with difficult rapids pretty much a certainty, there was the comforting sense that they would soon be back on relatively reassuring ground. Not only could the coastal strip be expected to be far more benign than just about any stretch of country they had so far traversed, but it was already to some extent a known quantity. The Corps of Discovery may have been pioneers in the western interior, but sections of the Pacific Coast had been explored and charted by a num-

Right: *The conical mass of Wind Mountain hints at the violent forces that built the Western Seaboard: It is, essentially, the basalt plug of an extinct volcano. Yet the gently lapping waters of the Columbia River in the foreground give a better sense of the region now, a place of mild temperatures and softly descending mist and rain.*

ber of previous seaborne expeditions. Since Bartolome Ferrello first came this way in 1542, several Spanish seafarers had explored these shores—most recently (and most methodically) Bruno de Heceta and Francisco de la Bodega y Quadra in 1775. The Englishman Captain James Cook (1729–89), whose voyages of exploration had been an inspiration to Thomas Jefferson in conceiving the idea for the Corps of Discovery, had sailed up parts of North America's Pacific Coast in 1776. During the return leg of that expedition, his third, he had been tragically killed. Great explorer though he might have been, Cook had by no means been infallible: Caught up in a violent storm, he had missed the mouth of the Columbia River altogether! Another Englishman, Captain George Vancouver, who sailed up the coast in 1792, discovering Puget Sound, would also turn out to be a somewhat erratic guide. That same year, the American trader Robert Gray had finally found and given a name to the Columbia River, so Lewis and Clark did at least have a clear idea of where they were headed. Even so, each of their predecessors had been restricted by his ship, his equipment, his manpower, and the conditions under which he had had to operate. The picture was by no means complete, and

was often actually erroneous. But this was what it meant to be at the cutting edge of early exploration, of course: each expedition having to learn by its predecessors' mistakes—sometimes the hard way. This appreciation lay some way ahead, though. For the moment, Lewis and Clark could find comfort in the assumption that, as far as they had come from their point of departure, for the first time in months they were approaching charted territory.

They also had the prospect of the winter to look forward to—for if that season held fears it also offered an opportunity for rest and recuperation. Not that the building and maintenance of winter quarters, the foraging for food and information, and the establishment of good relations with the native peoples could be managed without a great deal of hard work and energetic organization, nor that weeks of gales and rainstorms were likely to be conducive to the taking of their ease. But in the seven months since they had left their last winter quarters, there had scarcely been any letup in their regime. Up in the morning, striking camp, setting off for another day's arduous travel by water or overland trudge, then pitching camp for another night—and all to do again the next day, and the one after that,

Above *The Clearwater River, near Orofino, Idaho. The Expedition set off down this stretch of river on October 7, 1805, in its newly built canoes. Lewis was "very unwell, but obliged to attend everything," he reported. The explorers had left their horses with the Nez Percé at Canoe Camp.*

and so on. Winter, whatever its hardships, would at least bring a break in routine, a different daily cycle; there would be time, too, for reflection, for taking stock. A chance for cataloging specimens, writing up the notes, and for collecting one's thoughts, for thinking through the enormous significance of what had been achieved.

Right: A monument to the explorers at Station Camp, near Chinook, Washington, where the Corps stayed November 15–25, 1805.

As we have seen, Lewis and Clark had long since realized that the goal of an inland "northwest passage" had proved illusory—they would be reminded of this as they shot down the giddy rapids of the Columbia River day after day. There would be no big barges plying up and down this stream carrying the products of U.S. industry in return for the riches of Cathay; no neat little portage over the Continental Divide. On the other hand, their journey had given them an as yet unique opportunity to experience the vast scale of their continent, and to sense the enormous possibilities that were opening up before their country. Today it seems self-evident that the United States should occupy the full breadth of North America from the Atlantic to the Pacific; at the start of the nineteenth century, there was no inevitability about that fact at all. The idea of "Manifest Destiny" would not be formulated for another forty years, and even then would not be universally accepted. To many, it just meant new territories to administer and new "savages" to subdue—a new set of unwelcome responsibilities, in other words. In itself, the Lewis and Clark Expedition would do nothing to change the situation—indeed, its failure to find a viable water route arguably made the settlement of the far West that much less urgent a priority. Symbolically, however, its achievement would have more impact, as would the detail of the *Journals* when they afterwards emerged. For it is here that we find the first signs of an emotional investment in the West and everything it seemed to stand for, which would one day become a big part of what it meant to be an American.

Below: Washington's Lake Wallula is formed by the dammed waters of the Columbia River. The Corps of Discovery passed this point on October 18, 1805.

RAPID PROGRESS

"We passed today nine rapids," noted **Clark** in his journal on **October 11**. "We should make more portages if the season was not so far advanced and time precious with us." The temptation to get on as fast as possible, regardless of the risks, was understandable under the circumstances, but the risks were real, as Clark would discover:

***Above:** Making rapid progress down the Clearwater, and then the Snake River, the explorers reached what is now the Central Ferry State Park, near Dodge, Washington, by October 12, 1805.*

Passed rapids at 6 and 9 miles. At 12 miles we came to at the head of a rapid which the Indians told me was very bad. We viewed the rapid, found it bad. In descending, three stern canoes stuck fast for some time on the head of the rapid, and one struck a rock in the worst part. Fortunately, all landed safe below the rapid, which was nearly 3 miles in length. Here we dined, and for the first time for three weeks past I had a good dinner — of blue-winged teal.

After dinner we set out, and had not proceeded on two miles before our stern canoe, in passing through a short rapid opposite the head of an island, ran on a smooth rock and turned broadside. The men got out on the rock, all except one of our Indian chiefs, who swam on shore. The canoe filled and sank. A number of articles floated out, such as the men's bedding, clothes, and skins, the greater part of which were caught by 2 of the canoes, whilst a third was unloading and stemming the swift current, to the relief of the men on the rock, who could with much difficulty hold the canoe. However, in about an hour we got the men and canoe to shore, with the loss of some bedding, tomahawks, shot pouches, skins, clothes, etc., all wet. We had every article exposed to the sun to dry on the island. Our loss in provisions is very considerable. All our roots were in the canoe that sank, and cannot be dried sufficient to save. Our loose powder was also in the canoe and is all wet. This I think may be saved.

In this island we found some split timber, the parts of a house which the Indians had very securely covered with stone. We also observed a place where the Indians had buried their fish. We have made it a point at all times not to take anything belonging to the Indians, even their wood. But at this time we are compelled to violate that rule and take a part of the split timber we find here buried for firewood, as no other is to be found in any direction.

A WANAPAM VILLAGE

On **October 17**, **Clark** took a short detour to see a village of the Sokulk, or Wanapam, who lived in lodges of rush matting by the riverside:

I took two men in a small canoe, and ascended the Columbia River 10 miles to an island near the starboard shore on which two large mat lodges Indians were drying salmon (as they informed me by signs, for the purpose of food and fuel, and I do not think it at all improbable that those people make use of dried fish as fuel. The number of dead salmon on the shores and floating in the river is incredible to say—and at this season they have only to collect the fish, split them open and dry them on their scaffolds, on which they have great numbers. How far they have to raft their timber they make their scaffolds of I could not learn, but there is no timber of any sort except small willow bushes in sight in any direction....

One of those mat lodges I entered. Found it crowded with men, women and children, and near the entrance of those houses I saw many squaws engaged in splitting and drying salmon. I was fur-nished with a mat to sit on, and one man set about preparing me something to eat. First he brought in a piece of a drift-log of pine, and, with a wedge of the elk's horn and a mallet of stone curiously carved, he split the log into small pieces and laid it open on the fire, on which he put round stones. A woman handed him a basket of water and a large salmon about half dried. When the stones were hot he put them into the basket of water with the fish which was soon sufficiently boiled for use. It was then taken out, put on a platter of rushes neatly made and set before me. They boiled a salmon for each of the men with me. During those preparations I smoked with those about me who chose to smoke, which was but few, this being a custom those people are but little accustomed to, and only smoke through form.

Though a little perturbed at the scanty loincloths of the Wanapam women (which, he said, "barely… hide those parts which are so sacredly hid and secured by our women"), Clark was more favorably impressed by some of their attitudes:

Those people appear to live in a state of comparative happiness: they take a greater share in the labor of the women than is common among savage tribes, and as I am informed are content with one wife…. Those people respect the aged with veneration. I observed an old woman in one of the lodges which I entered. She was entirely blind, as I was informed by signs, had lived more than 100 winters. She occupied the best position in the house, and when she spoke great attention was paid to what she said….

Those people appear of a mild disposition and friendly disposed. They have in their huts—independent of their nets, gigs and fishing tackles— each bows and large quivers and arrows on which they use flint spikes. Their amusements are similar to those of the Missouri. They are not beggarly, and receive what is given them with much joy.

I saw but few horses. They appeared to make but little use of those animals, principally using canoes for the purposes of procuring food, etc.

*Opposite, top: Lodged high in a tree, these salmon caches should deter all but the most intrepid animal— or human—thieves. **Opposite, center:** A Chinook Tlakluit woman prepares salmon in this photograph by Edward Curtis. **Opposite, below:** The Corps reached the confluence of the Snake and Columbia Rivers on October 16, 1805. **Above:** Lake Wallula and (inset) the nearby basalt pillars known as the "Two Sisters"—according to legend, they were turned to stone by their jealous husband, the Coyote.*

An Indian Fish Factory

Just below the mouth of the Deschutes River, on **October 22**, **Clark** saw Indians preserving salmon on an all but industrial scale:

I observe great numbers of stacks of pounded salmon, neatly preserved in the following manner: i.e., after being sufficiently dried it is pounded between two stones fine, and put into a species of basket neatly made of grass and rushes better than two feet long and one foot diameter, which basket is lined with the skin of salmon stretched and dried for the purpose. In this it is pressed down as hard as is possible. When full, they secure the open part with the fish skins, across which they fasten through the loops of the basket that part very securely, and then on a dry situation they set those baskets the corded part up. Their common custom is to set 7 as close as they can stand, and 5 on top of them, and secure them with mats which is wrapped around them and made fast with cords and covered also with mats. Those 12 baskets of from 90 to 100 lbs. each form a stack. Thus preserved those fish may be kept sound and sweet several years, as those people inform me. Great quantities as they inform us are sold to the white people who visit the mouth of this river, as well as to the natives below.

He was just as impressed the next day to see on the river beach "two beautiful canoes."

[They were] of different shape and size to what we had seen above: wide in the middle, and tapering to each end; on the bow curious figures were cut in the wood, etc. Captain Lewis went up to the lodges to see those canoes and exchanged our smallest canoe for one of them by giving a hatchet and few trinkets to the owner, who informed that he purchased it of a white man below for horse. These canoes are neater made than any I have ever seen, and calculated to ride the waves and carry immense burdens.

There were still rough waters to be navigated, as they would be reminded the very next day:

Captain Lewis and myself walked down to see the place the Indians pointed out as the worst place in passing through the gut, which we found difficult of passing without great danger. But, as the portage was impractical with our large canoes, we concluded to make a portage of our most valuable articles and run the canoes through. Accordingly, on our return, divided the party: some to take over the canoes, and others to take our stores across a portage of a mile, to a place on the channel below this bad whorl and suck, with some others I had fixed on the channel with ropes to throw out to any who should unfortunately meet with difficulty in passing through. Great numbers of Indians viewing us from the high rocks under which we had to pass. The three first canoes passed through very well; the fourth nearly filled with water; the last passed through by taking in a little water. Thus, safely below what I conceived to be the worst part of this channel, felt myself extremely gratified and pleased.

*Above: "A good situation for winter quarters if game can be had." Viento State Park, Oregon, where the Corps spent the night of October 29. **Opposite, top:** "The hills are high and rugged," noted Clark on October 21, 1805, as the Expedition made its way downstream past what is now the John Day Dam, Washington. **Opposite, center:** A snow-capped Mount Hood appears in the distance, southwest of the explorers' campsite of October 22. At 11,235 feet, this is the highest peak in Oregon. **Below:** A Columbia River sunset, as seen from the Maryhill State Park, southern Washington.*

CULTURE SHOCKS

October 23, 1805
We purchased 8 small fat dogs for the party to eat, the natives not being fond of selling their good fish, compels us to make use of dog meat for food, the flesh of which the most of the party have become fond of from the habits of using for some time past.

On October 28, the Expedition members found themselves among the Chilluckittequaw, who were relations of the Chinook but who had clearly been exposed to a mix of cultural connections:

I entered one of the houses in which I saw a British musket, a cutlass and several brass tea kettles of which they appeared very fond. Saw them boiling fish in baskets with stones. I also saw figures of animals and men cut and painted on boards in one side of the house which they appeared to

prize, but for what purpose I will not venture to say. Here we purchased five small dogs, some dried berries and white bread made of roots.

Not far from North Bonneville, Washington, on **October 31**, however, **Clark** stumbled on a find that was more in keeping with native traditions:

"We purchased 8 small fat dogs for the party to eat, the natives not being fond of selling their good fish..."

In a very thick part of the woods is 8 vaults, which appeared closely covered and highly decorated with ornaments. Those vaults are all nearly the same size and form: 8 feet square, 6 feet high, sloped a little so as to convey off the rain, made of pine or cedar boards closely connected and securely covered with

wide boards, with a door left in the east side which is partially stopped with wide boards curiously engraved. In several of those vaults the dead bodies were wrapped up very securely in skins tied around with cords of grass and bark, laid on a mat, all east and west, and some of those vaults had as many as 4 bodies laying on the side of each other. The other vaults contained bones only. Some contained bones for the depth of 44 feet. On the tops and on poles attached to those vaults hung brass kettles and frying pans pierced through the bottoms; baskets; bowls of wood; seashells; skins; bits of cloth; hair; bags of trinkets and small pieces of bone, etc., and, independent of the curious engraving and paintings on the boards which formed the vaults, I observed several wooden images, cut in the figures of men and set up on the sides of the vaults all round. Some of these were so old and worn by time that they were nearly out of shape. I also observed the remains of vaults rotted entirely into the ground and covered with moss. This must be the burying place for many ages for the inhabitants of those rapids. The vaults are of the most lasting pine and cedar.

Top: The Columbia River at Cascade Locks, Oregon. The Expedition camped here between October 30 and November 1. Inset: Chinook craft take the choppy waters of the Columbia River in their stride.

TRADING RELATIONS

November 1, 1805

We got all our baggage over the portage of 940 yards, after which we got the 4 large canoes over by slipping them over the rocks on poles placed across from one rock to another, and at some places along partial streams of the river. In passing those canoes over the rocks etc., three of them received injuries which obliged us to delay to have them repaired. Several Indian canoes arrived at the head of the portage. Some of the men accompanied by those from the village came down to smoke with us. They appear to speak the same language with a different accent.

I cannot learn exactly as to the traffic those Indians carry on below, if white people or the Indians who trade with the whites who are either settled or visit the mouth of this river. I believe mostly with the latter, as their knowledge of the white people appears to be very imperfect, and the articles which they appear to trade mostly (i.e. pounded fish, beargrass and roots) cannot be an object of commerce with foreign merchants. However, they get in return for those articles blue and white beads, copper tea kettles, brass armbands, some scarlet and blue robes and a few articles of old clothes. They prefer beads to anything, and will part with the last mouthful or articles of clothing they have for a few of those beads. Those beads they traffic with Indians still higher up this river (for robes, skins…bread, beargrass, etc.), who in their turn traffic with those under the Rocky Mountains, for beargrass, quamash roots and robes, etc.

Below: The eroded core of an ancient volcano, Beacon Rock dominates the Columbia Gorge near North Bonneville, Washington, at 800 feet tall the world's greatest monolith after Gibraltar.

An Unpleasant Encounter

November 4, 1805
Several canoes of Indians from the village above came down, dressed for the purpose, as I supposed, of paying us a friendly visit. They had scarlet and blue blankets, sailor jackets, over-alls, shirts and hats, independent of their usual dress. The most of them had either muskets or pistols, and tin flasks to hold their powder. Those fellows we found assuming and disagree-able. However, we smoked with them and treated them with every attention and friendship.

During the time we were at dinner, those fellows stole my pipe tomahawk which they were smoking with. I immediately searched every man and the canoes, but could find nothing of my tomahawk. While searching for the tomahawk, one of those scoundrels stole a capotte [coat] of one of our interpreters, which was found stuffed under the root of a tree near the place they sat.

We became much displeased with those fellows, which they discovered, and moved off on their return home to their village, except two canoes which had passed on down.

November 6, 1805
We overtook two canoes of Indians going down to trade. One of the Indians spoke a few words of English and said that the principal man who traded with them was Mr. Haley, and that he had a woman in his canoe who Mr. Haley was fond of, etc. He showed us a bow of iron and several other things which he said Mr. Haley gave him.

Above: Rooster Rock, east of Troutdale, Oregon: Lewis and Clark passed by here on November 2, 1805. Below: The Columbia Valley near Cape Horn, Oregon. Opposite: The remains that erosion has left of Pillar Rock, in legend the stone-struck form of a local chief.

NEARING THE PACIFIC

Already, they could feel, they were making their way through tidal waters:

November 7, 1805

Encamped under a high hill on the starboard side, opposite to a rock situated half a mile from the shore, about 50 feet high and 20 feet in diameter. We with difficulty found a place clear of the tide and sufficiently large to lie on, and the only place we could get was on round stones on which we lay our mats. Rain continued moderately all day. Our small canoe, which got separated in a fog this morning, joined us this evening from a large island situated nearest the larboard [port] side, below the high hills on that side, the river being too wide to see either the form, shape, or size of the islands on the larboard side.

Great joy in camp. We are in view of the ocean, this great Pacific Ocean which we have been so long anxious to see, and the roaring or noise made by the waves breaking on the rocky shores (as I suppose) may be heard distinctly.

They had, it seems, seen only the edge of Gray's Bay rather than the "great Pacific Ocean" itself, yet it was already making its presence felt—sometimes quite inconveniently!

Some rain all day at intervals. We are all wet and disagreeable, as we have been for several days past, and our present situation a very disagreeable one inasmuch as we have not level land sufficient for an encampment, and for our baggage to lie clear of the tide, the high hills jutting in so close and steep that we cannot retreat back, and the water of the river too salt to be used. Added to this, the waves are increasing to such a height that we cannot move from this place. In this situation, we are compelled to form our camp between the height of the ebb and flood tides, and raise our baggage on logs. We are not certain as yet if the white people who trade with those people, or from whom they procure their goods, are stationary at the mouth, or visit this quarter at stated times for the purpose of

traffic, etc. I believe the latter to be the most probable conjecture. The seas rolled and tossed the canoes in such a manner this evening that several of our party were seasick.

November 9, 1805

At 2 o'clock p.m., the flood tide came in, accompanied with immense waves and heavy winds, floated the trees and drift which was on the point on which we camped and tossed them about in such a manner as to endanger the canoes very much. Every exertion and the strictest attention by every individual of the party was scarcely sufficient to save our canoes from being crushed by those monstrous trees, many of them nearly 200 feet long and from 4 to 7 feet through. Our camp entirely under water during the height of the tide, every man as wet as water could make them all the last night and today all day as the rain continued all day.… Notwithstanding the disagreeable situation of our party, all wet and cold (and one which they have experienced for several days past), they are cheerful and anxious to see further into the ocean.

But by November 14, it was evident to Clark that the Expedition's most formidable foe was not going to be the ocean waves but the almost uninterrupted rain:

The rain etc. which has continued without a longer intermission than 2 hours at a time for ten days past has destroyed the robes and rotted nearly one half of the few clothes the party has, particularly the leather clothes. Fortunately for us, we have no very cold weather as yet. And if we have cold weather before we can kill and dress skins for clothing, the bulk of the party will suffer very much.

He was as much on his guard against the Chinook, however, after what Private George Shannon had to say to him the next day:

Shannon informed me that he met Captain Lewis at an Indian hut about 10 miles below, who had sent him back to meet me. He also told me the Indians were thievish, as the night before they had stolen both his and Willard's rifles from under their heads, that they set out on their return and had not proceeded far up the beach before they met Captain Lewis, whose arrival was at a timely moment and alarmed the Indians, so that they instantly produced the guns.

Top: "*This dismal nitch where we have been confined for six days past.*" *Point Distress, Washington, where the explorers took refuge from storms between November 10 and 12, 1805.* ***Center:*** *A Chinook man on the bank of the Columbia.* ***Opposite, above:*** *Cape Disappointment, at the mouth of the Columbia River.* ***Opposite, below:*** "*This bay we call 'Haley's Bay,'*" *but it has been known as Baker's Bay in more recent times.*

NOT SO DISAPPOINTING

Cape Disappointment had been given its dismal name only a few years earlier, in 1788, when Captain John Meares had rounded Cape Roque in hopes of discovering the mouth of the great river believed to enter the ocean somewhere about here. Finding no way across the river bar, he gave up and continued in his quest, unaware of just how close to its object he had actually just come. It was in his chagrin at this failure that he gave the unoffending headland its new name. Robert Gray would not find it so disappointing four years later; he persevered, eventually passing through the admittedly tight entrance to the open estuary of the river he would name after his ship, the *Columbia*.

I told those Indians who accompanied Shannon that they should not come near us, and if anyone of their nation stole anything from us, I would have him shot, which they understood very well.

Clark had more to say on the Chinook's moral shortcomings in his journal for **November 17**:

Captain Lewis returned, having traversed Haley Bay to Cape Disappointment and the seacoast to the north for some distance. Several Chinook Indians followed Captain Lewis, and a canoe came up with roots, mats, etc. to sell. Those Chinooks made us a present of a root boiled much resembling the common liquorice in taste and size. In return for this root we gave more than double the value to satisfy their craving disposition. It is a bad practice to receive a present from those Indians, as they are never satisfied for what they receive in return if ten times the value of the article they gave.

To his obvious satisfaction, he found on **November 20** that the word had got around:

I met several parties of Chinooks which I had not before seen. They were on their return from our camp. All those people appeared to know my determination of keeping every individual of their nation at a proper distance, as they were guarded and reserved in my presence, etc. Found many of the Chinooks with Captain Lewis, of whom there was 2 chiefs, Comcommoly and Chillarlawil, to whom we gave medals and to one a flag. One of the Indians had on a robe made of 2 sea-otter skins, the fur of them more beautiful than any fur I had ever seen. Both Captain Lewis and myself

endeavored to purchase the robe with different articles. At length we procured it for a belt of blue beads which the squaw-wife of our interpreter Charbonneau wore around her waist.

November 21, 1805

An old woman and wife to a chief of the Chinooks came and made a camp near ours. She brought with her 6 young squaws—I believe for the purpose of gratifying the passions of the men of our party and receiving for those indulgences such small presents as she (the old woman) thought proper to accept of.

Those people appear to view sensuality as a necessary evil, and do not appear to abhor it as a crime in the unmarried state. The young females are fond of the attention of our men and appear to meet the sincere approbation of their friends and connections for thus obtaining their favors. The women of the Chinook nation have handsome faces, low and badly made with large legs and thighs, which are generally swelled from a stoppage of the circulation in the feet (which are small) by many strands of beads or curious strings which are drawn tight around the leg above the ankle. Their legs are also picked with different figures. I saw on the left arm of a squaw the following letters: *J. Bowman*. All those are considered by the natives of this quarter as handsome decorations, and a woman without those decorations is considered as among the lower class. They wear their hair loose, hanging over their back and shoulders. Many have blue beads threaded and hung from different parts of their ears and about their neck and around their wrists.

The Expedition members marked this, their definitive arrival at the Pacific Ocean by carving their names and dates on convenient trees.

Right: A Chinook afloat on the Columbia River, from an early twentieth-century photograph by Curtis.
Opposite: "Captain Clark and his men building a line of huts," as depicted in a drawing by Expedition member Patrick Gass.

THE CHINOOK: NATURAL ENTREPRENEURS

Living along the lower reaches of the Columbia River and up the nearby Washington Coast, the Chinook had been trading with white men for quite some time: hence, paradoxically, the fretful relationship that quickly developed between them and the Corps of Discovery. While they understood the exchange value of the goods he brought, the Chinook neither feared nor respected the white man overmuch—he was just another trader—hence their readiness to drive the hardest possible bargain (and in some cases actually to steal). The Chinook's reputation as traders would only grow in the decades that followed, after America's biggest furrier, John Jacob Astor, set up an outpost ("Astoria") close to Fort Clatsop in 1811. The Chinook became the main intermediaries between the white merchants and the other tribes, and their language formed the basis for a *lingua franca* (common trading language) spoken all along the Pacific seaboard from California to Alaska.

WINTER QUARTERS

"O! How horrible is the day," exclaimed the normally laconic **Clark** on **November 22**: it was clearly time for the Expedition to establish winter quarters. The explorers had been much taken with the Clatsop, from the southern shore of the estuary, who resembled their Chinook relatives "in every respect except that of stealing." This was a point in favor of their looking for somewhere on the other side of the river to set up their headquarters; more important, though, was the feeling that, as Clark put it:

[We needed] a convenient situation to procure the wild animals of the forest which must be our dependence for subsisting this winter. We have every reason to believe that the natives have not provisions sufficient for our consumption, and if they had, their prices are so high that it would take ten times as much to purchase their roots and dried fish as we have in our possession, including our small remains of merchandise and clothes, etc.

This certainly induces every individual of the party to make diligent inquiries of the natives for the part of the country in which the wild animals are most plenty. They generally agree that the most elk is on the opposite shore, and above, the elk being an animal much larger than deer, easier to kill and better meat (in the winter when poor), and skins better for the clothes of our party. Added to this a convenient situation to the seacoast, where we could make salt, and a probability of vessels coming into the mouth of the Columbia (which the Indians inform us "would return to trade with them in 3 months"), from whom we might procure a fresh supply of Indian trinkets to purchase provisions on our way home....

In the best American democratic traditions, the decision was put to a vote of all the party—even the call from "Janey" (Sacagawea) for "a place where there is plenty of potas" (wapato roots) was solemnly recorded. By overwhelming agreement, it was decided that the Expedition should look for a suitable site—somewhere near the coast, but rich in game—on the southern shore. Finding such a spot would, as it turned out, be more easily said than done. Far from offering a respite, their stay at the coast so far had brought them nothing but trouble, with no likely end in sight: a note of something like desperation enters Clark's journal entries.

> *"Those people appear to view sensuality as a necessary evil, and do not seem to abhor it as a crime of the unmarried state."*

November 28, 1805

We could find no deer. Several hunters attempted to penetrate the thick woods to the main south side without success. The swan and geese wild and cannot be approached, and wind too high to go either back or forward, and we have nothing to eat but a little pounded fish…. This is our present situation! Truly disagreeable. Added to this, the robes of our selves and men are all rotten for being continually wet, and we cannot procure others, or blankets in these places. About 12 o'clock, the wind shifted about to the northwest and blew with great violence for the remainder of the day. At many times it blew for 15 or 20 minutes with such violence that I expected every moment to see trees taken up by the roots. Some were blown down. Those squalls were succeeded by rain. O! How tremendous is the day. This dreadful wind and rain continued with intervals of fair weather, the greater part of the evening and night.

December 1, 1805

The immense seas and waves which break on the rocks and coasts to the southwest and northwest roars like an immense fall at a distance, and this roaring has continued ever since our arrival in the neighborhood of the seacoast, which has been 24 days since we arrived in sight of the Great Western (for I cannot say Pacific) Ocean as I have not seen one pacific day since my arrival in its vicinity, and its waters are forming and perpetually break with immense waves on the sands and rocky coasts, tempestuous and horrible.

After several days out scouting for a site, Lewis returned on December 5 with the news that he had found a place he thought would serve their purpose. "This was very satisfactory information to all the party," Clark notes. Two days later,

[We] have everything put on board the canoes and set out to the place Captain Lewis had viewed and thought well situated for winter quarters. We proceeded on against the tide…. We ascended a river which falls in on the south side of this bay 3 miles to the first point of high land on the west side, the place Captain Lewis had viewed, and formed in a thick growth of pine about 200 yards from the river. This situation is on a rise about 30 feet higher than the high tide's level, and thickly covered with lofty pine. This is certainly the most eligible situation for our purposes of any in its neighborhood.

December 11, 1805

Rained all the last night moderately. We are all employed putting up huts or cabins for our winter's quarters. Sergeant Pryor unwell from a dislocation of his shoulder; Gibson with the dysentery.

*Above: Clark called this Meriwether's Bay, believing that Lewis was the first to discover it, but Young's Bay had already been named for a commander of the British Royal Navy. **Opposite:** The Expedition's winter quarters, Fort Clatsop, Oregon, in modern reconstruction.*

December 23, 1805

Rained without intermission all the last night and today with thunder and hail the fore and after part of this day. Captain Lewis and myself move into our hut today unfinished.

December 24, 1805

Hard rain at different times last night and all this day without intermission. Men all employed in finishing their huts and moving into them.

Christmas Day, December 25, 1805

At daylight this morning we were awoke by the discharge of the firearms of all our party and a salute, shouts, and a song which the whole party joined in under our windows, after which they retired to their rooms. Was cheerful all the morning. After breakfast we divided our tobacco, which amounted to 12 carrots, one half of which we gave to the men of the party who used tobacco, and to those who do not use it we made a present of a handkerchief. The Indians left us in the evening. All the party snugly fixed in their huts. I received a present of Captain Lewis of a fleece hosiery shirt, drawers and socks, a pair of moccasins of Whitehouse, a small Indian basket of Goodrich, two dozen white weasels' tails of the Indian woman, and some black root of the Indians before their departure. Drewyer informs me that he saw a snake pass across the path today. The day proved showery, wet, and disagreeable.

We would have spent this day, the nativity of Christ, in feasting, had we had anything either to raise our spirits or even gratify our appetites. Our dinner consisted of poor elk, so much spoiled that we ate it through mere necessity, some spoiled pounded fish, and a few roots.

"Fort Clatsop," as it was called from its closeness to the village of the Clatsop people, was finished on December 30, just in time for the New Year's celebrations. **Lewis** wrote on **January 1, 1806,**

This morning I was awoke at an early hour by the discharge of a volley of small arms, which were fired by our party in front of our quarters to usher in the new year. This was the only mark of respect

which we had it in our power to pay this celebrated day. Our repast of this day, though better than that of Christmas, consisted principally in the anticipation of the 1st day of January 1807, when in the bosom of our friends we hope to participate in the mirth and hilarity of the day, and when, with the zest given by the recollection of the present, we shall completely, both mentally and corporeally, enjoy the repast which the hand of civilization has prepared for us. At present we were content with eating our boiled elk and wappato, and solacing our thirst with our only beverage, pure water.

REGULAR VISITORS

The Clatsop, like the Chinook, were old hands at trading with the white man: talking to them on **January 1**, **Clark** elicited a long list of regular visitors, some of whom include:

Moore: Visits them in a large 4-masted ship; they expect him in 2 moons to trade.

Mackey: In a ship; they expect him back in 1 or 2 moons to trade with them.

Mr. Haley: Visits them in a ship, and they expect him back to trade with them in 3 moons to trade. He is the favorite of the Indians (from the number of presents he gives) and has the trade principally with all the tribes.

Lemon: In a sloop, and they expect him in 3 moons to trade with them.

MAN'S BEST FOOD?

Accounts of dog meat being eaten in Korea have caused a storm of controversy in recent years, but this food is actually rather more American than apple pie. The dog appears to have come to America with the first peoples who came across the Beringia land bridge from east Asia over 13,000 years ago—and many Native American peoples seem to have retained the unsentimental attitudes of their Asian forebears. For them, as for other prehistoric communities, any animal companions would have had to pull their weight. Quite literally, in many cases: in a continent without the horse or any other possible beast of burden, dogs were often used to draw loads slung between trailing *travois* poles. And yes, they were eaten as food, as they still are in eastern Asia—and as horses, frogs, and snails still are in France. Cultures differ vastly in both their tastes and their taboos.

TASTES

Lewis noted in his journal on **January 3**:

At 11 a.m. we were visited by our near neighbors, Chief or Tiá Comowool, alias Conia, and six Clatsops. They brought for sale some roots, berries and three dogs; also a quantity of fresh blubber. This blubber, they informed us, they had obtained from their neighbors the Callamucks, who inhabit the coast to the southeast, near whose village a whale had recently perished. This blubber the Indians eat and esteem it excellent food. Our party from necessity having been obliged to subsist some length of time on dogs, have now become extremely fond of their flesh. It is worthy of remark that while we lived principally on the flesh of this animal, we were much more healthy, strong, and more fleshy than we had been since we left the buffalo country. For my own part, I have become so perfectly reconciled to the dog that I think it an agreeable food and would prefer it vastly to lean venison or elk.

One man's meat.... Captain Clark's journal, notoriously, copies Lewis's for long stretches, and does so just about word for word in the passage above. Aside from its conclusion, that is—his reads: "As for my own part, I have not become reconciled to the taste of this animal as yet!"

***Opposite:** "We are all employed putting up huts or cabins for our winter quarters," notes Clark in his journal for December 11, 1805. Today Fort Clatsop has been reconstructed in accordance with the explorers' drawings and descriptions. **Above:** The Whispering Giant at Astoria, Oregon. Since 1971, sculptor Peter Wolf Toth has set out to create some worthy monument to America's indigenous peoples in every one of the nation's fifty states.*

CORRUPTED BY CONTACT?

Had the natives of the coast been corrupted by their exposure to the outside world? Both Lewis and Clark made much of their untrustworthiness. **Lewis's** journal for **January 4** makes clear his feeling that they were insufficiently unworldly in their attitudes (though gratifyingly naïve in their business dealings):

These people, the Chinooks and others residing in this neighborhood and speaking the same language have been very friendly to us. They appear to be a mild, inoffensive people, but will pilfer if they have an opportunity to do so where they conceive themselves not liable to detection. They are great hagglers in trade, and if they conceive you anxious to purchase will be a whole day bargaining for a handful of roots. This I should have thought proceeded from their want of knowledge of the comparative value of articles of merchandise, and the fear of being cheated, did I not find that they invariably refuse the price first offered them and afterwards very frequently accept a smaller quantity of the same article. In order to satisfy myself on this subject, I once offered a Chinook my watch, two knives and a considerable quantity of beads for a small, inferior sea otter's skin which he did not much want. He immediately conceived it of much value, and refused to barter except I would double the quantity of beads. The next day, with a great deal of importunity on his part, I received the skin in exchange for a few strands of the same beads he had refused the day before. I therefore believe this trait in their character proceeds from an avaricious, all-grasping disposition. In this respect they differ from all Indians I ever became acquainted with, for their dispositions invariably lead them to give whatever they are possessed of, no matter how useful or valuable, for a bauble which pleases their fancy, without consulting its usefulness or value.

"It may appear somewhat extraordinary…that the flesh of the beaver and dog possess a great affinity in point of flavor."

THE FIRST SHIP

Recorded in 1894 by the great anthropologist Franz Boas, the Clatsop myth of "The First Ship" offers a striking sense of just how alien the first European merchants must have seemed in Indian eyes—and how extraordinary an opportunity their coming represented.

"An old woman was walking on the shore one day when she was pulled up short by the sight of a vast form she at first took for a whale—until she saw that it was topped by two great spruce trees. Ropes were tied to their trunks, and there was copper and iron everywhere. Then from the body of the monster emerged a bear—but with a face just like a man's. The woman ran back to her community, and all rushed out to behold this prodigious thing: there were two bears now, holding out copper kettles as though asking for water. One audacious man went into the ship, and found it full of boxes; the two bears, now clearly men, were captured and their vessel burned. The delighted Clatsop retrieved the copper, brass and iron from the gutted hulk, a veritable treasure: hearing of their good fortune, people flocked in from far upriver. The Clatsop grew rich, trading iron nails and copper strips for slaves; the white merchants, says the story, stayed with them as their prisoners."

QUESTIONS OF FOOD

But the Expedition members were slowly getting used to conditions on the coast, **Lewis** even able to muse, on **January 5**, on the difficulties of preparing salt right next to an ocean full of it, on the qualities of the whale meat they had been given by members of the Callamuck (or Tillamuck) tribe, from the same stranded carcass they had been told of two days before—and, indeed, on dietary matters more generally:

At 5 p.m., Willard and Wiser returned. They had not been lost as we apprehended. They informed us that it was not until the fifth day after leaving the fort that they could find a convenient place for making salt; that they had at length established themselves on the seacoast about 15 miles S.W. from this, near the lodge of some Killamuck families; that the Indians were very friendly and had given them a considerable quantity of the blubber of a whale which perished on the coast some distance southeast of them. Part of this blubber they brought with them: it was white and not unlike the fat of pork, though the texture was more spongy and somewhat coarser.

I had a part of it cooked and found it very palatable and tender. It resembles the beaver or the dog in flavor. It may appear somewhat extraordinary, though it is a fact, that the flesh of the beaver and dog possess a great affinity in point of flavor. These lads also informed us that J. Fields, Bratton and Gibson (the salt makers) had with their assistance erected a comfortable camp, killed an elk and several deer and secured a good stock of meat. They commenced the making of salt and found that they could obtain from 3 quarts to a gallon a day. They brought with them a specimen of the salt, of about a gallon. We found it excellent: fine, strong and white. This was a great treat to myself and most of the party, having not had any since the 20th ult. I say most of the party, for my friend Captain Clark declares it to be a mere matter of indifference with him whether he uses it or not. For myself, I must confess, I felt a considerable inconvenience from the want of it. The want of bread I consider as trivial, provided I get fat meat, for as to the species of meat I am not very particular, the flesh of the dog, the horse and the wolf having from habit become equally familiar with any other, and I have learned to think that if the cord be sufficiently strong which binds the soul and body together, it does not so much matter about the materials which compose it.…

*Opposite: A Chinook woman forages along a beach, in an early twentieth-century photograph by Edward S. Curtis. **Above**: Salt was important not just as a flavoring but as a mineral vital to life—and, potentially, as a commodity for trade during the return journey. Here, at Seaside, Oregon, is a modern reconstruction of the system of kettles that enabled Fields, Bratton, and Gibson, the Expedition's salt makers, to produce "from 3 quarts to a gallon a day."*

Captain Clark determined this evening to set out early tomorrow with two canoes and 12 men in quest of the whale, or at all events to purchase from the Indians a parcel of the blubber. For this purpose he prepared a small assortment of merchandise to take with him.

January 6, 1806

Captain Clark set out after an early breakfast with the party in two canoes as had been concerted the last evening. Charbonneau and his Indian woman were also of the party. The Indian woman was very importunate to be allowed to go, and was therefore indulged. She observed that she had traveled a long way with us to see the great waters and that, now that monstrous fish was also to be seen, she thought it very hard she could not be permitted to see either. (She had never yet been to the ocean.)

PACIFIC PEOPLES

Lewis goes on to consider the special characteristics of the Indians of the coast:

The Clatsops, Chinooks, Killamucks, etc. are very loquacious and inquisitive. They possess good memories and have repeated to us the names, capacities of the vessels, etc., of many traders and others who have visited the mouth of this river. They are generally low in stature, proportionably small, rather lighter complected and much more illy formed than the Indians of the Missouri and those of our frontier. They are generally cheerful but never gay. With us their conversation generally turns upon the subjects of trade, smoking, eating or their women. About the latter they speak without reserve in their presence, of their every part, and of their most familiar connection. They do not hold the virtue of their women in high estimation, and will even prostitute their wives and daughters for a fishing hook or a strand of beads. In common with other savage nations, they make their women perform every species of domestic drudg-

ery. But in almost every species of this drudgery, the men also participate. Their women are also compelled to gather roots and assist them in taking fish, which articles form much the greatest part of their subsistence. Notwithstanding the servile manner in which they treat their women, they pay much more respect to their judgement and opinions in many respects than most Indian nations. Their women are permitted to speak freely before them, and sometimes appear to command with a tone of authority. They generally consult them in their traffic and act in conformity to their opinion.

Clearly in reflective mood, he goes on to consider social organization—and human nature—more generally:

Top: Tsagiglalal, "She Who Watches," keeps vigil from a basalt rock beside the Columbia River near The Dalles, Oregon. She is believed to have been painted up to 300 years ago as part of a death cult that grew up in response to the ravages of smallpox among native communities.

ATTENTIVE MEMORIES

In Shakespeare's famous tragedy *Hamlet* (1601), the Prince at one point reels off a speech in verse, a dozen lines long—it has stayed in his memory, he explains, from a play he "once" enjoyed some years before. A fictional character has special privileges, of course, yet scholars have in any case pointed out that this feat of memorization is not, perhaps, so extraordinary in a young man of his time. In an age before books were widely available, people did not have what has been called "the luxury of inattention": they listened more effectively, and recalled much more of what they heard. That seems to be even more so in cultures that possess no written script at all, and where all knowledge, custom and myth are handed down over the generations by word of mouth—the "oral tradition." In many "primitive" cultures, bardic storytellers and chroniclers have held the most enormous epics in their memories—a basic human skill, it seems, that has been lost in the modern world.

I think it may be established as a general maxim that those nations treat their old people and women with most deference and respect where they subsist principally on such articles that these can participate with the men in obtaining them, and that that part of the community are treated with least attention when the act of procuring subsistence devolves entirely on the men in the vigor of life. It appears to me that nature has been much more deficient in her filial tie than in any other of the strong affections of the human heart, and therefore think our old men equally with our women indebted to civilization for their ease and comfort. Among the Siouxs, Assiniboins and others on the Missouri who subsist by hunting, it is a custom when a person of either sex becomes so old and infirm that they are unable to travel on foot from camp to camp as they roam in search of subsistence, for the children or near relations of such person to leave them without compunction or remorse. On those occasions they usually place within their reach a small piece of meat and a platter of water, telling the poor old superannuated wretch for his consolation that he or she had lived long enough, that it was time they should die and go to their relations, who can afford to take care of them much better than they could.

Below: A Nez Percé sweat lodge, used for purification rituals and photographed by Curtis around 1910.

GOING TO SEE THE WHALE

Clark, characteristically, had more down-to-earth concerns, though his journal for **January 8** finds him in obvious good humor:

Proceeded to the place the whale had perished. Found only the skeleton of this monster on the sand, between the villages of the Kilamox [Tillamuck] nation. The whale was already pillaged of every valuable part by the Kilamox Indians in the vicinity of whose villages it lay on the strand, where the waves and tide had driven up and left it. I returned to the village of 5 cabins on the creek, which I shall call Ecola or Whale Creek. Found the natives busily engaged boiling the blubber, which they performed in a large, square wooden trough, by means of hot stones. The oil, when extracted, was secured in bladders and the guts of the whale. The blubber, from which the oil was only partially extracted by this process, was laid by in their cabins, in large flitches for use. Those flitches they usually expose to the fire on a wooden spit, until it is pretty well warmed through, and then eat it either alone or with roots of the rush, shanataque, or dipped in the oil.

The Kilamox, although they possessed large quantities of this blubber and oil, were so penurious that they disposed of it with great reluctance and in small quantities only; insomuch that my utmost exertions, aided by the party, with the small stock of merchandise I had taken with me, were not able to procure more blubber than about 300 lb. and a few gallons of oil. Small as this stock is, I prize it highly, and thank Providence for directing the whale to us, and think Him much more kind to us than He was to Jonah, having sent this monster to be swallowed by us, instead of swallowing of us, as Jonah's did.

***Below and opposite:** Looking south down the Oregon coast to Haystack Rock in the distance. Expedition members explored this area on January 10, 1805.*

THE LOCAL CURRENCY

Lewis, meanwhile, was on **January 9** still wondering about the Indians' established trading relationships—if there was to be investment here, it would be well to understand the conditions currently prevailing.

The persons who usually visit the entrance of this river for the purpose of traffic or hunting, I believe are either English or Americans. The Indians inform us that they speak the same language with ourselves, and give us proofs of their veracity by repeating many words of English, as musket, powder, shot, knife, file, damned rascal, son of a bitch, etc. Whether these traders are from Nootka Sound, from some other late establishment on this coast, or immediately from the United States or Great Britain, I am at a loss to determine, nor can the Indians inform us.

This traffic on the part of the whites consists in vending guns (principally old British or American muskets), powder, balls and shot, copper and brass kettles, brass teakettles and coffeepots, blankets from two to three points, scarlet and blue cloth (coarse), plates and strips of sheet copper and brass, large brass wire, knives, beads and tobacco, with fishing hooks, buttons and some other small articles. Also a considerable quantity of sailors' clothes, as hats, coats, trousers and shirts. For these they receive in return from the natives dressed and undressed elk skins, skins of the sea otter, common otter, beaver, common fox, spuck [young sea otter], and tiger cat [bobcat]; also dried and pounded salmon in baskets, and a kind of biscuit which the natives make of roots, called by them *shappellel*. The natives are extravagantly fond of the most common cheap blue and white beads, of moderate size…. The blue is usually preferred to the white. These beads constitute the principal circulating medium with all the Indian tribes on this river. For these beads they will dispose of any article they possess. The beads are strung on strands of a fathom in length, and in that manner sold by the breadth or yard.

DRAMATIC DEVELOPMENTS

Clark, it transpired, had been having a more exciting time:

Last night about 10 o'clock, while smoking with the natives, I was alarmed by a loud shrill voice from the cabins on the opposite side. The Indians all ran immediately across to the village. My guide, who continued with me, made signs that someone's throat was cut. By inquiry, I found that one man, McNeal, was absent. I immediately sent off Sergeant N. Pryor and four men in quest of McNeal, whom they met coming across the creek in great haste, and informed me that the people were alarmed on the opposite side at something, but what he could not tell; a man had very friendly invited him to go and eat in his lodge; that the Indian had locked arms with him and went to a lodge in which a woman gave him some blubber; that the man invited him to another lodge to get something better, and the woman held him [McNeal] by the blanket which he had around him. This woman a Chinook, an old friend of McNeal's, and another, ran out and holloed, and his pretended friend disappeared.

I immediately ordered every man to hold himself in a state of readiness, and sent Sergeant Pryor and four men to know the cause of the alarm, which was found to be a premeditated plan of the pretended friend of McNeal to assassinate him for his blanket and what few articles he had about him.... This man was of another band, at some distance, and ran off as soon as he was discovered.

"I was alarmed by a loud shrill voice from the cabins... My guide...made signs that someone's throat was cut."

We have now to look back and shudder at the dreadful road on which we have to return, of 45 miles southeast of Point Adams and 35 miles from Fort Clatsop. I had the blubber and oil divided among the party, and set out about sunrise and returned by the same route we had gone out. Met several parties of men and women of the Chinook and Clatsop nations on their way to trade with the Kilamox for blubber and oil.

On the steep descent of the mountain, I overtook five men and six women with immense loads of the oil and blubber of the whale. Those Indians had passed by some route by which we missed them as we went out yesterday. One of the women, in the act of getting down a steep part of the mountain, her load by some means had slipped off her back, and she was holding the load by a strap which was fastened to the mat bag in which it was in, in one hand, and holding a bush by the other. As I was in front of my party, I endeavored to relieve this woman by taking her load until she could get to a better place a little below, and to my astonishment found the load as much as I could lift, and must exceed 100 pounds. The husband of this woman, who was below, soon came to her relief.

Top: Tsagiglalal, "She Who Watches," keeps vigil from a basalt rock beside the Columbia River near The Dalles, Oregon. She is believed to have been painted up

QUIET STUDY

As the men had hoped, once thoroughly at home in their winter quarters, there was time to dedicate to the tasks that had been so easily swept aside in the hurly burly of traveling, and to catch up on record-keeping and research. On **February 14**, **Clark** announced,

I completed a map of the country through which we have been passing from the Mississippi, at the mouth of the Missouri, to this place. On the map, the Missouri, Jefferson's River, the southeast branch of the Columbia or Lewis's River, Kooskooskee, and Columbia from the entrance of the southeast fork to the Pacific Ocean, as well as a part of Clark's River and our track across the Rocky Mountains, are laid down by celestial observations and survey. The rivers are also connected at their sources with other rivers, agreeably to the information of the natives and the most probable conjecture, arising from their capacities and the relative positions of their respective entrances, which last have, with but few exceptions, been established by celestial observations.

We now discover that we have found the most practicable and navigable passage across the continent of North America: it is that which we have traveled, with the exception of that part of our route from the foot of the Falls of the Missouri, or in the neighborhood of the entrance of the Rocky Mountains until we arrive on Clark's River.

Lewis, for his part, was turning his attention to the wonders of nature—and in particular, to the sea otter:

The sea otter is found on the seacoast and in the saltwater. This animal, when fully grown, is as large as a common mastiff dog. The ears and eyes are remarkably small, particularly the former, which is not an inch in length, thick, fleshy and pointed, covered with short hair. The tail is about 10 inches in length, thick where it joins the body and tapering to a very sharp point. In common with the body, it is covered with a deep fur, particularly on the upper side. On the under part fur is not so long. The legs are remarkably short, and the feet, which have five toes—each are broad, large and webbed. The legs are covered with fur and the feet with short hair. The body of this animal is long, and nearly of the same thickness throughout. From the extremity of the tail to that of the nose they will measure 5 feet or upwards. The color is a uniform dark brown, and when in good order and season perfectly black and glossy. It is the richest, and I think the most delicious, fur in the world—at least I cannot form an idea of any more so. It is deep, thick, silky in the extreme, and strong. The inner part of the fur when opened is lighter than the surface in its natural position. There are some fine black and shining hairs intermixed with the fur which are rather longer and add much to its beauty.

Below: *Clark's journal entry of March 2, 1806, with description and sketch of the "heath cock" (sage grouse).*

"DELICIOUS"

"More beautiful than any fur I had ever seen," had been Clark's response to the skin of the sea otter; Lewis could not even "form an idea" of anything more "delicious." Unfortunately, many in the eighteenth and nineteenth centuries shared the explorers' view, and sea otters were trapped and shot in their hundreds and thousands for their fur—only to take a further hammering from the effects of pollution in the twentieth century. The deep sensuousness of the sea otter's fur to the touch is the result of its incredible density: twice that of any other mammal, at almost 650,000 hairs per square inch. It confines itself to coastal waters, neither venturing upriver nor ranging any great distance out to sea. Sea urchins, crabs, clams, abalones, and other shellfish make up the bulk of the sea otter's daily diet (the smaller freshwater otter, by contrast, feeds mainly on fish). Lewis perhaps exaggerates its size—the average adult southern sea otter is no more than four feet long—but fails altogether to mention its amazing cuteness. Along with the world's most luxurious fur, the sea otter possesses a lively and frolicsome disposition, and has the most adorable way of lying back in the water and peering about it as it eats its food.

A WRITTEN TESTAMENT

With the weeks speeding by, and spring approaching, it was time to think seriously about preparations for the journey home—but to consider too the possibility that it might not be completed safely. As **Lewis** explains in his journal for **March 18**, they drew up several copies of what amounted to the Corps of Discovery's Last Testament, to be left in the care of local chiefs:

This morning we gave Delashelwilt a certificate of his good deportment etc., and also a list of our names, after which we dispatched him to his village with his female band. These lists of our names we have given to several of the natives, and also pasted up a copy in our room. The object of these lists we stated in the preamble of the same, as follows:

The object of this list is that, through the medium of some civilized person who may see the same, it may be known to the informed world that the party consisting of the persons whose names are hereunto annexed, and who were sent out by the government of the U. States in May 1804 to explore the interior of the continent of North America, did penetrate the same by way of the Missouri and Columbia rivers, to the discharge of the latter into the Pacific Ocean, where they arrived on the 14th of November, 1805, and from whence they departed the…day of March, 1806, on their return to the United States by the same route they had come out.

On the back of some of these lists we added a sketch of the connection of the upper branches of the Missouri with those of the Columbia, partic-

ularly of its main southeast branch, on which we also delineated the track we had come out and that we meant to pursue on our return where the same happened to vary. There seemed so many chances against our government ever obtaining a regular report through the medium of the savages and the traders of this coast, that we declined making any. Our party are also too small to think of leaving any of them to return to the United States by sea, particularly as we shall be necessarily divided into three or four parties on our return in order to accomplish the objects we have in view, and at any rate, we shall reach the United States, in all human probability, much earlier than a man could who must in the event of his being left here depend for his passage to the United States on the traders of the coast who may not return immediately to the United States, or if they should, might probably spend the next summer in trading with the natives before they would set out on their return.

Right: This bronze statue at Seaside, Oregon, proudly commemorates "The End of the Trail"—yet Washington indignantly disputes this title. Below: Looking out—as Lewis and Clark must have done—across Cannon Beach and the Seal Rocks, it's almost impossible not to be impressed by the wild grandeur of Oregon's rugged coastline.

READY TO RETURN

Two days later, Lewis was looking back on a winter more or less well spent, though his thoughts were obviously on the journey to come:

Although we have not fared sumptuously this winter and spring at Fort Clatsop, we have lived quite as comfortably as we had any reason to expect we should; and have accomplished every object which induced our remaining at this place, except that of meeting with the traders who visit the entrance of this river. Our salt will be very sufficient to last us to the Missouri, where we have a stock in store. It would have been very fortunate for us had some of those traders arrived previous to our departure from hence, as we should then have had it in our power to obtain an addition to our stock of merchandise, which would have made our homeward bound journey much more comfortable.

With several men sick, some canoes uncompleted, and food supplies not as substantial as had been hoped, the Expedition was not exactly in the best possible state of readiness. But there were many hundred miles to go, the weather was slowly but steadily improving and, as Lewis wrote on March 22, "the leafing of the huckleberry reminds us of spring."

RETRACING
STEPS

———— ✳ ———— ✳ ————

"The spurs of the Rocky Mountains which were in view from the high plain today were perfectly covered with snow. The indians inform us that the snow is yet so deep on the mountains that we shall not be able to pass them until the next full moon."

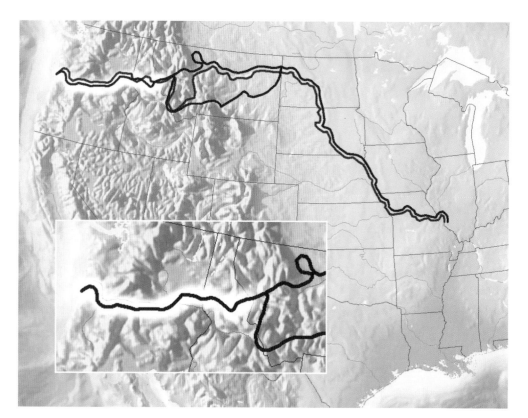

Opposite: *An enchantingly beautiful sight, but ultimately exasperating for the explorers: The mountain snows persisted well into the spring. The Bitterroot Mountains (seen here near the Lolo Pass, Montana) proved an impassable obstacle in the Expedition's path—even as conditions at lower altitudes became perfect for traveling.*

"What could they see but a hideous and desolate wilderness?" asked William Bradford, recalling the fears of his fellow pilgrim fathers (and mothers!) on landing in America in 1620.

"What could now sustain them but the Spirit of God and His grace? May not and ought not the children of these fathers rightly say: 'Our fathers were Englishmen, which came over this great ocean, and were ready to perish in this wilderness; but they cried unto the Lord, and He heard their voice and looked on their adversity,' etc."

Every American schoolchild knows the sequel: The settlers came through that first savage winter, surviving to celebrate the first Thanksgiving with an ample harvest. The *Journals* of Lewis and Clark offer an ironic update of this episode, the pilgrim fathers' sentiments finding an absurdly anticlimactic—and unwitting—echo in William Clark's words of relief on leaving winter quarters at Fort Clatsop in March of 1806:

At this place we had wintered and remained from the 7th of December 1805 to this day, and have lived as well as we had any right to expect, and we can say that we were never one day without 3 meals of some kind a day—either poor elk meat or roots—notwithstanding the repeated fall of rain which has fallen almost constantly.

The West Coast winter had been far less severe; of course, and the Expedition members much better prepared, yet the contrast between the two accounts is still revealing. The first and perhaps most obvious point is that, for Clark, the wilderness is no longer "hideous and desolate"; and the second is the apparent absence of gratitude to any God. Clark's note does read like a record of thanks; its simple style and solemn tone suggest a prayer, and that the Expedition has somehow been looked after is strongly implied. And yet we have the impression of a piety without an object; a reverence with no clear reference to religion.

The difference is accounted for by the disparity in backgrounds of America's pilgrim and founding fathers. The first group had crossed the ocean specifically to be able to worship God in their own way. Protestant Christians that they were, that way had included a passionately personal relationship with their creator, its intensity unmediated by the elaborate institutional structures that they felt enmeshed the Roman and Anglican Churches in worldliness and corruption. The pilgrims' scathing view of the old-established churches was shared by the generation that brought about the American Revolution of 1775, but these self-consciously forward-looking thinkers extended their contempt to include religion in general. Men like Thomas Paine, Benjamin Franklin, George Washington —and, especially perhaps, Lewis's friend and mentor Thomas Jefferson—had been formed in their attitudes by the European Enlightenment.

The Age of Reason, as it is often called, saw the thinkers of Europe developing many of the concepts and ideals that we in the modern world take for granted. The ideas of representative democracy and freedom of speech; the assumption that talent and energy matter more than high birth; these were radical notions in their day—and they date from this time.

The Enlightenment saw the introduction of what we still see as "enlightened" values into everything from medicine and education to law and order. The way men and women saw the world was transformed. Before, the only acceptable authorities for the scholar or scientist had been the scriptures and the writings of the medieval saints or the classical philosophers. Now, blind tradition gave way to common sense and free enquiry. Enlightenment thinkers set out to reinvent religion in a form that would seem more appropriate to a self-consciously scientific age. Some even went so far as to exclude from their theology the personalized deity of the Judeo-Christian scriptures. The real God, these "deists" suggested, was an impersonal force, His attitude to creation

Below: The world was Jefferson's church, his faith was in humanity, his reverence was for nature, and he had passed on these values to his protégé, Meriwether Lewis. The young explorer thrilled to the beauty of scenes like this one at Cannon Beach, on Oregon's coast.

that of the watchmaker who, having fashioned a perfect system of springs and cogwheels, simply winds it up and lets it tick on without further interference.

Thomas Jefferson was a deist. A man of the utmost seriousness of purpose, he was at the same time not religious in the usual sense. His creed was the capacity of humanity to strive and succeed: If he acknowledged any higher force, it was to be found in the grandeur and benignity of the universe. Meriwether Lewis, we know, shared many of his mentor's values: His journals testify to the extraordinary alertness and sheer enthusiasm of the Enlightenment mind. To the modern reader, though, they at times show some of the shortcomings of the era's way of thinking too—in particular, an element of intellectual snobbery. The Enlightenment's passionate promotion of democracy never sat entirely comfortably with an inbuilt elitism that set the enlightened few against the ignorant and superstitious masses.

Today, that sort of effortless superiority on the part of the intellectual simply cannot be sustained: The limitations of human thought and endeavor are all too evident. The role of science, though by no means discredited, has certainly been questioned; we no longer believe in a universe that runs like clockwork. And if many of the ideas of the Enlightenment have endured triumphantly in the democratic system of the United States, other attempts to impose its values have ended far less happily. The French Revolution of 1789 was only the first of a long series of utopian experiments to end in bloody and oppressive reigns of terror. Americans have learned to respect the many achievements of the Enlightenment without feeling obliged to follow its every prejudice, to emulate its idealism and enterprise without taking on its arrogance. The vast majority of modern Americans have chosen to embrace one or other of the world's great creeds, yet all have reason to be grateful to the founding fathers for their insistence on religious freedom. Their immediate aim may have been to protect their own freethinking philosophy, yet the benefits have been felt by those generations of immigrants from every corner of the earth who have helped make the United States the thriving multicultural nation it is today. Whatever our faith, in fact, we can respect the reverence a man like Meriwether Lewis felt in the face of creation; his love for a country as yet to be fully born.

STRIKING CAMP

Sunday, **March 23** saw the Expedition strike camp and start the long journey homeward, as Captain **Clark** related in his journal for that day:

The rain ceased and it became fair about Meridian [midday], at which time we loaded our canoes and at 1 p.m. left Fort Clatsop on our homeward-bound journey.

At this place we had wintered and remained from the 7th of December, 1805, to this day, and have lived as well as we had any right to expect, and we can say that we were never one day without three meals of some kind a day, either poor elk meat or roots, notwithstanding the repeated fall of rain which has fallen constantly since we passed the long narrows on the [   ] of November last.

Indeed, we have had only [   ] days' fair weather since that time. Soon after we had set out from Fort Clatsop, we were met by Delashelwilt and 8 men of the Chinook and Delashelwilt's wife, the Old Bawd, and his six girls. They had a canoe, a sea otter skin, dried fish, and hats for sale. We purchased a sea otter skin, and proceeded on.

Clark never did get round to checking back to confirm when they'd passed the particular narrows he'd had in mind: most likely, perhaps, it was the stretch just above Pillar Rock, Washington, which they'd passed on November 7. Neither did he do the math to establish exactly how many days they had been without rain in the preceding months: Scholars since have done it for him—and their answer? A miserable twelve!

THE SKILLUTES

On **March 27**, as **Lewis** describes, the Corps of Discovery entered the territory of another Indian people:

We set out early this morning and were shortly after joined by some of the Skillutes, who came alongside in a small canoe for the purpose of trading roots and fish. At 10 a.m. we arrived at two houses of this nation on the starboard side, where we halted for breakfast. Here we overtook our hunters. They had killed nothing. The natives appeared extremely hospitable: gave us dried anchovies, sturgeon, wappatoo [a plant native to the Columbia River valley], quamash [camas], and a species of small, white tuberous roots about 2 inches in length and as thick as a man's finger. These are eaten raw; are crisp, milky and agreeably flavored. Most of the party were served by the natives with as much as they could eat.

Left: Scientifically proven to be the furriest creature in the world (see page 162), and hunted accordingly, the sea otter is now a protected animal.

THE BALD EAGLE

"Our hunters joined us, having killed three eagles and a large goose," reports Lewis in his journal for March 26.

I had now an opportunity of comparing the bald with the grey eagle; I found that the grey eagle was about ¼ larger; its legs and feet were dark while those of the bald eagle were of a fine orange yellow. The iris of the eye is also of a dark yellowish brown while that of the other is of a bright silvery color with a slight admixture of yellow.

Not "bald" in the modern sense, of course, this raptor takes its name from an Old English word, balde, meaning "white": Its white head is indeed the bald eagle's most striking feature. Today a world-famous emblem of American pride and power, it seems undignified to see the bald eagle in these circumstances: To Lewis, of course, it was just another bird. In the 1800s, it had yet to take on its symbolic importance, while the idea of endangered species was still a century away. Abundant as the wilderness was in its wildlife, even a nature lover like Lewis thought nothing of shooting birds in order to study them. As time went by, indeed, hunters would blast away at the eagle to such effect that it seemed it might actually end up extinct outside of America's national crest. Fortunately, an energetic program of conservation appears to have brought the bald eagle back from the brink, and this majestic bird endures—a living, soaring symbol of strength and freedom.

They insisted on our remaining all day with them and hunting the elk and deer which they informed us were very abundant in their neighborhood. But as the weather would not permit us to dry our canoes in order to pitch them we declined their friendly invitation and resumed our voyage.

The principal village of these Skillutes reside on the lower side of the Coweliskee [Cowlitz] River a few miles from its entrance into the Columbia. These people are said to be numerous. In their dress, habits, manners and language they differ but little from the Clatsops, Chinooks, etc. They have latterly been at war with the Chinooks, but peace is said now to be restored between them, but their intercourse is not yet resumed. No Chinooks come above the marshy islands, nor do the Skillutes visit the mouth of the Columbia. The Clatsops, Cathlahmahs and Wahkiakums are the carriers between these nations, being in alliance with both.

Late in the evening we passed our camp of the 5th of November and encamped about 4½ miles above…. We had scarcely landed before we were visited by a large canoe with eight men. From them we obtained a dried fruit which resembled the raspberry and which I believe to be the fruit of the large-leafed thorn [salmonberry] frequently mentioned. It is rather acid, though pleasantly flavored. I preserved a specimen of this fruit. I fear that it has been baked in the process of drying, and if so the seed will not vegetate. Saw the cottonwood, sweet willow, oak, ash and the broad-leafed ash, the growth which resembles the beech, etc. These form the growth of the bottom lands while the hills are covered almost exclusively with the various species of fir heretofore described. The black alder appears as well on some parts of the hills as the bottoms.

AN OMINOUS ENCOUNTER

April 1, 1806

We were visited by several canoes of natives in the course of the day, most of whom were descending the river with their women and children. They informed us that they resided at the great rapids and that their relations at that place were much straitened at that place for want of food; that they had consumed their winter store of dried fish and that those of the present season had not yet arrived. I could not learn whether they took the sturgeon, but presume if they do it is in but small quantities, as they complained much of the scarcity of food among them. They informed us that the nations above them were in the same situation, and that they did not expect the salmon to arrive until the full of the next moon, which happens on the 2nd of May.

We did not doubt the veracity of these people, who seemed to be on their way with their families and effects in search of subsistence, which they find it easy to procure in this fertile valley. This information gives us much uneasiness with respect to our future means of subsistence. Above the falls or through the plains from thence to the Chopunnish there are no deer, antelope or elk on which we can depend for subsistence. Their horses are very poor most probably at this season, and if they have no fish their dogs must be in the same situation. Under these circumstances there seems to be but a gloomy prospect for subsistence on any terms. We therefore took it into serious consideration what measures we were to pursue on this occasion.

Above: Hat Rock, Umatilla, Oregon. Opposite: Unexpected rock formations punctuate the line of the Columbia Valley, strange relics of volcanic cataclysms past, including Rooster Rock, near Latourell Falls.

It was at once deemed inexpedient to wait the arrival of the salmon, as that would detain us so large a portion of the season that it is probable we should not reach the United States before the ice would close the Missouri, or at all events would hazard our horses which we left in charge of the Chopunnish [Nez Percé], who informed us they intended passing the rocky mountains to the Missouri as early as the season would permit them, which is as we believe about the beginning of May.

April 2, 1806

This morning we came to a resolution to remain at our present encampment or somewhere in this neighborhood until we had obtained as much dried meat as would be necessary for our voyage as far as the Chopunnish; to exchange our pirogues for canoes with the natives on our way to the great falls of the Columbia, or purchase such canoes from them for elkskins and merchandise as would answer our purposes. These canoes we intend exchanging with the natives of the plains for horses as we proceed until we obtain as many as will enable us to travel altogether by land. At some convenient point, perhaps at the entrance to the southeast branch of the Columbia, we purpose sending a party of four or five men ahead to collect our horses, that they may be in readiness for us by our arrival at the Chopunnish, calculating by thus acquiring a large stock of horses we shall not only secure the means of transporting our baggage over the mountains but that we will also have provided the means of subsisting, for we now view the horses as our only certain resource for food — nor do we look forward to it with any horror, so soon is the mind which is occupied with any interesting object reconciled to its situation.

Mine and Thine

The journey up the Oregon Gorge afforded **Lewis** another insight (**April 9**) into the contrast between the baseness of men and the sublime magnificence of nature:

John Colter, one of our party, observed the tomahawk in one of the lodges which had been stolen from us on the 4th of November last as we descended this river. The natives attempted to wrest the tomahawk from him, but he retained it. They endeavored afterwards to exculpate themselves from the odium of having stolen it; they alleged that they had bought it from the natives below, but their neighbors had several days previously informed us that these people had stolen the tomahawk and then had it at their village.

"The natives attempted to wrest the tomahawk from him, but he retained it."

We passed several beautiful cascades which fell from a great height over the stupendous rocks which close the river on both sides nearly, except a small bottom on the south side in which our hunters were encamped. The most remarkable of these cascades falls about 300 feet perpendicularly over a solid rock into a narrow bottom of the river on the south side…. Several small streams fall from a much greater height, and in their descent become a perfect mist which, collecting on the rocks below, again become visible, and descend a second time in the same manner before they reach the base of the rocks.

"The Great Mart of All This Country"

The need for horses was growing desperate so, as **Clark** records in his journal for **April 16**:

About 8 o'clock this morning I passed the river with the two interpreters and nine men, in order to trade with the natives for their horses, for which purpose I took with me a good part of our stock of merchandise.

Great numbers came from both villages and delayed the greater part of the day without trading a single horse. Drewyer returned with the principal chief of the Skillutes, who was lame and could not walk. After his arrival, some horses were offered for sale, but they asked nearly half the merchandise I had with me for one horse. This price I could not think of giving. The chief informed me if I should go to his town with him, his people would sell me horses. I therefore concluded to accompany him to his village 7 miles distant.

This is the great mart of all this country. Ten different tribes who reside on the Tapteet [Yakima] and Cataract Rivers visit those people for the purpose of purchasing their fish, and the Indians on the Columbia and Lewis's River quite to the Chopunnish [Nez Percé] nation visit them for the purpose of trading horses [and] buffalo robes for beads and such articles as they have not. The Skillutes procure the most of their cloth, knives, axes and beads from the Indians of the north of them who trade with white people who come into the inlets to the north at no great distance from the Tapteet.

April 17, 1806
I rose early after a bad night's rest, and took my merchandise to a rock which afforded an eligible situation for my purpose, and at a short distance from the houses, and divided the articles of merchandise into parcels of such articles as I thought best calculated to please the Indians. Many of the natives from different villages on the Columbia above offered to trade, but asked such things as we had not and double as much of the articles which I had as we could afford to give.

GREAT JOY!

Gradually, though, the Expedition's luck started to show signs of changing—over the days that followed, Clark managed to procure a horse here, another there. And at last, as **Lewis** reports on **April 19**, another momentous event took place, which brought the hope at least of easier times to come.

THE SALMON RUN

Every spring, far out in the Pacific, the salmon marshal in their millions before—at some mysterious signal—advancing in overwhelming force up the estuaries and rivers of the West. As summer begins, they surge upstream in their silvery shoals, leaping rapids, driven on by the compulsion to find their way home and breed. For the region's bears, otters, mink, and other predators—including humans—the salmon run is a deluge of delicious and easily procured protein, just there for the taking. Yet those who fail to take it while it lasts—and at times only a few days may separate the pioneers from the stragglers—will find themselves having to wait another twelve months. For the peoples of the Northwest, the salmon run was the pivotal event of the year. Whole communities worked frantically to maximize the harvest. Most of the harvest was quickly gutted, cleaned, filleted, and dried, to help see the village through the long, hungry seasons that follow. So vast and mysterious a gift was the salmon run—and so wholly did the Indians depend on it—that it is no surprise that it should have given rise to its own rituals and taboos. Why would the fish return to a community that had not greeted them with the requisite courtesies? The consequences of offending them were quite unthinkable.

There was great joy with the natives last night, in consequence of the arrival of the salmon. One of those fish was caught. This was the harbinger of good news to them. They informed us that these fish would arrive in great quantities in the course of about five days. This fish was dressed and, being divided into small pieces, was given to each child in the village. This custom is founded on a superstitious opinion that it will hasten the arrival of the salmon. With much difficulty we obtained four other horses from the Indians today. We were obliged to dispense with two of our kettles in order to acquire those. We now have only one small kettle to a mess of eight men.

By April 27, tired and footsore, the Expedition members were nearing the Walla Walla village of Chief Yellept, whose offer of hospitality they had had to pass up the previous fall.

He appeared much gratified at seeing us return, invited us to remain at his village three or four days, and assured us that we should be furnished with a plenty of such food as they had themselves, and some horses to assist us on our journey. After our scanty repast we continued our march, accompanied by Yellept and his party, to the village…. This chief is a man of much influence not only in his own nation but also among the neighboring tribes and nations. Yellept harangued his village in our favor, entreated them to furnish us with fuel and provision, and set the example himself by bringing us an armful of wood and a platter of three roasted mullets. The others soon followed his example with respect to fuel, and we soon found ourselves in possession of an ample stock. They burn the stems of the shrubs in the plains, there being no timber in their neighborhood of any description. We purchased four dogs of these people on which the party supped heartily, having been on short allowance for near two days.

WITH THE WALLA WALLA

Lewis and Clark were anxious to be on their way, but, as **Clark** notes (**April 28**), Yellept's generous hospitality was hard to resist—and there was, after all, a need to amass supplies for the next stage of their journey.

This morning early the Great Chief Yellept brought a very elegant white horse to our camp and presented him to me, signifying his wish to get a kettle, but, being informed that we had already disposed of every kettle we could possibly spare, he said he was content with whatever I thought proper to give him. I gave him my sword, 100 balls and powder and some small articles, of which he appeared perfectly satisfied. It was necessary before we entered on our route through the plains, where we were to meet with no lodges or resident Indians, that we should lay in a stock of provisions and not depend altogether on the gun.... Being anxious to depart, we requested the chief to furnish us with canoes to pass the river, but he insisted on our remaining with him this day at least, that he would be much pleased if we would consent to remain two or three, but he would not let us have canoes to leave him today. That he had sent for the Chimnapums [Yakima], his neighbors, to come down and join his people this evening and dance for us....

We found a Shoshone woman, prisoner among these people, by means of whom and Sacagawea, Charbonneau's wife, we found the means of conversing with the Wallawallas. We conversed with them for several hours and fully satisfied all their inquiries with respect to ourselves and the objects of our pursuit. They were much pleased.

"A little before sunset, the Chimnapums arrived...they waited very patiently to see our party dance"

They brought several diseased persons to us for whom they requested some medical aid. One had his knee contracted by the rheumatism, another with a broken arm, etc., to all of whom we administered, much to the gratification of those poor wretches. We gave them some eye-water, which I believe will render them more essential service than any other article in the medical way which we had it in our power to bestow on them. Sore eyes seem to be a universal complaint among these people. I have no doubt but the fine sand of those plains and the river contribute much to the disorder. The man who had his arm broken had it loosely bound in a piece of leather without anything to support it. I dressed the arm which was broken short above the wrist, and supported it with broad stick to keep it in place, put it in a sling and furnished him with some lint bandages etc. to dress it in future.

A little before sunset, the Chimnapums arrived. They were about 100 men and a few women. They joined the Wallawallas, who were about the same number, and formed a half circle around our camp, where they waited very patiently to see our party dance. The fiddle was played and the men amused themselves with dancing about an hour. We then requested the Indians to dance, which they very cheerfully complied with....They were much gratified in seeing some of our party join them in their dance.

Top: Oregon's Columbia River Gorge, a place of stunning natural beauty, but for the Expedition the scene of a grueling—and frequently perilous—struggle upriver.

FRUSTRATIONS

Having taken leave of the Walla Walla on **May 1, Lewis** gives them a glowing testimonial—albeit at others' expense:

Some time after we had encamped, three young men arrived from the Wallawalla village, bringing with them a steel trap belonging to one of our party which had been negligently left behind. This is an act of integrity rarely witnessed among Indians. During our stay with them they several times found the knives of the men which had been carelessly lost by them and returned them. I think we can justly affirm to the honor of these people that they are the most hospitable, honest and sincere people that we have met with in our voyage.

The next few days' travel would bring out the more difficult undercurrents of a relationship in which mutual goodwill always seems to be accompanied by distrust—at times open hostility. Ill-temper was the inevitable companion to ill nourishment at a time when winter supplies were exhausted and the full salmon season had yet to arrive. Even the most humanitarian of activities, the highest gratitude, were compromised by suspicion on both sides, as is illustrated by **Lewis's** journal for **May 5**:

We passed an Indian man who gave Captain Clark a very elegant gray mare, for which he requested a phial of eyewater, which was accord-

"...they are the most hospitable, honest and sincere people that we have met with in our voyage."

ingly given him. While we were encamped last fall at the entrance of the Chopunnish River, Captain Clark gave an Indian man some volatile liniment to rub his knee and thigh for a pain of which he complained. The fellow soon after recovered, and has never ceased to extol the virtues of our medicines, and the skill of my friend Captain Clark as a physician. This occurrence, added to the benefit which many of them experienced from the eyewater we gave them about the same time, has given them an exalted opinion of our medicine.

My friend Captain Clark is their favorite physician and has already received many applications. In our present situation, I think it pardonable to continue this deception, for they will not give us any provision without compensation in merchandise, and our stock is now reduced to a mere handful. We take care to give them no article which can possibly injure them.

Their next encounter with the Nez Percé, later that evening, was no better.

We arrived here extremely hungry and much fatigued, but no articles of merchandise in our possession would induce them to let us have any article of provision, except a small quantity of bread of cous and some of those roots dried. We had several applications to assist their sick, which we refused unless they would let us have some dogs or horses to eat. A chief, whose wife had an abscess formed on the small of her back, promised a horse in the morning, provided we would administer to her…. Captain Clark soon had more than fifty applications. I prepared some doses of flower of

Above: The Snake River, now a reservoir, in what is now the Central Ferry State Park, near Dodge, Washington.
Opposite: The Nez Percé's Feast Lodge for the dead Chief Joseph, photographed by Curtis, 1904.

sulphur and cream of tartar, which were given with directions to be taken on each morning.

A little girl and sundry other patients were offered for cure, but we postponed our operations until morning. They produced us several dogs, but they were so poor that they were unfit for use.

Grudging and uneasy as relations with these Nez Percé were, the Expedition had to adjust themselves to the fact that they were going to have to spend a good deal longer in their company, as **Lewis** explains in his journal for **May 7**:

The spurs of the Rocky Mountains which were in view from the high plain today were perfectly covered with snow. The Indians inform us that the snow is yet so deep on the mountains that we shall not be able to pass them until the next full moon or about the first of June; others set the time at a still more distant period. This is unwelcome intelligence to men confined to a diet of horsebeef and roots, and who are as anxious as we are to return to the fat plains of the Missouri, and thence to our native homes.

KINDER HOSTS

Things began to look up for the Expedition three days later, though, when they reached Commearp (or Lawyer's Canyon) Creek, and met some Nez Percé friends they had made on their outward journey:

At four in the afternoon, we descended the hills to Commearp Creek and arrived at the village of Tunnachemootoolt, the chief at whose lodge we had left the flag last fall. This flag was now displayed on a staff placed at no great distance from the lodge. Underneath the flag, the chief met my friend Captain Clark, who was in front, and conducted him about 80 yards to a place on the bank of the creek where he requested we should encamp. I came up in a few minutes and we collected the chiefs and men of consideration, smoked with them, and stated our situation with respect to provision. The chief spoke to his people, and they produced us about two bushels of the quamash roots, dried, four cakes of the bread of cows, and a dried salmon trout.

We thanked them for this store of provision but informed them that, our men not being accustomed to live on roots alone, we feared it would make them sick, to obviate which we proposed exchanging a horse in rather low order for a young horse in tolerable order with a view to kill. The hospitality of the chief revolted at the idea of an exchange. He told us that his young men had a great abundance of young horses, and if we wished to eat them we should be furnished with as many as we wanted. Accordingly, they soon produced us two fat young horses, one of which we killed. The other we informed them we would postpone killing until we had consumed the one already killed.

This is a much greater act of hospitality than we have witnessed from any nation or tribe since we have passed the Rocky Mountains. In short, be it spoken to their immortal honor, it is the only act which deserves the appellation of hospitality which

we have witnessed in this quarter. We informed these people that we were hungry and fatigued at this moment, that when we had eaten and refreshed ourselves we would inform them who we were, from whence we had come and the objects of our researches.

A principal chief, by name Hohastillpilp, arrived with a party of fifty men mounted on elegant horses. He had come on a visit to us from his village, which is situated about six miles distant near the river. We invited this man into our circle and smoked with him. His retinue continued on horseback at a little distance. After we had eaten a few roots, we spoke to them as we had promised, and gave Tunnachemooltoolt and Hohastillpilp each a medal….

We explained to them the design and the importance of medals in the estimation of the whites as well as the red men who had been taught their value. The chief had a large conic lodge of leather erected for our reception, and a parcel of wood collected and laid at the door; after which he invited Captain Clark and myself to make that lodge our home while we remained with him.

Above: The Expedition's campsite of May 31, 1806, was drowned with the damming of the Snake River. Opposite: The Clearwater (Kooskooskee) River, Idaho: The Expedition camped near here from May 15–June 10, 1806.

A Healing Touch

Tunnachemooltoolt ("Broken Arm") and Hohastillpilp would be the Expedition's hosts for the best part of a month, but thanks to their generosity the delay was anything but irksome. As **Clark** explains (**May 12**), he and Lewis were asked to give medical assistance and help heal diplomatic rifts between the Nez Percé and their neighbors:

A fine morning. Great numbers of Indians flock about us as usual. After breakfast I began to administer eyewater and in a few minutes had near 40 applicants with sore eyes, and many others with other complaints….The Indians had a grand council this morning, after which we were presented each with a horse by two young men at the instance of the nation. We caused the chiefs to be seated and gave them each a flag, a pint of powder, and 50 balls; to the two young men who had presented the horses we also gave powder and ball. The Broken Arm, or Tunnachemooltoolt, pulled off his leather shirt, and gave me. In return, I gave him a shirt.

We retired into the lodge, and the natives spoke to the following purpose: i.e., they had listened to our advice and that the whole nation were determined to follow it; that they had only one heart and one tongue on this subject. Explained the cause of the war with the Shoshones. They wished to be at peace with all nations, etc. Some of their men would accompany us to the Missouri, etc., etc., as a great number of men, women, and children were waiting and requesting medical assistance, many of them with the most simple complaints which could be easily relieved, independent of many with disorders entirely out of the power of medicine—all requesting something.

We agreed that I should administer, and Captain Lewis hear and answer the Indians. I was closely employed until 2 p.m., administering eyewater to about 40 grown persons, some simple cooling medicines to the disabled chief, to several women with rheumatic affections, and a man who had a swelled hip, etc., etc.

Despite a congenial stay with the Nez Percé, **Lewis** was plainly in a hurry, as his journal for **May 17** reveals:

I am pleased at finding the river rise so rapidly. It no doubt is attributable to the melting snows of the mountains, that icy barrier which separates me from my friends and country, from all which makes life esteemable—patience, patience!

Clark echoed these sentiments on the same day:

I frequently consult the natives on the subject of passing this tremendous barrier which now present themselves to our view for a great extent. They all appear to agree as to the time those mountains may be passed, which is about the middle of June. At the distance of 18 miles from the river, and on the eastern border of the high plain the Rocky Mountain commences and presents us with… Winter! Here we have summer, spring and winter in the short space of twenty or thirty miles.

As we have seen, Lewis and Clark's expertise as doctors commanded the regard (not to say amazement) of the Indians. Now, as **Lewis** tells us (**May 22**), they had to apply their skills rather closer to home:

Charbonneau's child is very ill this evening. He is cutting teeth, and for several days past has had a violent lax, which having suddenly stopped he was attacked with a high fever and his neck and throat are much swollen this evening. We gave him a dose of cream of tartar and flower of sulphur and applied a poultice of boiled onions to his neck, as warm as he could well bear it.

"Charbonneau's child is very ill this evening.…We gave him a dose of cream of tartar and flower of sulphur and applied a poultice of boiled onions to his neck."

MEDICAL MATTERS

The doctoring skills of Lewis and Clark may have amazed the Native Americans: to us, though, they often seem all but barbaric in their crudeness. In fact, both had been given some training by the "American Hippocrates," Benjamin Rush. Though advanced in his understanding of the need for hygiene, his emphasis on the use of bleeding—literally the draining of blood from the patient's body to increase its "purity"—for a range of ailments already seemed old-fashioned. But Rush was an extraordinary figure, even by the standards of the Enlightenment, and he transcended his time in his open-mindedness: He had for decades been a keen student of native medicine.

The following night, Clark saw encouraging signs, but a day later, Jean-Baptiste (or "It"!) was giving **Lewis** cause for concern (**May 24**):

Above: Long Camp, near Kamiah, Idaho, where the Expedition waited (May–June 1806) for the mountain snows to clear.

The child was very restless last night. Its jaw and the back of its neck are much more swollen than they were yesterday, though his fever has abated considerably. We gave it a dose of cream of tartar and applied a fresh poultice of onions….

Another, grown-up patient whose joints had been so badly inflamed that he could scarcely sit up straight, let alone stand or walk, was also showing signs of responding to some (rather drastic!) treatment:

John Shields observed that he had seen men in a similar situation restored by violent sweats. Bratton requested that he might be sweated in the manner proposed by Shields, to which we consented. Shields sunk a circular hole of 3 feet diameter and four feet deep in the earth. He kindled a large fire in the hole and heated well, after which the fire was taken out, a seat placed in the center of the hole for the patient with a board at the bottom for his feet to rest on. Some hoops of willow poles were bent in an arch crossing each other over the hole; on these several blankets were thrown, forming a secure and thick awning of about 3 feet high.

The patient being stripped naked was seated under this awning in the hole and the blankets well secured on every side. The patient was furnished with a vessel of water which he sprinkles on the bottom and sides of the hole and by that means creates as much steam or vapor as he could possibly bear. In this situation he was kept about 20 minutes, after which he was taken out and suddenly plunged in cold water twice and was then immediately returned to the sweat hole where he was continued three quarters of an hour longer then taken out covered in several blankets and suffered to cool gradually. During the time of his being in the sweat hole, he drank copious draughts of a strong tea of horse mint…. This experiment was made yesterday. Bratton feels himself much better and is walking about today and says he is nearly free from pain.

THE "PRAIRIE BUFFALO"

"A species of lizard called by the French engagés prairie buffalo are native of these plains as well as of those of the Missouri," notes Lewis in his journal for May 29. "I have called them the horned lizard," he goes on. Naturalists have settled on "short-horned lizard," to distinguish this curious creature from the better-known horned lizards of the arid Southwest. Lewis's imagination appears to desert him completely as he indignantly upbraids his men: "I cannot conceive how the engagés ever assimilated this animal with the buffalo, for there is not greater analogy than between the horse and the frog." Scientific literalism was, perhaps, the besetting sin of the Enlightenment mind.

ONWARD—AND UPWARD

The persistence of snows in the high mountains was frustrating. By **June 14** they had resolved to push on—though not, **Lewis** reveals, without trepidation:

We had all our articles packed up and made ready for an early departure in the morning. Our horses were caught, and most of them hobbled and otherwise confined in order that we might not be detained. From hence to Traveler's Rest we shall make a forced march. At that place we shall probably remain one or two days to rest ourselves and horses and procure some meat. We have now been detained near five weeks in consequence of the snows—a serious loss of time at this delightful season for traveling. I am still apprehensive that the snow and the want of food for our horses will prove a serious embarrassment to us as at least four days' journey of our route in these mountains lies over heights and along a ledge of mountains never entirely destitute of snow. Everybody seems anxious to be in motion, convinced that we have not now any time to delay if the calculation is to reach the United States this season. This I am determined to accomplish if within the compass of human power.

By **June 17** they had made good progress, nearing the ridge between the Kooskooskee (North Fork Clearwater) and Chopunnish (Lochsa) rivers, but the way was getting both harder and more confusing, as **Clark** describes:

***Below:** The Bitterroot Mountains, near Lolo, Montana, deep in snow.*

We found ourselves enveloped in snow from 8 to 12 feet deep, even on the south side of the mountain. I was in front and could only pursue the direction of the road by the trees which had been peeled by the natives for the inner bark of which they scraped and ate. As those peeled trees were only to be found scattered promiscuously, I with great difficulty pursued the direction of the road one mile further to the top of the mountain, where I found the snow from 12 to 15 feet deep.... Here was winter with all its rigors: the air was cold, my hands and feet were benumbed. We knew that it would require four days to reach the fish weir at the entrance of Colt [Whitesand] Creek—provided we were so fortunate as to be enabled to follow the proper ridge of the mountains to lead us to that place. Of this all of our most expert woodsmen and principal guides were extremely doubtful. Short of that point, we could not hope for any food for our horses—not even underwood itself, as the whole was covered many feet deep in snow. If we proceeded and should get bewildered in those mountains, the certainty was that we should lose all of our horses and consequently our baggage, instruments, perhaps our papers, and thus eventually risk the loss of our discoveries which we had already made if we should be so fortunate as to escape with life.

"The snow bore our horses very well," Clark continued, "and the traveling was therefore infinitely better than the obstruction of rocks and fallen timber which we met with in our passage over last fall, when the snow lay on this part of the ridge in detached spots only." It being

TALE OF TEARS

The Nez Percé story has been one of almost continuous injustice, ever since they were named by the first French trappers for the pierced noses some other tribes in the region had, but which they never had themselves. Their own name, Nimipu, just means "people," and they do seem to have been an unassuming nation, content to gather quamash in spring, fish the Clearwater and Snake Rivers for salmon in summer, and cross the mountains to hunt buffalo on the Missouri Plains for a few weeks before the snows returned each year. But even by the time they met the Corps of Discovery, they were coming under pressure from better-armed neighbors like the Blackfeet, Hidatsa, and Crow, and their troubles would deepen as the nineteenth century wore on. Gold strikes in the 1860s brought miners streaming into Nez Percé lands, dislodging many. In 1877, those who remained were formally evicted from their ancestral territories. Led by Chief Joseph (above), the survivors set out in hopes of linking up with Sitting Bull's Lakota, then exiled in Canada, to carry on the resistance; harassed by government forces across 1,700 miles, they were forced to a standstill 30 miles from the frontier. "Hear me, my chiefs," said Joseph, famously: "I am tired; my heart is sick and sad. From where the sun now stands, I will fight no more forever."

Lewis and Clark's judgment that rapid progress could be made just so long as the Expedition could be sure of its direction in the trackless snow, they decided that it made sense to delay again, just so long as it took to get a native guide. A small party was sent out to find someone suitable. By **June 23** they were back, as **Lewis** reports:

At 3 p.m., Drewyer, Shannon and Whitehouse returned. Drewyer brought with him three Indians who had consented to accompany us to the Falls of the Missouri for the compensation of two guns…. These are all young men of good character and much respected by their nation. We directed the horses to be brought near camp this evening and secured in such manner that they may be readily obtained in the morning.

June 25, 1806

Last evening the Indians entertained us with setting the fir trees on fire. They have a great number of dry limbs near their bodies which, when set on fire, creates a very sudden and immense blaze from bottom to top of those tall trees. They are a beautiful object in this situation at night. This exhibition reminded me of a display of fireworks. The natives told us that their object in setting those trees on fire was to bring fair weather for our journey.

June 27, 1806

The road still continued on the heights of the same dividing ridge on which we had traveled yesterday for nine miles or to our encampment of the 17th of September last. About one mile short of this encampment, on an elevated point, we halted by the request of the Indians a few minutes and smoked the pipe. On this eminence the natives have raised a conic mound of stones of 6 or eight feet high, and on its summit erected a pine pole of 15 feet long…. From this place we had an extensive view of these stupendous mountains principally covered with snow like that on which we stood. We were entirely surrounded by those mountains, from which, to one unacquainted with them, it would have seemed impossible ever to have escaped. In short, without the assistance of our guides, I doubt much whether we who had once passed them could find our way to Traveler's Rest in their present situation, for the marked trees on which we had placed considerable reliance are much fewer and more difficult to find than we had apprehended. These fellows are most admirable pilots. We find the road wherever the snow has disappeared, though it be only for a few hundred paces.

After having smoked the pipe and contemplating this scene sufficient to have dampened the spirits of any except such hardy travelers as we have become, we continued our march.

A Welcome Break

By **June 28**, **Clark's** journal makes clear, they were making their way with much more confidence:

We find the traveling on the snow not worse than without it, as the easy passage it gives us over rocks and fallen timber fully compensates for the inconvenience of slipping. Certain it is that we travel considerably faster on the snow than without it. The snow sinks from 2 to 3 inches with a horse, is coarse and firm and seems to be formed of the larger particles of the snow. The surface of the snow is rather harder in the morning than after the sun shines on it a few hours, but it is not in that situation so dense as to prevent the horses from obtaining good foothold.

As **Lewis** describes, in his journal for **June 29**, the hot springs near Lolo, Montana—"Traveler's Rest"—provided welcome relaxation for weary bones:

The principal spring is about the temperature of the warmest baths used at the hot springs in Virginia. In this bath, which had been prepared by the Indians by stopping the river with stone and gravel, I bathed and remained in 19 minutes. It was with difficulty I could remain thus long, and it caused a profuse sweat. Two other bold springs adjacent to this are much warmer, their heat being so great as to make the hand of a person smart extremely when immersed. I think the temperature of those springs about the same as that of the hottest of the hot springs of Virginia.

Both the men and the Indians amused themselves with the use of a bath this evening. I observed that the Indians, after remaining in the hot bath as long as they could bear it, ran and plunged themselves into the creek, the water of which is now as cold as ice can make it. After remaining here a few minutes, they returned again to the warm bath, repeating this transition several times, but always ending with the warm bath.

By the end of the month the Expedition had safely completed the descent to Traveler's Rest. "Our horses have stood the journey surprisingly well," wrote Captain Clark. While the hunters went out for meat, it was resolved, Lewis would take a party to the Missouri Falls to recover the caches and canoes they had left behind the previous fall. The Corps would split up for the next stage of the journey, Lewis striking north with one group to explore the Marias River, while Clark and his company cut across country to the upper reaches of the Yellowstone River.

Below: The valley of the Bitterroot River, near Traveler's Rest, Lolo, Montana: The Expedition paused here before pushing on homeward.

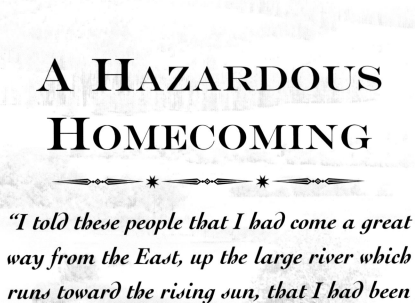

A Hazardous Homecoming

✸

"I told these people that I had come a great way from the East, up the large river which runs toward the rising sun, that I had been to the great waters where the sun sets and had seen a great many nations."

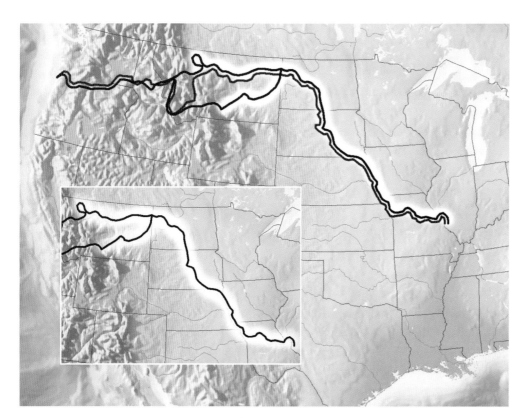

Opposite: *"We ascended a small rise and beheld an open, beautiful, level valley or plain of about 20 miles wide and near 60 long…around which I could see high points of mountains covered with snow." The Big Hole River, near Wisdom, Montana, where the returning Corps of Discovery arrived on July 6, 1806.*

A continent successfully crossed, the highest of the Western mountains traversed for the second time, the prospect of fine weather and a following current to sweep them safely down the Missouri. The Corps of Discovery could take comfort now: The worst of the journey must surely be over—yet we have no sense of Lewis and Clark relaxing in their brief break at "Traveler's Rest." Still less do we see any signs of complacency or triumph. There was much to do, of course: game to be procured, maps to be refined, and observations to be taken—yet there would have been time, too, for reflection if the explorers so desired. Such time as he had for thought, however, seems only to have increased the fearfulness that Lewis felt. For one, he admits to his "concern" on parting with Clark a few days later. His anxieties are understandable: Both men were experienced enough wayfarers to know that nothing could ever be taken for

granted in the Western wilderness. Just as many dangers as they had encountered on the outward leg of their journey might await them on their return home. Yet there must have been more to Lewis's trepidation than that. Hardened backwoodsmen by now, Lewis and Clark did not lightly give way to the sort of worries that could only be unproductive. The answer is surely that, with success in sight, the stakes were suddenly so much higher. Having achieved so much, they had that much more to lose in the event of failure. Should they be denied their triumph at the eleventh hour, it would be a cruel conclusion indeed to all their labors; the journey's actual perils paled into insignificance beside this unshakable anxiety.

The Lewis and Clark Expedition can itself be seen as marking a comparable moment in American history: the point at which the New Republic came of age. If the explorers' journey to the Pacific Coast opened up the horizons of the former colonies, it also

Below: The route of the Red River Expedition, as revealed by John H. Robinson's map of Mexico, Louisiana, and the Missouri Territory (1819). "The exploring party stopped here commanded by Major Sparks," explains an annotation on the map; the Spanish camp is indicated a little farther to the south.

represented their transition to a more complex and—in many ways—more dangerous age. Thrown in with the Louisiana Purchase had been a whole host of native peoples, and native problems, while new borders meant new conflicts with the European powers. Britain, by now, was an old adversary, of course, yet America's apparent expansionism lent a new twist to long-standing tensions. It also brought the country into direct confrontation with the fading—yet still formidable—power of Spain. It had been mainly for the sake of discipline and efficiency that the Corps of Discovery had been organized along military lines, yet this should not disguise the fact that the whole undertaking had been, in a certain sense, an act of war. The lands bought from France under the terms of the

Louisiana Purchase extended only as far as the high Cordillera, and the Corps' descent to the Pacific had been an incursion into Spanish territory. Mexico, or "New Spain," still covered a great deal of what is now the western part of the United States: The territorial gains of the Mexican Wars lay several decades in the future. Spain claimed not only California and the Southwest, but also what would later become the states of Oregon and Washington—all the way up to the border with the British-controlled territories of western Canada.

This far north, of course, the Spanish presence was largely notional, yet the U.S. incursion had been by no means a technicality as far as the Spanish crown was concerned. Just how seriously it was taken—and just how gravely it might all

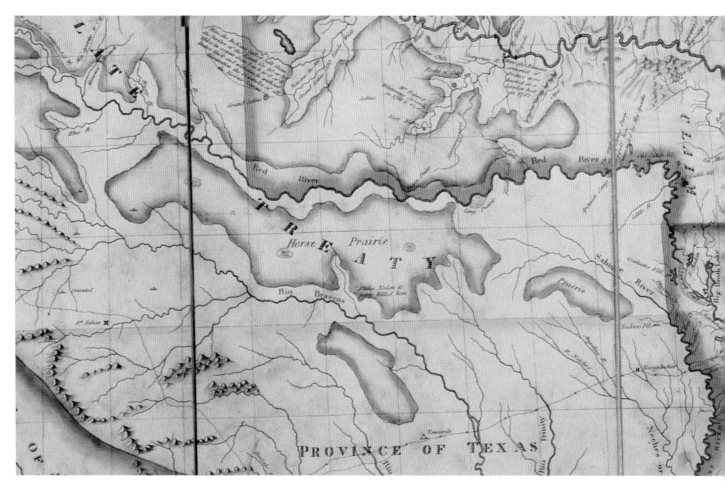

have ended for Lewis and Clark—was hinted at by events unfolding at about the same time, several hundred miles to the south. In one of the great might-have-beens of American history, Jefferson had sent another party out to explore the Louisiana Purchase, this one to explore territories in Texas and the Southwest. The "Great Excursion," as it was called, should have been every bit as important as the Lewis and Clark Expedition. Led by civil engineer and surveyor Thomas Freeman and the young doctor and naturalist Peter Custis, with Captain Richard Sparks as the ranking military officer, this party has become known—in so far as it is known by a posterity that has always been forgetful of failure—as the "Freeman and Custis" or "Red River" Expedition. Setting

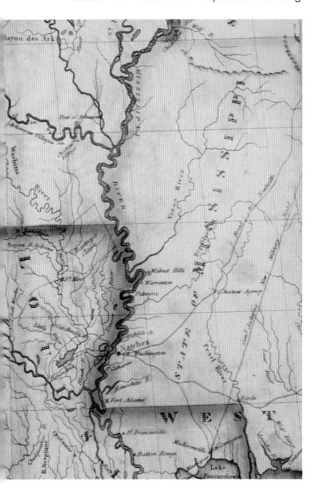

off from the Mississippi up the Red River in the Spring of 1806, its aim was to cross Louisiana, Arkansas, and Oklahoma into Texas. The explorers did make it some 600 miles upstream, and Custis (cautious though he was in his identifications) recorded twenty-one new plant and animal species, and provided fresh data on many more that were already known. The stage was set for a historical triumph to surpass even that of the Lewis and Clark Expedition when, on July 28, at what is now known as Spanish Bluff, near New Boston, Bowie County, Texas, they met an expeditionary force 700 strong led by Spanish Captain Francisco Viana, an experienced commander. The leaders of the "Great Excursion"—like Lewis and Clark—had strict instructions from the President that, "if at any time a superior force authorized or not authorized by a nation should be arrayed against your further passage and inflexibly determined to arrest it, you must decline its further pursuit and return." Viana's little army clearly comprised just such a superior force, and the expedition had no alternative but to turn on its heels and slink ignominiously home. The Spanish had, it seems, hoped to intercept both American parties, but Lewis and Clark were obviously well clear of their pursuers by this time. Even so, the fate of the Great Excursion underlines the seriousness with which Spain regarded such violations of its territorial integrity: The West was not the "empty," "ownerless" wilderness it may have seemed.

Not, of course, that the colonial powers were the only ones with an interest in these territories: Native peoples actually had a rather better title to the land. Up until now, the Corps of Discovery had enjoyed what, with hindsight, may seem like

Below: *Despite decades of upheaval and fierce conflict, many native peoples would manage to maintain their traditional ways well into the twentieth century, when this photograph was taken on a Blackfoot reservation.*

extraordinarily warm relations with the peoples they encountered. As we have seen, they had been welcomed precisely because they were outsiders. Their mediation was constantly being sought to help heal old conflicts and to arbitrate quarrels. With no history of his own in the region, the white man could enjoy a sort of "honeymoon," his uninvolved neutrality the key to his ready welcome. This could hardly be

expected to go on indefinitely, though: If Americans were going to start trading more seriously in the West—and certainly if they were going to begin settling there in any numbers—this neutral status could never be sustained. In fact, as it turned out, the honeymoon would be over before the Expedition was: Within a few weeks of their departure from Traveler's Rest, Expedition members had killed two Blackfoot men. This was no battle. In fact, it was little more than a brawl—a stabbing and shooting in a fight over a stolen gun—yet the incident set the tone for the history of the West over half a century and more. The image of the Indian as a thievish, murderous "savage" who was best dead, and the native view of the white American as a ruthless occupier and bringer of violence, were both confirmed. The War for the West would, at times, appear to be no more than a series of variations on this basic theme, and there were bigger battles to come, and crueler slaughters, before an uneasy peace was finally achieved.

Any sense of foreboding the explorers felt, then, as they set out on their homeward journey, seems only too amply justified in hindsight. At the same time, however, it is possible to find inspiration in their indomitable courage, their clear love of the land they were traversing. And of its people, too; for, if Lewis and Clark's condescension toward their Native American contacts at times seems alien, we are struck as well by the respect—and even affection—they so often felt for them. That their *Journals* set a paradigm of distrust and oppression can hardly be disputed, yet at the same time it would be perverse to ignore the precedent for cooperation—and even friendship—they establish, too.

THE PARTING OF THE WAYS

On **July 3**, as previously agreed, the Expedition divided into two parties. "I took leave of my worthy friend and companion Captain Clark and the party that accompanied him," wrote **Lewis**:

I could not avoid feeling much concern on this occasion, although I hoped this separation was only momentary. I proceeded down Clark's River [the Bitterroot] seven miles with my party of nine men and five Indians. Here the Indians recommended our passing the river, which was rapid and 150 yards wide…. We busied ourselves collecting dry timber for the purpose of constructing rafts; timber being scarce, we found considerable difficulty in procuring as much as made three small rafts.

We arrived at 11 a.m. and had our rafts completed by 3 p.m., when we dined and began to take over our baggage which we effected in the course of 3 hours, the rafts being obliged to return several times. The Indians swam over their horses and drew over their baggage in little basins of deer

"I took leave of my worthy friend and companion Captain Clark and the party that accompanied him."

skins which they constructed in a very few minutes for that purpose. We drove our horses in after them and they followed to the opposite shore. I remained myself with two men who could scarcely swim until the last; by this time the raft, by passing so frequently, had fallen a considerable distance down the river to a rapid and difficult part of it crowded with several small islands and willow bars which were now overflown. With these men I set out on the raft and was soon hurried down with the current a mile and a half before we made shore. On our approach to the shore the raft sunk and I was drawn off the raft by a bush and swam on shore. The two men remained on the raft and fortunately effected a landing at some little distance below. I wet the chronometer by this accident which I had placed in my fob as I conceived for greater security….

The mosquitoes were so excessively troublesome this evening that we were obliged to kindle large fires for our horses. These insects tortured them in such a manner until they placed themselves in the smoke of the fires that I really thought they would become frantic. About an hour after dark the air became so cold that the mosquitoes disappeared.

Top: *"Clark's River," now known as the Bitterroot, not far from Lolo, Montana—Lewis's party had a difficult time crossing near here on July 3, 1806.*

PESTS GREAT AND SMALL

July 15, 1806

A little before dark McNeal returned with his musket broken off at the breech, and informed me that…he had approached a white bear within ten feet without discovering him, the bear being in the thick brush. The horse took the alarm and, turning short, threw him immediately under the bear. This animal raised himself on his hind feet for battle and gave him time to recover from his fall which he did in an instant and with his clubbed musket he struck the bear over the head and cut him with the guard of the gun and broke off the breech. The bear, stunned with the stroke, fell to the ground and began to scratch his head with his feet. This gave McNeal time to climb a willow tree which was near at hand and thus fortunately made his escape. The bear waited at the foot of the tree until late in the evening before he left him, when McNeal ventured down and caught his horse (which had strayed off to the distance of

"The mosquitoes continue to infest us in such a manner that we can scarcely exist."

2 miles) and returned to the camp. These bear are a most tremendous animal. It seems that the hand of providence has been most wonderfully in our favor in respect to them, or some of us would long since have fallen a sacrifice to their ferocity…. The mosquitoes continue to infest us in such manner that we can scarcely exist…. My dog even howls with the torture he experiences from them: they are almost insupportable. They are so numerous that we frequently get them in our throats as we breathe.

Above: *Clark's group journeyed this way down the Shield River Valley on their way to the Yellowstone on July 15, 1806, past the present-day situation of Clyde Park, Montana.* ***Opposite:*** *"Captain Lewis shooting an Indian," as depicted by Patrick Gass, who must have used artistic license in representing his leader in full dress uniform.*

An Unfortunate Encounter

July 26, 1806

I had scarcely ascended the hills before I discovered to my left, at the distance of a mile, an assemblage of about 30 horses. I halted and used my spyglass, by the help of which I discovered several Indians on the top of an eminence just above them, who appeared to be looking down toward the river—I presumed, at Drewyer. About half the horses were saddled.

This was a very unpleasant sight. However, I resolved to make the best of our situation and to approach them in a friendly manner. I directed Joseph Fields to display the flag which I had brought for that purpose and advanced slowly toward them…. I told the two men with me that I apprehended that these were the Minnetarees of Fort de Prairie [Blackfeet], and from their known character I expected that we were to have some difficulty with them; that if they thought themselves sufficiently strong, I was convinced that they would attempt to rob us, in which case, be their numbers what they would, I should resist to the last extremity, preferring death to being deprived of my papers, instruments, and gun; and desired that they would form the same resolution, and be alert and on their guard….

I now asked them by signs if they were the Minnetarees of the North, which they answered in the affirmative. I asked if there was any chief

"I was convinced that they would attempt to rob us…in which case, I should resist to the last extremity"

among them, and they pointed out three. I did not believe them. However, I thought it best to please them and give to one a medal, to a second a flag, and to the third a handkerchief, with which they appeared well satisfied…. As it was growing late in the evening, I proposed that we should remove to the nearest part of the river and encamp together. I told them that I was glad to see them and had a great deal to say to them.

We mounted our horses and rode toward the river, which was at but a short distance…. We descended a very steep bluff about 250 feet high to the river, where there was a small bottom of nearly ½ a mile in length. In this bottom, there stand three solitary trees, near one of which the Indians formed a large semicircular camp of dressed buffalo skins and invited us to partake of their shelter, which Drewyer and myself accepted, and the Fieldses lay near the fire in front of the shelter.

With the assistance of Drewyer I had much conversation with these people in the course of the evening. I learned from them that…from hence to the establishment where they trade on the Saskatchewan River is only 6 days' easy march, or such as they usually travel with their women and children, which may be estimated at about 150 miles; that from these traders they obtain arms, ammunition, spirituous liquor, blankets, etc., in exchange for wolves and some beaver skins.

I told these people that I had come a great way from the East, up the large river which runs toward the rising sun, that I had been to the great waters where the sun sets and had seen a great many nations, all of whom I had invited to come and trade with me, on the rivers on this side of the mountains; that I had found most of them at war with their neighbors and had succeeded in restoring peace among them. That I was now on my way home and had left my party at the Falls of the Missouri with orders to descend that river to the entrance of Maria's River and there wait my arrival, and that I had come in search of them in order to prevail on them to be at peace with their neighbors, particularly those on the west side of the mountains, and to engage them to come and trade with me when the establishment is made at the entrance of this river; to all of which they readily gave their assent, and declared it to be their wish to be at peace with the Tushepaws

Below: The Yellowstone River at Pompey's Pillar, northeast of Billings, Montana. Clark added his name to the ancient images inscribed on this "remarkable rock" on July 25, 1806.

[Flatheads], who they said had killed a number of their relations lately, and pointed to several of those present who had cut their hair, as an evidence of the truth of what they had asserted....

I took the first watch tonight and sat up until half after eleven. The Indians by this time were all asleep. I roused up Reuben Fields and lay down myself. I directed Fields to watch the movements of the Indians, and if any of them left the camp, to awaken us all, as I apprehended they would attempt to steal our horses.

This being done, I fell into a profound sleep and did not wake until the noise of the men and Indians awoke me a little after light, in the morning.

A TRAGIC OUTCOME

July 27, 1806
This morning at daylight the Indians got up and crowded around the fire. Joseph Fields, who was on post, had carelessly laid his gun down behind him, near where his brother was sleeping. One of the Indians—the fellow to whom I had given the medal last evening—slipped behind him and took his gun and that of his brother unperceived by him. At the same instant, two others advanced and seized the guns of Drewyer and myself. Joseph Fields, seeing this, turned about to look for his gun and saw the fellow just running off with her and his brother's. He called to his brother, who instantly jumped up and pursued the Indian with him, whom they overtook at the distance of 50 or 60 paces from the camp, seized their guns and wrested them from

him—and Reuben Fields, as he seized his gun, stabbed the Indian to the heart with his knife. The fellow ran about fifteen steps and fell dead. Of this I did not know until afterward. Having recovered their guns they ran back instantly to the camp.

Drewyer, who was awake, saw the Indian take hold of his gun and instantly jumped up and seized her and wrested her from him, but the Indian still retained his pouch. His jumping up and crying "Damn you, let go my gun!" awakened me. I jumped up and asked what was the matter, which I quickly learned when I saw Drewyer in a scuffle with the Indian for his gun. I reached to seize my gun, but found her gone. I then drew a pistol from my holster and, turning myself about, saw the Indian making off with my gun. I ran at him with my pistol and bid him lay down my gun, which he was in the act of doing when the Fieldses returned and drew up their guns to shoot him, which I forbade as he did not appear to be about to make any resistance or commit any offensive act. He dropped the gun and walked slowly off.

I picked her up instantly. Drewyer, having about this time recovered his gun and pouch, asked me if he might not kill the fellow, which I also forbade as the Indian did not appear to wish to kill us. As soon as they found us all in possession of our arms, they ran and endeavored to drive off all the horses.

I now hollered to the men and told them to fire on them if they attempted to drive off our horses. They accordingly pursued the main party who were driving the horses up the river, and I pursued the man who had taken my gun, who, with another, was driving off a part of the horses which were to the left of the camp.

I pursued them so closely that they could not take twelve of their own horses, but continued to drive one of mine with some others. At the distance of three hundred paces, they entered one of those steep niches in the bluff with the horses

BLACKFOOT BLUES

How the Blackfeet got their name is a matter of speculation: Did they dye their moccasins black? They themselves used the name *Amskapi Pikuni*, which means "spotted robes." Speaking an Algonquian language, the Blackfeet had migrated to this area from farther east, around the Great Lakes, pushing westward into Saskatchewan and northern Montana some centuries before the Expedition.

Prior to their first, fateful meeting with Lewis and his men, the Blackfeet had enjoyed good relations with Europeans for several decades—British and French-Canadian traders had frequently stayed with them as guests. And, as they themselves told Lewis, they could take furs direct to the traders: Both the Hudson Bay and North West Fur companies had posts along the Saskatchewan. The guns they had been given in exchange down the years had given them an advantage over their Shoshone and Nez Percé neighbors and rivals, giving them a regional dominance they were determined to protect at any cost.

Hence their hostility toward Lewis when he outlined his vision for partnership and peace among the native peoples—a vision he had naively imagined would be seen as reassuring. Quite the reverse: To the Blackfeet, it meant the end of a monopolistic relationship with the white man. Were the Shoshone and Nez Percé to get guns as well, the era of Blackfoot dominance would be at an end.

before them. Being nearly out of breath, I could pursue no further. I called to them, as I had done several times before, that I would shoot them if they did not give me my horse and raised my gun. One of them jumped behind a rock and spoke to the other, who turned around and stopped at the distance of thirty steps from me, and I shot him through the belly. He fell to his knees and on his right elbow, from which position he partly raised himself and fired at me and, turning himself about, crawled in behind a rock, which was a few feet from him. He overshot me. Being bareheaded, I felt the wind of his bullet very distinctly.

"Being bareheaded, I felt the wind of his bullet very distinctly."

Not having my shot pouch I could not reload my piece, and as there were two of them behind good shelters from me, I did not think it prudent to rush on them with my pistol, which had I discharged. I had not the means of reloading until I reached camp. I therefore returned leisurely toward camp. On my way, I met with Drewyer who, having heard the report of the guns, had returned in search of me and left the Fieldses to pursue the Indians. I desired him to hasten to the camp with me and assist in catching as many of the Indian horses as were necessary, and to call to the Fieldses, if he could make them hear, to come back, that we still had a sufficient number of horses. This he did, but they were too far to hear him. We reached the camp and began to catch the horses and saddle them and put on the pack…. We had caught and saddled the horses and begun to arrange the packs when the Fieldses returned with four of our horses. We left one of our horses

and took four of the best of those of the Indians.

We took some of their buffalo meat and set out, ascending the bluffs by the same route we had descended last evening, leaving the balance of nine of their horses, which we did not want…. Having ascended the hill, we took our course through a beautiful level plain…. My design was to hasten to the entrance of Maria's River as quick as possible, in the hope of meeting with the canoes and party at that place, having no doubt but that the Indians would pursue us with a large party. No time was therefore to be lost, and we pushed our horses as hard as they would bear…. By dark, we had traveled about 17 miles further. We now halted to rest ourselves and horses about two hours. We killed a buffalo cow and took a small quantity of the meat.

After refreshing ourselves, we again set out by moonlight and traveled leisurely. Heavy thunderclouds lowered around us on every quarter but that from which the moon gave us light. We continued to pass immense herds of buffalo all night, as we had done in the latter part of the day. We traveled until 2 o'clock in the morning, having come, by my estimate, after dark about 20 miles. We now turned out our horses and laid ourselves down to rest in the plain, very much fatigued, as may be readily conceived. My Indian horse carried me very well—in short, much better than my own would have done—and leaves me with but little reason to complain of the robbery.

July 28, 1806

The morning proved fair. I slept sound, but fortunately awoke as day appeared. I awakened the

men and directed the horses to be saddled. I was so sore from my ride yesterday that I could scarcely stand. And the men complained of being in a similar situation; however, I encouraged them by telling them that our own lives as well as those of our friends and fellow travelers depended on our exertions at this moment…I now told them that it was my determination that if we were attacked in the plains on our way to the point, that the bridles of the horses should be tied together and we would stand and defend them, or sell our lives as dear as we could.

CATCHING CLARK

Out of danger, the party made good time and were soon on the point of catching up with Clark, as **Lewis** records in his journal for **August 7**:

We arrived at the entrance of the Yellowstone River. I landed at the point and found that Captain Clark had been encamped at this place, and from appearances had left it about 7 or 8 days. I found a paper on a pole at the point, which merely contained my name in the handwriting of Captain Clark. We also found the remnant of a note which had been attached to a piece of elk's horn in the camp. From this fragment I learned that game was scarce at the point and mosquitoes troublesome, which were the reasons given for his going on. I

*Opposite: The Missouri at Fort Benton, Montana: Lewis's party stopped here in the small hours of July 28, after riding all evening to shake off any pursuing Blackfoot party. **Above, main picture:** The Fort Peck Reservoir is the centerpiece of the Charles M. Russell Wildlife Refuge, Montana. **Inset:** Not all man-made changes to the landscape involve bridges, roads, and towns: the Russian Olive (Elaeagnus angustifolia) was introduced by gardeners in the 1900s but has now run rife through valley bottoms across the Western states.*

also learned that he intended halting a few miles below, where he intended waiting for my arrival….

I instantly re-embarked and descended the river in the hope of reaching Captain Clark's camp before night. About 7 miles below the point on the southwestern shore, I saw some meat that had been lately fleeced and hung on a pole. I directed Sergeant Ordway to go on shore and examine the place. On his return, he reported that he saw the tracks of two men which appeared so recent that he believed they had been there today. The fire he found at the place was blazing and appeared to have been mended up afresh or within the course of an hour past. He found at this place a part of a Chinook hat, which my men recognized as the hat of Gibson. From these circumstances we concluded that Captain Clark's camp could not be distant, and pursued our route until dark with the hope of reaching his camp. In this, however, we were disappointed; and night coming on compelled us to encamp.

In the event, Clark and his contingent would remain tantalizingly out of reach—one jump ahead, it seemed, however fast Lewis's party went. Not until **August 12** would **Lewis** at last be able to report:

At 1 p.m. I overtook Captain Clark and party and had the pleasure of finding them all well.

"WE PROCEEDED ON ALL TOGETHER"

Reunited again, the Corps of Discovery pushed on down the Missouri; with the current behind them, they were making excellent time. As **Clark** relates, the native communities on either bank were now old friends—with the Expedition, if not with one another:

August 14, 1806

Set out at sunrise and proceeded on. When we were opposite the Minnetarees' grand village, we saw a number of the natives viewing us. Soon after we came to at a crowd of the natives on the bank opposite the village of the Shoe Indians, or Mahas, at which place I saw the principal chief of the little village of the Minnetarees and the principal chief of the Mahas. I proceeded on to the Black Cats' [Mandan] village, where I intended to encamp, but the sand blew in such a manner that we determined not to continue on that site. I walked up to the Black Cats' village.

I had, as soon as I landed, dispatched Charbonneau to the Minnetarees, inviting the chiefs to visit us, and Drewyer down to the lower village of the Mandans to ask Mr. Jessaume to come and interpret for us.

After assembling the chiefs and smoking one pipe, I informed them that I still spoke the same words which we had spoken to them when we first arrived in their country. We then invited them to visit their Great Father, the President of the United States, and to hear his own counsels and receive his gifts from his own hands, as also to see the population of a government which can, at their pleasure, protect and secure you from all your enemies and chastise all those who will shut their ears to his counsels…. I urged the necessity of their going on with us as it would be the means of hastening those supplies of merchandise which would be sent to their country and exchanged as before mentioned for a moderate price in pelts and furs, etc.

The great chief of the Minnetarees spoke. He said he wished to go down and see his great father very much, but that the Sioux were in the road and would most certainly kill him or any others who should go down. They were bad people and would not listen to any thing which was told them. When he saw us last we told him that we had made peace with all the nations below. Since that time the Sioux had killed 8 of their people and stolen a number of their horses. He said that he had opened his ears and followed our counsels; he had made peace with the Cheyenne and Rocky Mountain Indians, and repeated the same objections as mentioned: that he went to war against none and was willing to receive all nations as friends…. If the Sioux were at peace with them and could be depended on, he as also other chiefs of the villages would be glad to go and see their great father, but as they were all afraid of the Sioux they should not go down.

> **Above:** *Its distinctive horns bedecked with vegetation after vigorous browsing, a pronghorn stands alert for any danger.* **Opposite:** *A war party of the Sioux, photographed by Curtis around 1910.*

DOWN THE YELLOWSTONE

Captain Clark's journey across country to the upper Yellowstone and thence down to the Missouri had been uneventful by comparison, the greatest peril his party had faced being the "very troublesome" mosquitoes. Joseph Potts was, he reported (July 3), "very unwell...owing to riding a hard trotting horse." But the "pill of opium" Clark administered "soon relieved him." A "sumptuous dinner of a fat saddle of venison and mush of cows" marked out July 4, "the day of the Declaration of Independence of the United States, and a day commonly celebrated by my country." Other than that, the month went by more or less without incident. Though the trail was often unclear, Sacagawea was on her home ground here: "The Squaw" was, Clark acknowledged, "of great service to me as a pilot." Thanks to her, the party found its way over the Bozeman Pass, Montana, from where it was a relatively easy journey down the Yellowstone River.

TETON TROUBLE

On **August 30**, as **Clark** describes, the Expedition came upon a party of Teton Sioux, the cause of so much agitation farther upriver:

80 or 90 Indian men all armed with fusils and bows and arrows came out of a wood on the opposite bank about ¼ of a mile below us. They fired off their guns as a salute. We returned the salute with two rounds.... I determined to find out who they were without running any risk of the party and Indians.... I then directed the man who could speak a few words of Sioux to inquire what nation or tribe they belonged to. They informed me that they were Tetons....

They belonged, as it turned out, to the same band the explorers had come so close to fighting with on their way upriver in September 1804:

I told those Indians that they had been deaf to our counsels, and ill-treated us as we ascended this river two years past, that they had abused all the whites who had visited them since.... We viewed them as bad people, and no more traders would be suffered to come to them, and whenever the white people wished to visit the nations above, they would come sufficiently strong to whip any villainous party who dared to oppose them, and words to the same purpose.

I also told them that I was informed that a part of all their bands were going to war against the Mandans, etc., and that they would be well whipped, as the Mandans and Minnetarees, etc. had a plenty of guns, powder and ball, and we had given them a cannon to defend themselves. And directed them to return from the sand bar and inform their chiefs what we had said to them, and to keep away from the river or we should kill every one of them.... After they had informed the chiefs, etc., as I suppose, what we had said to them, they all set out on their return to their camps back of a high hill. Seven of them halted on the top of the hill and blackguarded us, told us to come across and they would kill us all, etc., of which we took no notice.

NEWS OF HOME

As **Clark** reports, though, just a few days later, on **September 3**, they would find themselves in altogether more congenial company:

JOHN COLTER, MOUNTAIN MAN

As though the excitements of the Lewis and Clark Expedition were not enough, John Colter turned back just as the Corps of Discovery was heading home in triumph, taking off with two trappers into the wilderness. His arrangement with Forest Hancock and Joseph Dickson of Illinois actually lasted only a few weeks before the three fell out, but Colter remained in the woods and mountains of the Three Forks region, trapping on his own. In 1807 he joined Manuel Lisa's expedition up the Bighorn River: Sent out alone to trap and trade, he single-handedly explored much of what is now the Yellowstone National Park. But it was in 1809, when he was working out of Fort Raymond on the Upper Missouri, that he once more found himself entering the annals of American legend. He and another trapper, John Potts, were captured by a party of Blackfeet—still angry at the ending of their cozy arrangement with the Canada-based fur companies. Potts was executed on the spot, but Colter was stripped naked and set to run for his life, in what he eventually realized was a cruel parody of the hunt. Killing his closest pursuer with his own spear, he took his robe and ran on, escaping the other "hunters" and finally making it back to Fort Raymond eleven days later.

At half past 4 p.m. we spied two boats and several men. Our party plied their oars, and we soon landed on the side of the boats. The men of these boats saluted us with their small arms. I landed and was met by a Mr. James Aird from Mackinaw by way of Prairie du Chien and St. Louis. This gentleman is of the house of Dickson and Co. of Prairie du Chien, who has a license to trade for one year with the Sioux. He has two bateaux loaded with merchandise for that purpose. This gentleman received both Captain Lewis and myself with every mark of friendship. He was himself at the time with a chill of the ague on him which he has had for several days.

Our first inquiry was after the President of our country, and then our friends, and the state of politics of our country, etc., and the state of Indian affairs, to all of which inquiries Mr. Aird gave us as satisfactory information as he had it in his power to have collected in the Illinois, which was not a great deal....

This gentleman informed us of many changes and misfortunes which had taken place.... Three hundred of the American troops had been cantoned on the Missouri a few miles above its mouth. Some disturbance with the Spaniards in the Natchitoches country is the cause of their being called down to that country.

This "disturbance," though they could hardly have known it, was a part of the ongoing dispute with Spain over the boundaries of the Louisiana Purchase that had prompted the dispatch of Francisco Viana and his men to intercept the "Great Excursion"—and, had it proved possible, Lewis and Clark themselves. One way or another, they were coming back to a world of conflict, great and small:

The Spaniards had taken one of the United States' frigates in the Mediterranean. Two British ships of the line had fired on an American ship in the port of New York and killed the captain's brother. Two Indians had been hanged in St. Louis for murder, and several others in jail. And that Mr. Burr and General Hamilton fought a duel, the latter was killed, etc., etc.

On September 20, they had final confirmation that they were close to civilization:

The party, being extremely anxious to get down, ply their oars very well. We saw some cows on the bank, which was a joyful sight to the party and caused a shout to be raised for joy.

And at 4 p.m. on September 21, over two years since they had passed through previously on their way upstream,

We arrived in sight of St. Charles. The party, rejoiced at the sight of this hospitable village, plied their oars with great dexterity, and we soon arrived opposite the town. This day being Sunday, we observed a number of gentlemen and ladies walking on the bank. We saluted the village by three rounds from our blunderbusses and the small arms of the party, and landed near the lower part of the town. We were met by great numbers of the inhabitants. We found them excessively polite. The inhabitants of this village appear much delighted at our return, and seem to vie with each other in their politeness to us all.

Two days later, their epic journey was at last complete:

Set out, descended to the Mississippi and down that river to St. Louis, at which place we arrived about 12 o'clock. We suffered the party to fire off their pieces as a salute to the town. We were met by all the village and received a hearty welcome from its inhabitants.

Above: One legacy of Lewis and Clark: By the 1850s St. Louis was utterly unrecognizable as the "village" from which they had set out. Opposite, inset: A Blackfoot reservation scene early in the twentieth century. Opposite, below: The magnificent Montana elk.

EPILOGUE

❖ ✦ ❖ ✦ ❖

"Every person…seemed to express great pleasure at our return, and acknowledged themselves much astonished…we were supposed to have been lost long since."

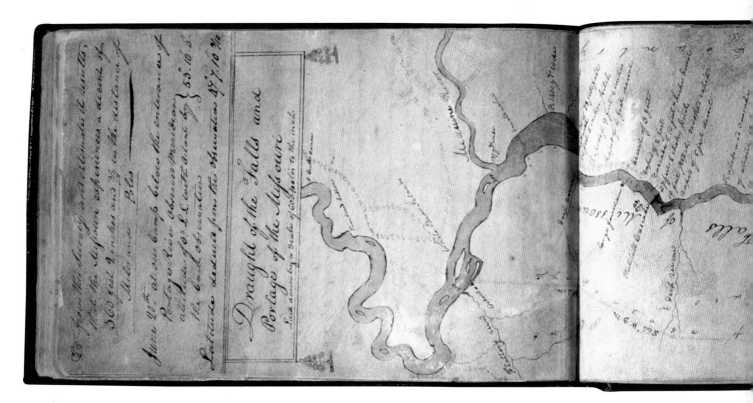

"I slept but little last night," wrote Clark in his journal for September 24—hardly surprisingly; the extraordinary thing is that he was managing to write at all amid the homecoming celebrations. But writing he was: That very day he would settle down to pen letters to "Governor Harrison and all my friends in Kentucky." Actually, it seems, he would simply be copying out a letter that was drafted by his friend Lewis, the more confident writer—for both men knew that it would quickly find its way into the press. Lewis had already, the previous afternoon, written his initial report to President Jefferson—having held back the day's post, a horseback messenger, until it was ready.

The explorers' return to "civilization" meant a return to what, in hindsight, seems a strikingly modern media and political culture: Lewis and Clark both knew the importance of "spinning" their success as effectively as possible. Hence Lewis's letter to the president has some of the sober portentousness of the political position paper—though enlivened by its author's at times uncontainable enthusiasm. (It also takes pains to be tactful, letting Jefferson down as easily as possible over the failure to find a viable waterway to the West.) "Clark's" letter to his "friends in Kentucky," as composed by Lewis with a careful eye on the Frankfort, Kentucky, *Western World* as well as the rest of the nation's press, dwelt more on giddy precipices, raging torrents, warlike savages, and angry grizzlies. Both letters may be seen, historians have suggested, as parts of Lewis's attempts to set out the Expedition's stall: He was eager that his friend Clark and the other Corps members would be fairly recompensed for what they had been through. Moreover, by raising the Expedition's profile as far as possible all the way from the White House down to the nation's kitchens and barrooms, he hoped to ensure that both his scientific findings and his vision for the West would be taken seriously.

Above: *"Draught of the Falls and Portage of the Missouri," as recorded by Clark on June 26, 1805.*

Opposite: *The lower (69-foot) section of Oregon's Multnomah Falls; the Columbia River plunges an awesome 621 feet in all over a glacially formed shelf. Today, though the scenery remains spectacular, the cascades of the Columbia Gorge have largely been tamed by modern river management—and some even entirely drowned by damming.*

FIRST THINGS FIRST: THE BOOK DEAL

Lewis was, perhaps, also concerned that there would be a ready market for his own proposed "Book of the Expedition" when it eventually appeared. Lewis's instinct for media management would let him down here, as his insistence on keeping his counsel until his own magisterial account was ready for publication opened the way for hastier memoirs from more junior members of the Corps of Discovery: Private Robert Frazier and Sergeant Patrick Gass. The scramble to publish, and the unseemly squabbling that resulted, as authors and publishers attempted to do down each other's books to the advantage of their own, will not surprise anyone accustomed to the cut-and-thrust of today's celebrity culture. But this really shouldn't have surprised Lewis either: In an age before movies and TV, books were a major source of sensation and entertainment, as well as of enlightenment. Publishing was an industry with high rewards and even higher risks. Lewis not only lost the battle of the books, but was left looking a little cheap and opportunistic himself, his attempts to police the publications of his men being viewed with a cynicism that, when all was said and done, may not have been entirely unjustified. Whatever the truth of the matter, Lewis's sense that he had lost control of how "his" Expedition would be viewed seems to have shaken his confidence, and ultimately drawn him down into depression.

THE CELEBRATIONS

For the moment, though, he and other Expedition members were free to enjoy their triumph: The cream of St. Louis society turned out for a banquet and ball on the night of September 25. The explorers continued to be celebrated as they made their triumphant—but distinctly leisurely—return to Washington in the weeks and months that followed. They were in no hurry, of course: There was administrative business to take care of in St. Louis before they could even depart, and then there was the fact that every community en route wanted to see the returning heroes. Yet it has to be remembered, too, that—even in the settled area of the United States—travel was still a difficult and time-consuming business. (For example, Lewis's letter to Jefferson of September 23 took a month to arrive.) Suffice it to say that it was not until November 9 that they reached Clark's sister's house at Locust Grove, Louisville, Kentucky, where there were further festivities. Clark stayed on in that neighborhood to pay court to Julia Hancock, his future bride, leaving Lewis to push on to Washington alone. Lewis arrived on December 28 to as warm a reception as could possibly be imagined—a welcome in which pride and patriotism were compounded by relief, as one observer explained:

"Never did a similar event excite more joy through the United States. The humblest of its citizens had taken a lively interest in the issue of the journey and looked forward with impatience for the information it would furnish. Their anxieties too, for the safety of the Corps had been kept in a state of excitement by lugubrious rumors circulated, from time to time, of uncertain authorities and uncontradicted by letters or direct information from the time they had left the Mandan towns."

THE HANGOVER

Even before the celebrations were over, the backlash was beginning—and Joel Barlow's proposal that the Columbia River be renamed after Lewis did not help. No matter that the suggestion appalled Lewis himself, and was dismissed out of hand by Jefferson: The President's political enemies were only too delighted to think the worst. From being a feather in Jefferson's cap, the Expedition was becoming a stick to belabor him with, the whole affair taking on a party-political dimension neither he nor Lewis had ever imagined, still less

A FLORAL TRIBUTE

Founded in 1743 by John Bartram and Benjamin Franklin, the American Philosophical Society was famous the world over; America's leading scientists came to its regular meetings in Philadelphia. Jefferson was almost as proud of his presidency of the APS as he was of his presidency of the country, and he saw his Expedition as a natural extension of the society's activities. John Bartram had established America's first scientifically organized botanical garden, and the APS was the obvious recipient for the plant specimens the explorers had gathered in the West. Despite the rigors of the trail, Lewis and Clark had taken the utmost care with their specimen sheets: For the most part, they had made it back safe, sound, and stunningly beautiful.

Some had not yet finished their journey: Frederick Pursh, the German botanist given the task of ordering and cataloging the collection, took some with him when he went off to a new job in England. This was technically theft, but no one felt inclined to quibble when they were subsequently restored, having been meticulously recorded and written up—and beautifully illustrated—in Pursh's book *Flora Americae Septentrionalis (The Flora of North America)*. Far from stealing Lewis and Clark's thunder, or that of the APS, Pursh had done American science proud. Only very belatedly would this be appreciated, though—not because Pursh was condemned, but because the collection was forgotten, having been caught up in the blanket amnesia that came to surround the entire undertaking of Lewis and Clark. Eventually, botanists came to see the priceless value of the resource they had hidden away, its lovingly preserved specimens as freshly beautiful as they had ever been. Today, tourists flock to see the Academy of Natural Science's Lewis and Clark Herbarium, in Philadelphia, which is acknowledged as one of the great glories of American science.

Above: Rose Paintbrush (Castilleja rhexifolia) lends a tint of delicate beauty to the harsh terrain of the Lost Trail Pass. Lewis and Clark redrew not only the geographical but the botanical map of North America.

intended. And as a House committee considered the land grants and cash payments to be made to Corps members by a grateful nation, the haggling and the horse trading only made matters worse. Lewis's attempts to get the best deal possible for his men were a mark of his integrity, but—taken along with the wrangling still going on over the publication of Expedition memoirs—allowed more prejudiced observers to insinuate that the heroes of the hour may have been driven by mercenary motives. The announcement of February 28, 1807, that he had been appointed governor of Louisiana must have been especially gratifying for Lewis in his present circumstances. Not only would the position give him considerable influence on the government of a territory for which he had the greatest enthusiasm and on which he had come to hold strong, well-informed views, but it would remove him from a Washington where he was coming to feel increasingly beleaguered. Even better, his friend Clark was appointed Superintendent for Indian Affairs for Louisiana: The "Lewis and Clark" partnership was back in business.

"It seemed as if those scenes of visionary enchantment would never have an end," enthused Lewis, quite transported by the otherworldly beauty of White Cliffs, Montana (May 31, 1805).

But business, it transpired, was not to be Lewis's strength: He seems to have been hopeless when it came to money. Indeed, the man who had faced down the dangers of the wild and crossed the continent, an inspirational leader, proved ill-equipped for what should have been far less taxing responsibilities. Like the veteran back from the wars, for whom peace holds more terrors than the battlefield ever did, Lewis found life in St. Louis far tougher than his existence on the trail. Confident that he would have his fortune when his *Journals* went on sale, he made no actual effort to get them ready for publication. In the meantime he speculated rashly, often borrowing money from friends (including Clark). As a public administrator, too, Lewis was ineffectual—with Jefferson arguably doing him no favors by his indulgence and generosity, allowing him to spend public money freely, with little accountability and to no obvious advantage. Increasingly lonely and unhappy, Lewis could not but compare his life with Clark's: His friend loved his work with the Native Americans and was serenely contented in his marriage. Envying him his lot, Lewis looked about with increasing urgency for a wife of his own, but was to be no luckier in love than he had been in money. He plunged deeper and deeper into depression, and seems to have consoled himself by drinking heavily—to the further detriment of his work. He also appears to have become increasingly dependent on drugs, especially opium. This was a great deal less shocking in the early nineteenth century than it would be now—illustrious opium addicts of the day included the English writers Samuel Taylor Coleridge and Thomas de Quincey—yet it was hardly the mark of a man in control of his destiny.

THE BITTER END

By the fall of 1809, Thomas Jefferson was no longer in office. His successor, James Madison, shared neither his interest in the West nor his regard for Lewis. Angry at the Governor of Louisiana's free-spending waywardness, his Secretary of War William Eustis decided abruptly to pull the rug: He refused point-blank to honor drafts for public expenditure that Lewis had signed. These promptly became the personal liability of a man already up to his ears in debt. On his way to Washington to plead his case, eluding the vigilance of friends who had already thwarted two earlier attempts, Lewis shot himself in the early hours of October 11.

With him, for several decades, died the heroic story of the Lewis and Clark Expedition. Suicide was then deemed the most dishonorable of crimes. It loomed large enough in the nineteenth-century mind to eclipse the great achievements of Lewis's lifetime: America's hero had become a source of shame. With the start of the twentieth century, though, public attitudes began to change: Suicide was regarded with more sympathy, even when not actually condoned. More and more, Americans felt able to see past the manner of Meriwether Lewis's death to the incredible story of his life—and the extraordinary achievements of his traveling companions. Clark had thrived, as we have seen, and won wide respect—apparently on both sides of the ethnic divide—with his work as Superintendent of Indian Affairs. But his good fortune did nothing to soften his attitude to York, his slave, whose repeated requests for freedom he refused for years. In 1815 he finally acquiesced, and York set himself up with his own haulage business—but the venture failed, and he died shortly after of cholera. Clark showed more enlightenment in his treatment of Sacagawea's son, Jean-Baptiste, and daughter, Lisette (who was born later), formally adopting them after their mother died in 1812.

Below: Journey's end for Lewis — Grinder's Inn, on the Natchez Trace in Tennessee.

BELATED RECOGNITION

Lewis's journals were with him when he died: They never had made his fortune, as he had always hoped. They would, however, one day restore his historic reputation. That they did owes much to the research of the distinguished scholar Reuben Thwaites, who prepared

A MONUMENTAL INJUSTICE?

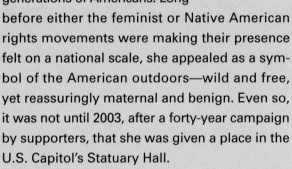

There are more statues of Sacagawea in the United States than of any other woman— something in the Shoshone woman's story seems to have caught the imagination of generations of Americans. Long before either the feminist or Native American rights movements were making their presence felt on a national scale, she appealed as a symbol of the American outdoors—wild and free, yet reassuringly maternal and benign. Even so, it was not until 2003, after a forty-year campaign by supporters, that she was given a place in the U.S. Capitol's Statuary Hall.

Clark's personal slave, York, has not received anything like the same sculptural recognition, though in recent years he has had a supporting role in several monuments to the Expedition as a whole. At first, it seems, he suffered from the African-American's general invisibility in U.S. society: It simply did not occur to officialdom that he was a fit subject for commemoration. Later, his contribution would be acknowledged, but his status as slave was an uncomfortable reminder of an oppressive institution white America preferred to forget. Ed Hamilton's 8-foot bronze statue in Louisville, Kentucky (2003), is believed to be the first monument exclusively to honor York.

the first full edition of the *Original Journals of the Lewis and Clark Expedition* in time for the centenary in 1904–05. All subsequent studies of Lewis and Clark have been in Thwaites's debt—and the present book is certainly no exception. Yet it is difficult to believe that, had Thwaites not come along, somebody else would not have undertaken the task: The Expedition's significance could hardly go on being ignored indefinitely. Americans were starting to see not only the historic importance of the journey the Corps of Discovery had made, but the power of the journals as a narrative, a work of literature.

Today, 200 years after they were written, they have assumed, for many, a place as the U.S. national epic: what Homer's *Iliad* and *Odyssey* were for the Greeks, what Virgil's *Aeneid* was for ancient Rome. Like the great epics of antiquity, the *Journals* are about much more than an exciting story—though they certainly do tell a stirring tale of action and adventure. Describing a decisive episode in the foundation of the civilization to which they belong, they enshrine the heroic values by which that civilization has since sought to live. Had their authors set out consciously to do that, they never would have succeeded: Only in hindsight have their prosaic observations come to resonate so strongly.

Resonate they do, however: Here, first and foremost perhaps, are the unassuming courage and quiet resolve we now know as the hallmarks of America's greatest heroes. Here, too, are the powers of friendship, compassion, and humanity, an unforced admiration for the qualities of other cultures—and a deep, abiding love for the American way. An intellectual curiosity that won't be satisfied, a practical intelligence that finds a way around any obstacle: These, surely, are among the great strengths of the American mind. And, last but certainly not least, the love of nature, its plants and animals, its majestic scenery and its wide open spaces: Nowhere have these things found more unforgettable expression than they have in the *Journals* of Lewis and Clark.

Above: *An emblem of courage, endurance and loyalty, Sacagawea's face has become an American icon.*